Bello:

hidden talent rediscovered

Bello is a digital only imprint of Pan Macmillan,
established to breathe new life into previously published,
classic books.

At Bello we believe in the timeless power of the imagination,
of good story, narrative and entertainment and we want to use
digital technology to ensure that many more readers
can enjoy these books into the future.

We publish in ebook and Print on Demand formats
to bring these wonderful books to new audiences.

www.panmacmillan.co.uk/bello

B E L L

Winston Graham

Winston Mawdsley Graham OBE was an English novelist, best known for the series of historical novels about the Poldarks. Graham was born in Manchester in 1908, but moved to Perranporth, Cornwall when he was seventeen. His first novel, The House with the Stained Glass Windows was published in 1933. His first 'Poldark' novel, Ross Poldark, was published in 1945, and was followed by eleven further titles, the last of which, Bella Poldark, came out in 2002. The novels were set in Cornwall, especially in and around Perranporth, where Graham spent much of his life, and were made into a BBC television series in the 1970s. It was so successful that vicars moved or cancelled church services rather than try to hold them when Poldark was showing.

Aside from the Poldark series, Graham's most successful work was Marnie, a thriller which was filmed by Alfred Hitchcock in 1964. Hitchcock had originally hoped that Grace Kelly would return to films to play the lead and she had agreed in principle, but the plan failed when the principality of Monaco realised that the heroine was a thief and sexually repressed. The leads were eventually taken by Tippi Hedren and Sean Connery. Five of Graham's other books were filmed, including The Walking Stick, Night Without Stars and Take My Life. Graham wrote a history of the Spanish Armadas and an historical novel, The Grove of Eagles, based in that period. He was also an accomplished writer of suspense novels. His autobiography, Memoirs of a Private Man, was published by Macmillan in 2003. He had completed work on it just weeks before he died. Graham was a Fellow of the Royal Society of Literature, and in 1983 was honoured with the OBE.

Winston Graham

MEMOIRS OF A PRIVATE MAN

BELL

First published in 2003 by Macmillan

This edition published 2013 by Bello
an imprint of Pan Macmillan, a division of Macmillan Publishers Limited
Pan Macmillan, 20 New Wharf Road, London N1 9RR
Basingstoke and Oxford
Associated companies throughout the world

www.panmacmillan.co.uk/bello

ISBN 978-1-4472-5676-2 EPUB
ISBN 978-1-4472-5675-5 POD

A CIP catalogue record for this book is available from the British Library.

Visit www.panmacmillan.com to read more about all our books
and to buy them. You will also find features, author interviews and
news of any author events, and you can sign up for e-newsletters
so that you're always first to hear about our new releases.

Preface

I was in Pratt's Club one evening recently and sat next to Patrick Leigh Fermor. Talk came round to the subject of autobiographies, and I told him I had written a large part of mine some few years ago but then, self-doubting, had put it away in my safe pending further thought. Only four people had read it, and of those the only 'outsider' was an old friend who had been the chief editor at a large London publishing firm. Her view was one of general approval of what I had written, with one proviso – she felt that my life, at least as I had depicted it, was a little too 'exemplary' to attract attention these days.

When I told him this, Paddy looked at me with a quizzical scrutiny. 'Surely you must have committed *some* sins?'

'Of course,' I replied, 'but these are all *ordinary* sins, which only *just* come into that category now. No one is interested in reading about them. The trouble is, I have not committed any of the fashionable sins, such as murder, burglary, buggery, sodomy, child abuse, gang rape, necrophilia—'

He interrupted firmly: 'Have you ever committed simony?'

'Um – er – what's that?' I asked.

He lowered his voice, his eyes globular with tidings. 'Church bribery,' he said.

This closed the conversation for a while, but after another glass of wine he returned to the subject.

'When I get back to Greece I'll send you a letter listing all the sins I think you *might* have committed.'

'Fair enough,' I said, 'but put it in a brown envelope, won't you.'

'Of course,' he agreed. He finished his wine. 'But I shall print SINS on the corner.'

I have waited hopefully, but so far have heard nothing. Perhaps he has forgotten. (Of course he is always the despair of his publisher for writing his books so slowly.) Or perhaps it was all the fantasy of a jolly evening.

Anyway, this tells the reader what to expect.
   'May it please Your Lordship ...'

BOOK ONE

Chapter One

About five years ago I met a well-dressed stranger at the Savile Club who, in the course of conversation, asked me what my profession was. I said I was a novelist. 'Oh, really?' he said. 'But what do you do for a living?'

This is an extreme case of one of the amiable misconceptions that exist in the minds of the public about the rewards of authorship. At the other extreme are those who assume that, after beginning one's writing life in an attic smoking pot in company with a dandruffed girlfriend, one only has to write one successful book and one is able to buy a lemon-yellow Rolls-Royce and escape to the Bahamas to avoid tax. (This pretty well happened to Michael Arlen many years ago when he wrote *The Green Hat*, but it is still rare.) Between these extremes are as many gradations as there are authors writing.

I am, I suppose, what is generally called a popular novelist. So I am not particularly regarded by the literary trend-makers of our time. When my first Poldark book, *Ross Poldark*, was published it was a Book Society Recommendation. (Much later, another Cornish novel, *The Grove of Eagles*, was a Book Society Choice.) But when the *Poldark* novels were put on as a series on television, most critics disliked them. Some absolutely hated them. When the series became an enormous success they just preferred to avoid reference to it. Like people in a Victorian drawing room when someone has loudly and vulgarly broken wind, they tried to pretend it hadn't happened.

But I have been successful, yes. And very lucky too. When my father died I was nineteen and my mother knew there was only one thing I wanted to do in life, and as she could just afford to support me if I lived at home, she offered to do so. It suited her well, for my elder brother was married, and she didn't like the thought of living alone. It suited me, for I could dream and write the days away, madly anxious, of course, to justify my existence by making a living out of this chosen profession but not having to depend on it for bed and board. The novelist George Gissing, when told of some rising young writer of whom everyone had great hopes, would look out from under his heavy brows and say: 'Has he *starved*?' By that criterion I never qualified.

But one lived on a *tight* rein. There was never money to spare for being adventurous. Money for all essentials, but little else. When at the age of twenty-five I gathered together enough money for my first ever trip abroad – to Paris – I came home with seven shillings left. And by then I was a fully-fledged novelist, with two books published.

I was born in Victoria Park, Manchester, before the First World War. My mother's grandfather had started his own business as a wholesale grocer in Gorton, Manchester, in 1825, and later moved to Shudehill, where the firm remained until it was bombed out in 1941. In the Thirties it began to expand into the pharmaceutical trade, and gradually this took over so that by the 1950s the grocery side had been altogether dropped. Mawdsley's is now the largest privately owned pharmaceutical firm in England.

My mother's father was a big man – 6 ft and at his heaviest weighed 21 stone 7 lbs, or 301 lbs. His wife was tiny, and they had nine children, of whom five survived. One of my mother's earliest memories was of *her* mother sitting beside the fire in tears, her long black hair down, weeping for the loss of another baby. My grandmother – this same one – became very delicate between pregnancies and frequently felt faint. The doctor prescribed a teaspoon of brandy, and she followed his advice. When that doctor died the new doctor found that she was getting through four bottles a week. He forbade all spirits. My grandmother desperately and loudly proclaimed that she would *die*, but she did not, and thereafter recovered.

She was a Greenhow, and I know very little about her family except that her grandfather had five wives – a considerable achievement in the days when divorce was scarcely to be thought of and the average man did not have Henry VIII's advantage of being able to send them to the block. My grandfather was a Mawdsley – a name of minor consequence in the city of Manchester. His father, Thomas Mawdsley (1800–1880), was a Chartist and helped to found one of the first trade unions, the Amalgamated Association of Operative Cotton Spinners, in 1845. I do not know what his business was – presumably to do with cotton – but by the time he was forty he had made enough money to retire, thereafter spending his time and energies on schemes for educating the working man. For ten years he was secretary of the Lancashire Short Time Committee, working with his counterparts in Yorkshire and under the Earl of Shaftesbury to get the Ten Hours Bill on the statute books.

In 1849 he led a delegation to London, where he stayed six months, testifying about conditions in the cotton mills of Lancashire to a select committee of the House of Commons. When the Ten Hours Act was finally passed in 1850, a dinner was held in London to celebrate the great occasion and he was invited to speak. He refused, saying that he was 'only good at pot-hooks'. It is a good Lancashire expression and is the only evidence I can find in my ancestry that anyone else may have had some aptitude for writing. It also shows a peculiarly Mawdsley sense of humour.

When he died he was given a public funeral, and a flattering, if not altogether grammatical, tribute to his activities was put on his tall gravestone, which is in Harpurhey Cemetery.

My grandfather's cousin, James Mawdsley (1848–1902), was also prominent in the trade union movement, taking over the Secretaryship of the Amalgamated Association of Operative Cotton Spinners in 1878, but always on the side of moderation and tending to deplore the politicizing of the trade unions. So in 1899 he stood for Parliament for the double constituency of Oldham as a 'Tory Trade Unionist', opposing two Liberals. His running mate was that famous Socialist, Winston Churchill, fighting his first election; but in spite of all they could do the issues became so confused that the electorate played safe and voted for the Liberals, Alfred (later Baron) Emmott and Walter Runciman (later Viscount Runciman of Doxford).

Mr Churchill and Mr Mawdsley remained friends until James died, but by the time I was born Mr Churchill had himself become a Liberal and my mother, having imbibed Liberalism at her father's knee, decided it would be a good idea if I bore his name.

My grandfather had a substantial house in Dickenson Road, and a carriage and pair for when he took his wife out. But a tramway was laid down the road, and, still in the days of horse trams, he would run after a tram, in spite of his great bulk, and jump on it to take him to his business in the mornings. When he was transferring his business from Gorton to the more central and larger premises at Shudehill his sons were still at school, and his eldest daughter had run away from home to marry a sailor, so he came to rely on my mother, his second daughter, who managed the Gorton premises for him while he was establishing the other. Perhaps this was how my mother came to have such a good business head, though, after she was married, she did not employ it gainfully.

My mother was looked on as 'delicate'. As a girl she was pretty but very slight – 'like a yard of pump water', as her elder sister tartly observed – and although she had a number of suitors, it was not until she met my father at a church outing, when she was twenty-seven, that the magic worked. As very much the younger son (my brother Cecil was ten years older), I was not able to observe my parents through all their married life; but they did seem to be completely devoted to each other for the whole of the thirty years they had together. If it is true in marriage that one is always the lover and one the loved, he was certainly the lover.

My father always gave me the impression of having more cultural and intellectual interests than the Mawdsleys (who by this generation had lost all the public-spirited zeal of their forebears), but he was of a slightly lower social status. His father had kept a shop of some sort, and his mother was a sturdy, benign, broad-spoken, vigorous Blackburn woman who had somehow surprisingly produced three children of unmistakable gentility and ambition, all of them with educated voices, though their schooling had been slight. My father when he married was with a firm of tea importers in Sheffield. He played the cello. His younger brother, who worked on a Liverpool newspaper, played the violin. Their sister was intensely musical, and for a time ran her own orchestra. Though no performer herself – I remember some excruciating evenings – she was a good teacher both of the piano and the violin. (For a short time she taught the young Kathleen Ferrier.)

My mother played the piano extremely well but with a restricted repertoire of things she knew and had long practised. As a girl she would practise four hours a day. She was no sight-reader. Some of the pleasantest memories of my youth were the Sunday evenings when I would sit in the drawing room reading a book and humming or whistling the familiar Mozart or Schubert. She didn't seem to mind my accompaniment.

Before my parents married, my mother's mother told my father that they could never have children: 'Anne is too delicate.' Yet in fact Anne lived to be eighty and produced two sons, both of whom have handsomely exceeded their mother's age.

At the reception after their wedding my mother remembers that her old sweetheart, Will Bowker, who had a good tenor voice, was singing 'Son of my Soul' as she came down the stairs in her going-away costume. Later, catching the train to take them on their honeymoon, my father leaned out to wave goodbye to those who had come to see them off, and sat back on his silk hat.

They went to Llandudno, and no doubt made gentle love in the long September evenings. When she was old I took her back there. She had not been to Llandudno in the interval, but with characteristic reserve forbore to make any comment other than the casual remarks she had made in other places we had visited.

Eventually I volunteered the question that coming to this town again after so long must bring back many memories. She said: 'Everything I look at is like a stone in my heart.'

I don't know where my parents lived when they were first married, but after a while they moved to Huby, near Sheffield, so that my father should be near his business. But the hard water did not suit my mother, who was living up to her reputation of being delicate, and they moved back to Manchester. About this time the tea firm went into liquidation, and my grandfather invited my father to join him in running the firm of D. Mawdsley & Co. This aroused intense jealousy on the part of his eldest son, Tom, who by now had left school and was expecting to inherit control of the firm. Tom had all the makings of an excellent engineer but had no talent for commerce, and when eventually he did come into the firm, followed by his ineffectual but well-meaning brother Daniel, the jealousy continued. My father, who did not suffer fools gladly (or even silently), could certainly have been a more tactful man; but it meant that for about twenty years this incompatible partnership, constantly engendering petty backbiting and rancour, continued, until it was broken by my father's premature illness – at fifty-four – and death – at sixty.

I was born at 66 Langdale Road, Victoria Park – film producer Monja Danischewsky later suggested there should be a plaque put on the house marked 'Watch this Space' – but when I was two my parents moved to a somewhat better house in Curzon Avenue – No. 18. One of my first memories is of being allowed into the front door of the empty house, toddling the length of the long hall into the dining room and trying to peer out of the windows at the back garden. But the window sills were too high for me to see out. I soon learned my new address but it came out as 'Eighteen Cur-daddy Addy'.

Victoria Park was something of an anachronism even in those days, being a partly independent, self-ruling small district only three miles from the centre of Manchester. One paid the city rates, of course, but an additional rate was levied to cover the special facilities offered – manned barricades at all entry points, to keep out beggars and other undesirables, park-keepers to see that a decent order was maintained inside the confines, no public transport nearer than the gates, which was a considerable disadvantage to the frail and the elderly. Motor cars and carriages of course went in and out, when the frontier barriers had to be raised for them. This was no park in the ordinary sense of being a publicly owned place of recreation. For that one went to Birch Park, just outside the confines.

Victoria Park had been initiated by a group of wealthy merchants – building their heavy-stuccoed, porticoed, sash-windowed Victorian mansions set amid heavy Victorian trees – who wanted privacy and privilege and were prepared to pay for it by forming a quiet enclave within the noisy city; and this was precisely what they had achieved. By about the turn of the century part of the original park was developed and a number of avenues of smaller houses built to accommodate a much less well-to-do but still fairly select type of city dweller who shared and helped to pay for the amenities of the park.

18 Curzon Avenue was a tall, narrow semi-detached house with a long hall flanked by a sizeable drawing room and a kitchen and scullery, with a dining room at the back. Stairs led up to five bedrooms, a bathroom, a lavatory, and there was also an outside lavatory, and fairly extensive cellars, one of which, I think, was intended for wine. If so, it was sadly neglected during our occupancy. Not that my family was ever teetotal on principle, but we scarcely ever drank liquor of any sort, and certainly not wine.

We kept one living-in maid – or a succession of them, for my mother was not easy to please. All the same, some of them stayed a long time and became long-suffering members of the family. There was one, Patty, an Irish girl, who used to stand in front of the mirror in her bedroom and say to herself: 'Aren't I beautiful? Aren't I beautiful!' A precocious eight-year-old, I was sometimes present at these self-adulatory sessions. In the end too many young men were in agreement with her, and my mother decided that she was not best fitted for domestic service in a God-fearing household.

Were we God-fearing? Not really. My mother kept steadily, if quietly, to her beliefs all her life, but *her* father was very much a free-thinker and associated with atheists and agnostics, one of whom, a Mr Jack Slaney, used to greet my mother when she came in from Sunday school with: 'Well, Annie, have you seen Jesus Christ today?' My father was pretty well a non-believer too – at least until his last and only illness, when he began to dabble in Christian Science and spiritualism. My brother never went to church, and I would go perhaps twice a year with my mother. The long walk was something that my mother – still relentlessly delicate – only essayed on special dates such as Christmas and Easter. One of the maids –

I've forgotten which one – taught me to say my prayers, and later a fiercely religious headmaster indoctrinated a lot that had been missing at home.

I always shied away from what might be termed overt religion. When I was twelve a curate from the church took to calling, with the aim of persuading me to attend confirmation classes. With equal persistence I would bolt into the garden at the sound of him so that my mother could truthfully – though ruefully – inform him that I was out.

I often wonder why religious teaching was totally missing at home. I think perhaps my mother was so lacking in energy that she just couldn't be bothered. But at least our household was the very reverse of one in which religion is practised but remains a sham (an enduring theme with novelists). With my parents it was 'do as I do, not do as I say'. (Never spoken but implicit.) I never heard a swear word – even from my older brother – nor an obscenity, nor really ever a vulgarism. Even if we didn't go to church, we never played cards on Sundays.

It is often said that only children make bad mixers. I was not an only child, but a worse mixer could hardly have been found. The fact that my brother Cecil was ten years the elder may have resulted in my being an only child in all but name, and the fact that he was more often at home than my busy and preoccupied father resulted in my taking my cue and my beliefs – or lack of them – from him rather than from someone who was older and wiser. Cecil combined a mild, inoffensive good nature – and a strong sense of humour – with curiously aggressive views, downright philistine and arrogant. He had no interest in religion (not even in his last days, when some hitherto unbelievers have second thoughts), little interest in books outside certain narrow spheres, no real interest in music or painting or poetry – though he would quote *Omar Khayyam* with relish. His interests were in the fresh air, the sun, the sea, the sands – and in his beloved Cornwall, where he made his home for nearly sixty years.

His comically misanthropic view of life, his pessimism, his philistinism all had a strong influence on me, and although my passionate preoccupation with books from the age of eight soon helped me to throw off the last of the three blights, the former two – or at least the pessimism – have stayed with me in milder form all my life. Of course it would be very unfair to put all the blame on him for what I suspect may be a family predisposition.

Among the maids we had, the one I remember most was called Evelyn – a bouncy, jolly, generous-minded girl from Northumberland, who came when she was seventeen (she told my mother she was eighteen in order to get the job) and stayed with us about five years, seeing us through all the traumas of those sickly years of the Twenties, when my father had his severe stroke, my mother had double pneumonia, and I followed with lobar pneumonia.

Evelyn had had a bitterly hard life. Her father and mother had had to get married when she was on the way, and her father's parents had taken against their new daughter-in-law. Her father, a miner, had a brother who worked on the roads, and one Sunday was called out to clear a blocked drain. Because this brother was drunk, Evelyn's father went instead, climbed down the manhole and was overcome by poisonous fumes and died. Evelyn and her mother and sister lived in direst poverty, receiving the barest help from their relatives until her mother married another miner, who heard there were better prospects of work in Lancashire and so moved. When war came he volunteered, and his family had to try to live on the 10/6 a week allowed them by the government. Towards the end of the war Evelyn's mother died of peritonitis and malnutrition, and Evelyn and her sister were about to be taken to an institution when the war ended and her stepfather came home. But he quickly married again, another child came along, and the new stepmother said there was simply not room in their cottage for them all. Evelyn's grandparents said they would take the younger sister only, and Evelyn was on her own. She found work at a button factory and boarded out. Her wages were 10/- a week and she paid 9/6 a week for her bed and board.

When a friend told her there was a lady in Victoria Park looking for a living-in maid to whom she would pay 10/- a week including food and a *bedroom to herself* she borrowed money from her landlady to buy a new dress, called to see her new mistress and was engaged. Every Wednesday afternoon off thereafter she would take the long tram ride and walk to her old landlady's and pay her back sixpence of the money she had borrowed. Later she was to take me in the afternoons to the local cinema – a fleapit indeed – where we were thrilled together by films like *Intolerance* and *The Exploits of Elaine* and *Way Down East*. I imagine my mother must have connived at these secretive ventures, for Evelyn could not have afforded the price out of her own pocket.

Inevitably, of course, a young man, Arthur, came along, a sober, frail young man who wanted to marry her. My mother, naturally, was against it – they were far too young – hadn't she been twenty-eight herself when she married? – but inevitably the young man got his way. Poor Evelyn. She was dogged by ill-luck and her own warm, overflowingly generous nature. Perhaps she was plunged into marriage prematurely because by then my family was sick to death – almost literally – of the illnesses of Victoria Park – my father crippled and prematurely old at fifty-six, my mother saddled with bronchitis every winter, and I apparently threatened with further attacks of pneumonia – a lethal disease then, before the dawn of antibiotics – and my brother, the only healthy one, desperately wanting to get married himself and move to Cornwall, which he had lost his heart to after one visit.

So Evelyn left us and married, and since they could not afford a house of their own she moved in with Arthur's widowed father and four brothers, for whom she then became a permanent scrubber and cook and housekeeper. Eventually a child came – a boy – and they were able to afford rooms of their own, then a tiny house. They could do this because Evelyn got work at Lewis's, the big Manchester store, first as an assistant in the dress department, then in the accounts department, where she established a reputation for efficiency and integrity. So began what must have been the best part of her life. Eventually they were even able to afford a small car; but her husband Arthur was always ailing – he worked in the cotton industry, and the flying dust affected his chest and made him a martyr to bronchitis. They always said that some day they would retire – like us – to the sea.

Their son John was just too young for World War II but was conscripted at the end of it and drafted out to Egypt. When he was free he returned to England and to his work as a draughtsman. But a year after his return he developed a rare kidney disease and began to lose his abounding good health. The doctors could do nothing for him, and the War Office would accept no responsibility, as there had been a sufficient lapse between his discharge and the onset of the complaint for them to deny liability. Aware that he was dying, Evelyn put the situation to her boss at Lewis's, saying that she had worked there for twenty-four years and could not afford to miss her pension, due when she had been there twenty-five. Her boss told her to take six months off to nurse her son. Which she did. And when he died she went back to Lewis's to work out the final year. When it came to settling her pension she was summoned before the board of the company and told that, alas, although she had worked the full length of time, because there had been a break in the time, company rules made her ineligible for a pension. So she got no pension at all.

I do not know if Lord Woolton, who by then was owner of Lewis's, ever heard of this case, but I hope that whoever was responsible for that decision rots in Hell.

A few years later Arthur died, but when I came to meet her again, Evelyn was in her mid-seventies, a cheerful, God-fearing, church-going, hard-working widow – her life in ruins behind her but not a trace of bitterness in her disposition. She lived from hand to mouth, helping other people, respectable, a lady of some small dignity. She had never owed a penny that she hadn't repaid, never, I'm sure, committed a mean act or a petty one. Her main concern was that when she died she would leave enough money behind for a proper funeral. This in fact occurred recently.

Then he that patiently wants burden bears
No burden bears,
But is a King, a King.

13

Chapter Two

My brother went to the Hulme Grammar School and I was destined for the Manchester Grammar, but at seven I got meningitis, and when I began to recover the doctor said, 'Don't worry about schooling, just concentrate on keeping him alive.' So I was sent to Longsight Grammar School, which had moved into a vast house in Victoria Park and therefore was only five minutes' walk away. I hated it.

Whether such schools could exist today, with the Department for Education maintaining a supervisory interest, I don't know. It was presided over by an extremely brilliant, extremely religious, extremely eccentric clergyman called Arthur Frederick Fryer who ran the school almost on his own, with the aid of his wife, a couple of women teachers, another man whose name I can't remember – only his nickname, Snowball – and a couple of masters who came in occasionally.

Running the school was almost literally true of A. F. Fryer. My memories of him seem chiefly to consist of seeing him in flight from one place to another, mortar board perilously perched, gown fluttering like the Witch of Endor. He was also immensely kind when his poisonous little charges gave him the opportunity to be. At the annual school concert the school song ended on a very high note, and each year someone screamed his way well above the others. It was darkly whispered among small boys that Old Fryer was responsible.

Teaching at the school was chaotic but moderately sound – the bright sparks came to the surface, the dullards sank without trace. I was a bright spark and floated upwards easily enough without having to exert myself. I won prizes every year – not because of any supreme cleverness on my part, but because the competition was so mediocre. The only reason I can imagine people sent their children to Longsight Grammar was because it was fee-paying and because it carried some small cachet by being both a grammar school and 'within the Park'. Or because of proximity – as in my case.

I was taken to meet the high master of the Manchester Grammar School – a man called Paton – and was accepted for the school, but then pneumonia arrived, the doctor told my parents I would not live the night, and, when I did, they decided to play safe and not commit me to a three-mile trip in all weathers, half of it walking, twice a day. So I stayed where I was.

The fact that I hated school need not be taken in itself as a criticism of the school I went to. I would have hated any school. Many years later it dawned on me, looking back over the evidence, that my mother badly wanted a girl when I was born, and although she mostly disguised her feelings she would dearly have loved to dress me up in buttons and bows. When it turned out that I was 'delicate' – unlike my brother, who ailed nothing – she was able to sublimate her mixed feelings on my mistaken gender by lavishing every care and attention on me, guarding me against every chill or ill, ministering to my every want. So I was a spoiled brat. She even somehow delayed sending me to school until I was seven; but when I did go I did not at all care for the new and abrasive life it offered me.

My mother was a very strong character. Even when I criticize her I never forget her many sterling qualities. She was a faithful and loyal wife, a devoted mother, generous and guardedly warm-hearted, struggling always with debility rather than real ill-health, a singularly *pure* woman – as indeed my father was pure. (I have written a little about them in a short story called 'The Island'.) It was not so much that they didn't see the evils of life as that they chose to ignore them. Both born and brought up in Victorian times, they seem to exemplify so much that was best in that age. They believed in English liberal democracy, and in the perfectibility of man. My home was always warm and sheltering.

Loving too, but in a very undemonstrative way. Kissing was almost unknown – as indeed was praise. Praise might make you get above yourself, and that would *never* do. Self-esteem was the cardinal sin. '*Side*', as we called it. It's ingrained in me even today.

I remember when I was about nine finding my mother in tears because of the racking uncertainty of having her eldest son in the trenches and liable to be killed or maimed at any time. My father said: 'Go and comfort your mother.' I went across and perched on the arm of her chair, and kissed her and stroked her face. I did this willingly and sympathetically, but I was horribly embarrassed in the act. It wasn't quite the sort of thing that happened in our family. We loved, but we didn't demonstrate our love.

Despite her virtues, my mother, as the custodian of a highly strung, oversensitive and over-imaginative child, had a number of signal disadvantages. She loved to make your flesh creep – and God, did she not make mine! It was not of ghosts of which she spoke but of *ill-health*. Her brilliant china-blue eyes would focus on you when she told you for the tenth time about her cousin Ernest, who went to a danceand, coming home in the train, when still very hot from his exertions, gave up his seat to a lady and stood with his back to the open window. He was dead within a week, of pneumonia. And of his brother Henry who died the following year from the same thing: they were twenty-one and twenty-two. And of Cousin Essie, who when playing in the garden used to say to my mother, 'Feel my heart, cousin, feel how it beats so fast.' And she too died, at nineteen. Speaking of our doctor, that eminent man who when much younger had saved my grandmother by taking her off the bottle, she would say to some visiting friend, 'Of course our doctor, Dr Scotson, is a very good man, but' – in lowered voice but never too low for me to hear – 'far too fond of the *knife*.' Her attitude to me was embodied in the words: 'Wrap up, Winston', 'Take a scarf, Winston', 'Put your other coat on, it's a nasty east wind', etc., etc., *da capo*.

Of course there was some reason for the concern. For a year after my bout of meningitis I would start screaming in the middle of the night, and my father would pick me up and carry me about the room, eyes open, still screaming, but not awake. I had the most ghastly dreams, some of which I could recall even into middle life. There is one I still remember about breaking knuckles. For most of my early youth if I ran fifty yards I would begin to cough like a broken cab horse. After the lightest, most casual rough and tumble with a friend I would feel sick for an hour. Although naturally high-spirited, all this was a constant brake on high spirits, so that I often appeared even more reserved and more shy than I actually wanted to be.

Not that I didn't have friends. I was not unpopular at school – except with a few hearty oafs – and had my own coterie of four or five boys, with whom I had a lot of fun. Also there were another four or five, who lived in Curzon Avenue but did not go to Longsight Grammar School, who formed another circle of which I was the sort-of leading spirit. *Never* the leading spirit when it came to any kind of athletic prowess, but almost always so in other things. I used to read some book of adventure and then they would sit round in a circle while I retold them the story – this often at great length. They would shout with annoyance if I tried to break off too soon. They adopted names I invented and games I devised.

A few girls used to be about too, though they were never part of the group. I remember kissing Hilda Carter fifty-four times in one day, which was considered a world record. But it was all very matter of fact, and she didn't seem to mind.

What was not matter of fact was a meeting with a girl called Amy Warwick in Morecambe when I was thirteen. It took me five years to get over that. I think it was Edith Wharton who wrote somewhere: 'One good heartbreak will provide the novelist with a succession of different novels, and the poet with any number of sonnets and lyric poems, but he *must* have a heart that can break.'

The last two or three years at school were not so dislikeable. Freed of the necessity of making a new life in a new and better school, I continued to coast along, doing just enough work to come top, growing much taller and a *bit* stronger, senior to the majority of the chaps in the school, and eventually a prefect. The number in my class lessening until there were only seven, avoiding school sports but taking up tennis; it was not such an agony turning out every day. All the same, the tuition was eccentric and sometimes inefficient.

But in the early school years, alongside my many genuine ailments were psychosomatic indispositions fostered by my dislike of school and the fact that on a day-school basis one could have a day off or even a morning off without too much difficulty. Compare the horrors of an early breakfast, a five-minute tramp through the rain, an uncongenial desk and an uncongenial task with a group of fairly uncongenial boys, an irascible master or mistress, scribbling in exercise books, learning verses from the Bible or from poetry, struggling with French, then wild affrays in the passages and all the other undesirable moments in a tedious and tiring day – compare it to a day at home: reading over a more leisurely breakfast, reading in the lavatory, reading in the dining room in a comfortable armchair before a blazing fire, reading over dinner, reading in the afternoon, reading over supper, reading in bed – the only discomfort being that I didn't know what prep I should have been doing for the following day. It's little wonder that a feverish headache or a bout of morning vomiting occurred too often to be true.

I saw little of my father at these times – he was away in the mornings before I woke – but my mother, though she no doubt suspected part of my ailments were sham, could never be absolutely sure the symptoms were not the onset of some dire genuine illness, and it was very much in her nature to pamper her children anyhow.

Perhaps she comfortably argued that I was 'educating myself'. It was partly true. My parents didn't have a big collection of books: a few novels, Dickens, Thackeray, Lytton, some good general books on such things as Evolution, Botany, and Astronomy; but above all there was a ten-volume 'New Edition' of *Chambers' Encyclopedia*. This was a goldmine. I read the volumes endlessly, hopping from one subject to another like a honey-drunk bee. They opened new worlds for me.

But in addition to these I had a daily diet of 'comics' – six a week – and when a lending library was discovered I was able to borrow sensational novels which I lapped up at a phenomenal rate, thereby debasing my taste. I remember winning a handsomely bound Walter Scott novel – *The Talisman* – as a prize and making a great effort on it but finding it completely unreadable. Perhaps there really is a trace of the philistine in me, for I have not read it even yet.

When I met Sybille Bedford for the first time a few years ago, in addition to congratulating her on her magnificent books, including her just published and semi-autobiographical novel *Jigsaw*, I said how bitterly, bitterly I envied her her childhood. 'Why?' she said. 'It was not particularly happy.' 'I know,' I said, 'but it was so *rich* in every sort of literary and artistic influence. You lived and breathed in a world where great literature came more naturally to you than the daily paper. In spite of all your vicissitudes, shortage of money, treks across Europe and the rest, everything was put before you, in art, in music, in writing. You accepted the best because you knew no other.'

It must be said, though, that in my early writing years I remember being thankful not to have been to a university, where one was taught to have the opinions of one's mentors. (Surely F. R. Leavis's unforgivable sin was teaching the young to sneer.)
   Instead I came in wading through the trash, picking my own path, making my own discoveries and choices which for better or worse were not imposed from without.

But one of the greatest drawbacks in not going to a university, though I did not realize it then, was not in missing the tuition but in not meeting students of my own age, of like or different opinion (on whom I could sharpen my own mind), and of making friendships which would last all through the years.

In my early twenties I was invited, with two others, under the auspices of the WEA, to go to a summer school being held at Wadham College, Oxford. As an introductory task, I was invited to write an essay on Charles Morgan's *The Fountain*, which was a book greatly admired by the critics. I wrote an essay so adverse that I was not at all popular with my tutors when I got there. So maybe some contrariness in my nature might have enabled me to preserve an independent judgement anyhow.

Saturday the 8th of August 1914 was a warm summery day, but towards noon the sky clouded over and it was beginning to rain, as it sometimes does in Manchester.

I had wandered in from outside; my mother was in the kitchen with the maid, so I went into the drawing room. This was unoccupied – only the piano looked tempting; but I went back into the hall and thence to the dining room. My father, sober and grave, was standing on one side of the fireplace and my brother, rosy cheeks and eyes glinting, was on the other. They were discussing an event which had occurred the previous Tuesday; Britain, in defence of Belgium, had declared war on Germany.

I remember exactly what my brother excitedly said as I came in. 'It'll be a regular flare up!' My father gravely shook his head. But neither of them dreamed that my brother would eventually grow to be old enough to be drawn in. When he was, in late 1917, he was drafted into the South Wales Borderers and began his training at Kinmel Park, North Wales. It was known locally as Kill'em Park, because of the dozens of young men who died there from pneumonia and allied diseases before they got anywhere near a German. I remember going to see him once, trailing with my mother across what seemed like miles to a great flat camp where he appeared abruptly at the door of a wooden hut, pale and suddenly thin and with an appalling cough.

Later he was transferred to Newmarket, and in the early spring of 1918 was sent to France. People said to my mother, 'Oh, they won't put him in the firing line – they'll keep him in the rear, he's far too young.' In fact he went straight in and was in the thick of the great Ludendorff Offensive that sent the Allies reeling and prompted Haig's famous 'Backs to the Wall' message. One day my mother got a telegram from the War Office. With terrified fingers she fumbled it open to see that her lance corporal son had been 'wounded but remained on duty'. In fact a shell splinter had cut his face just below the eye. Had it been an inch higher it would probably have killed him and so altered not only his destiny but mine and that of scores of other people, since without his pressure we might not have moved to Cornwall. So all one's destiny is controlled and decided by the direction of a flying splinter.

In September 1918, to his family's profound relief, he was sent home to train for a commission. It was to be in the Machine Gun Corps, which was known in the army as the Suicide Club; but before he could go back to France the Armistice came.

It must all have been a shattering experience for a boy just out of school, a genteel boy who had never been away from home. I remember the maid picking the lice off his shirt when he came home. He was so inured to maiming and death that during a nine-hour German bombardment at the beginning of the Ludendorff Offensive, he sat all the time on a box of Mills bombs in a mud-filled trench listening to a solitary British gun, an eighteen-pounder, persisting with its lonely reply. His only company was two members of his platoon, and they were dead.

Yet when he himself lay dying nearly seventy years later I sat by his bed and somehow the question of the war came up, and he said: 'I wouldn't have missed it for anything.' Such is the oddity of human nature.

By the end of the war he was just twenty and his natural destination in a dishevelled civilian world would have been a position with his father at D. Mawdsley & Co. But the objections of my uncle, who had four sons coming on, blocked this, so he took a position with a firm of cotton shippers called Jones, London & Garrard, who shortly offered him a post as their chief representative in Hong Kong. It was a brilliant opportunity, with high pay and fine prospects, but he turned it down; his nine months in France had convinced him that he wanted no more travel. So he worked for the firm for several years in England in what was, because of the collapse of the Indian and Chinese markets, to become a dead-end job. As it happened, the man who went out to Hong Kong in his place was murdered, so it was not altogether an ill decision.

He soon wanted to marry, could not possibly afford to on his then salary, and my uncle had succeeded in introducing his two eldest sons into D. Mawdsley & Co.

Cecil said he owed a great debt of gratitude to Uncle Tom for his jealousy, for otherwise he would probably never have come to live in *Cornwall*. Taking a holiday there with his fiancée in September 1924, at a place he chose at random out of the *Great Western Railway Holiday Guide*, he fell instantly in love with the county and the village of Perranporth. Having got there eighteen months later, he never wanted to move again, even after he had retired, and never did move again, for all the rest of his long life.

When my father was fifty-four he took his bath one November Sunday morning, came down and sat in the drawing room to read the *Sunday Chronicle*. But after a few minutes he found he could not hold the paper; he was losing the use of his right hand and arm. Then he lost the use of his right leg. Then he lost his speech. Then he lost consciousness. Coming chattering in as a noisy schoolboy, I was stopped by the maid, who said: 'Hush, your father's ill!' I stared at her and said: 'D'you mean Mother?'

My father in my eyes was never ill. He never had been. The apostle of fitness, he used to jump gates instead of opening them. He was never known to be tired. The year before this, taking one of his regular walks with his men friends, they found on reaching the station to go home that they had walked twenty-four miles. So while waiting for the train he ran up and down the platform so that he could say he had done twenty-five.

It was a strange mixture – of this relentlessly energetic man and this delicate woman who was always tired and had no stamina at all. (Perhaps I am a fair mix of the two.) If he ever felt impatient with her he never for a second showed it. Nothing was too good for her, nothing too much trouble. If there was ever impatience in his heart it showed only with his sons – much more particularly towards me, whom his wife was bringing up as a mollycoddle. For, except with my mother, he was not really a sensitive man. When he took Cecil to an indoor swimming pool for the first time he told him to jump in at the deep end and he'd paddle his way easily back to safety. Instead Cecil was hauled out half-drowned, and as a result never learned to swim in his life.

During my childhood and early youth I saw my father only at weekends and sometimes briefly in the evenings, and his attitude towards me always seemed to be one of abruptness and slight disparagement. When I was thirteen I went down with lobar pneumonia, and the doctor, finding me unable even to cough, warned my parents that I was not likely to live the night. In the bedroom, after he had gone, my father rounded on my mother, blaming her bitterly for allowing me to go back to school when I hadn't properly recovered from influenza. I remember listening to this and thinking: 'Good Lord, he's *fond* of me!'

On that sad Sunday morning when *he* was taken ill they sent a maid hurrying for the doctor. Our own doctor was out, so another man came. He made a brief examination, lifted my father's eyelid, and shook his head. He left a note at our own doctor's, saying his patient would be dead before nightfall.

But the patient did not die. Instead a bed was brought down to the drawing room and a day nurse and a night nurse were engaged. These women were stiff and starched and demanding. The night nurse's first insistence was that our new drawing-room carpet must be washed with carbolic soap. For six months they ruled the house while my father climbed slowly back to life and, to the doctor's astonishment and delight, began to move his right arm and leg again. Presently he was able to go out in a wheelchair, then to walk with a stick – a few steps, and ever a few steps further. But physically he was a ruined man, and such had been the damage to his brain that he began to have fits – sometimes twice a month, sometimes at longer intervals. In them he would go purple and grey, and as the fit reached its climax he would scream at the top of his voice. No sedative was able to cure or prevent them. Sometimes a handkerchief tied and tightened around the right arm would check them and the attack would pass off with only a brief aguelike shaking.

It was at this early stage of his convalescence that we bought a wheelchair, which he could steer by means of a long iron handle at the front, and during the first summer holidays I used to push him as far as Birch Park where, on a quiet afternoon, he would get out and sit on a park seat, sometimes chatting – so far as he was able – with a friend. During these peaceful interludes I raised his ire more than once by standing on the chair, steering with the bar and

23

pushing with the other leg. This way one could get up a fine turn of speed and go careering round the park paths with the wheelchair going backwards.

It was the following summer that I went with my parents for a prolonged stay at Morecambe. My father by then could walk short distances with a stick; we stayed at a small hotel at the end of Regent Road and walked every morning to the front, on to the pier and along to its end where every day a concert party called 'Jack Audley's Varieties' performed. No doubt a more adventurous boy would have struck out on his own, but, apart from absenting myself when there was a rough sea to watch – and sometimes the sea can be spectacularly rough there – I went along and listened and, of course, read. Because the concert party was not geared to people staying more than two weeks the programmes repeated fairly frequently, so that in the end I could, without conscious effort, remember and sing, with all the words, their entire repertoire. Even today I can remember twenty songs, and when my children were young I would sometimes entertain them with these. Reference was then sometimes made to 'Daddy's music-hall days'. Alas, all my music-hall days were spent reclining in a deckchair.

Of course after his illness my father was quite incapable of any form of work, and within four months my Uncle Tom called to say regretfully that the firm could no longer afford to pay his salary. I listened, convinced that destitution stared us in the face, not knowing that my father for years had taken a derisory salary in order to bolster the profits of the firm, of which my mother, being a partner with her two brothers, took a third share.

Tom's eldest son, the younger Tom, whom I much liked, presently joined the firm. Young Tom was a very strange character (an extreme example of the kind of eccentric the Mawdsley family occasionally throws up): an intellectual, a lover of music and the arts, a dilettante, and a neurotic. Like his three brothers he was brought up under the iron hand of his irritable, ill-tempered, jolly, uncultured, weathercock of a father, and when the boys were at home they did everything they were told, exactly as they were told, and no questions asked. (My mother said they crept around the

24

house like white mice.) May, *their* mother, was an easygoing, even-tempered but astute woman who alone knew how to manage Tom senior. The boys, when they possibly could, kept out of his way.

But young Tom, although he did not marry and continued to live at home, developed a life of his own, joined the Manchester Athenaeum, went to concerts and read widely. In a way he was a sad young man – and there are many such about – a person with a passion for culture and no creative talent at all. At the age of twenty-four, having read deeply in psychiatry, he went to an analyst and for the rest of his short life visited him five times a week. In the mid-Thirties he began to take an active interest in the persecution of the Jews in Hitler's Germany and Austria, and by various contrivances – such as finding or inventing jobs for them in the firm – was able to get a half-dozen of them to the safety of England. Because of his work in this field he convinced himself that he was a marked man whose name would be in the Nazi Black Book, which would condemn him to a concentration camp if Hitler were to win the war. When France collapsed and the British army straggled back weaponless from Dunkirk, Tom thought the war lost and committed suicide by jumping from a third-floor window of the warehouse. He left a note saying: 'I have died for democracy.'

The second son, Harry, was much more normal, a typical thrusting unintellectual North Country good-timer, good-looking and a smart dresser. He would probably have done well in the firm and for the firm, but decided one fine June morning to drive with a friend to Wimbledon in his new Riley. At five o'clock in the morning, racing along the empty roads, they met a bus on the wrong side of the road, the driver having gone to sleep. Both young men were killed instantly.

Tom's youngest son, Denis, was eventually drafted in to the firm, so fortunately it remained a family concern.

Chapter Three

The year I was to be fourteen, after I had been seriously ill with pneumonia, my mother had double pneumonia and also nearly died. I remember being sent to the cinema one night when she was gravely ill. When I got back, having separated from my friend Ernest Emery at the gate, I looked up and saw the front bedroom bay windows in darkness. This was where my mother was. I crept up the path and peered in at the drawing-room window where there was a light, and saw my crippled father sitting in conversation with the nurse and the doctor. Their faces were all grave, and I thought all was lost. If my mother was dead it was the end of the world for me. All mothers at the age I was then are no doubt dearly precious, but my own mother, in her love for me, had kept me so close that I could see no future for myself without her. I have long thought that psychologically her attitude was a terrible blunder; but if one assesses the outcome I suppose it cannot be criticized too drastically. (What is it that makes an author?)

Anyway, that night I was afraid to go in to the house, so fell on my knees, the doormat scratching them, to pray to a God I had never properly been introduced to that she was still alive – that somehow she was still alive. When eventually I summoned the courage to go in I discovered that my mother was dozing and the doctor and the nurse had turned the gas down and come downstairs to discuss the situation with my father. I should have learned from that that the imagination – my imagination – can always put two and two together and make six. It has been doing so ever since.

All this made my parents ready for a move. My mother with catarrh all the year and bronchitis every winter because of the 'dampness' of Victoria Park; my father a restive, frustrated cripple still only in his mid-fifties but forcibly retired by ill-health; and now my near-death and hers – there was nothing any longer to keep us in Manchester. The idea was to move to Southport, or perhaps to St Anne's, which is the better, residential end of Blackpool, and which they knew suited my mother's health. Together they could find a pleasant bungalow and face a long retirement. But behold my brother, frustrated beyond measure in his dead-end job, desperately wanting to marry, and now, suddenly, totally besotted in his desire to live in Cornwall. He didn't mind *what* he did, however menial, so long as it was in Cornwall.

So in September 1925 we all took a holiday in Perranporth – Cecil's fiancée Elsie with us – and stayed at the Tywarnhayle Hotel for two weeks, in the little undeveloped village with its fantastic cliff formations – mostly man-made, by miners seeking tin – and its three miles of golden sands and its apparently balmy climate. The whole family saw the light and was converted. Cecil and Elsie desperately sought opinions of the possibility of work in the district or some opening that they might jointly or individually seize on. There was nothing. Simply nothing. As many have found before them, and since.

But eventually it became evident that opening a shop catering for the villagers in one form or another might provide an opportunity. It was an acknowledged fact that almost all the people in the village went to Truro on Wednesdays for market day and did all their real shopping there. In Perranporth there was a big grocer's called The Red House which, although badly run, was surely going to prosper in due time. There was a corner shop opposite run by a man called Samuel Harvey Mitchell, which in its small way sold everything from paraffin to Cornish cream; one or two other small village shops, old-fashioned in habit and long-established, and a group of wooden huts on the way to the promenade in which you could buy newspapers, toys, sweets and some primitive beach equipment. But in the newly developing part of the village, overlooking the recently opened Boscawen Park and boating lake, a chemist called Polgreen had recently built a fine-looking house and shop, next to which was a solitary plot of land as yet unsold and undeveloped. There would be no more shops built beyond.

It still startles me to think what happened in two weeks. In that time a builder called Healey, owner of the plot and of the Red House, and the father of Donald Healey, the only man in the last fifty years to give his name to a British-designed and built motor car, had been approached, a sketch plan produced by his architect, Pitkeathley, and discussed and amended and agreed, and the deal done, for the building of a similar shop and premises to the Polgreens'. So far nobody had any firm idea as to what *sort* of shop it was going to be, but opinion in the village was earnestly canvassed, and a decision was precipitately taken, that what was most lacking in Perranporth was a go-ahead ladies' and gentlemen's outfitters. Elsie was clever with her needle but knew nothing more of the business than that, having worked in an insurance office. Cecil was good at figures but knew nothing more of the retail business either. Within the last three days of our stay my parents found a furnished bungalow on rising ground 300 yards from the proposed shop, and took it for twelve months from the 1st of November.

Thereupon everyone returned in triumph to Manchester where, burdened with a sick husband and still as delicate as ever herself, my mother set about leaving all her friends, selling up all our furniture and effects and moving 300 miles to a new life in the depths of an unknown Celtic county by the sea.

The decision was made to sell everything, even to pots and pans and pictures and beds and brooms and baking tins – retaining only the piano, a bookcase full of books and our silver and china, personal clothing and effects.

I don't remember much of that time except the wrench of selling many things we had grown attached to. We were leaving other things behind, apart from friends. After his stroke, my father had a ragingly high blood pressure, and in those days there were no pills to control it. In a desperate clutch at anything, anything to make him better, he had taken first to Christian Science, in which his gentle brother-in-law Dan had long been a believer, and then to spiritualism. Seances were held at our house at which a young medium while under the 'control' of one of her spirits would massage my father's arm and leg, trying to bring back the muscle strength. One has to record that she was the first person to make him walk across the room without a stick, and in the nine months under her care he never had a fit. Later it was whispered that she had been exposed as a fraud. I can only speak of the improvement she brought in him and the fact that she refused any payment for her visits.

We must have seemed a strange crew arriving in that Cornish village where most people were still Cornish and new blood from up-country was then mercifully rare – I and my parents in the October, my brother and sister-in-law, newly married, the following April. We were semi-genteel, middle-middle-class, rather modest and retiring but with an underlying sense of position. This was particularly so in my mother's case, who never forgot that she had been Miss Anne Mawdsley. It scarcely existed in my brother, who was the most un-class-conscious person I have ever met. I was not far behind – at that time – being almost totally unaware that there were people either superior or inferior to myself.

I remember saying to a woman called Dorothy Hunt, whose bungalow we eventually bought: 'It's a bit difficult among all these new faces. I can't remember who I'm supposed to know and who I'm not supposed to know.' She said stiffly: 'I think the Cornish are just as good as we are, so there's no reason to pick and choose one's friends.' I stared at her in total astonishment. I suppose I could have phrased it better, making it clear that I was talking solely about recognition, since in a city one would have looked a damned fool saying good afternoon to everyone one passed. But the idea that 'supposed to know' implied some sort of social discrimination was utterly foreign to me.

Maybe at that time I was a bit of a *literary* snob – though snob is the wrong word. I had virtually nothing whatever to contribute to ordinary gossipy family chat, but if books were mentioned I came awake. So far as the company I kept was concerned, it might be said that although I had no great opinion of my own literary abilities, I had less of theirs.

From the very earliest days I had wanted to write. At the age of five I dictated a story to my mother which began: "Oh, look," said

Tom to his mother, "There is a dead man on the doorstep!" That was as far as the story went. I can't remember whether it was inspiration that dried up first or my mother's patience. I won a special essay prize, open to a number of schools, the subject being 'The Horrors of War'. It was my first meeting, aged ten, with the high master of the Manchester Grammar School, Mr Paton, who had helped to judge and who presented the prize. He made the now-expected joke about my Christian name, since by then my namesake had become famous. There was an occasion when our doctor came to see me and, being in a rarely jovial mood, stuck his stethoscope on the end of my nose and said: 'I hope you're not capable of a terminological inexactitude.' It was shortly after Winston Churchill in the Commons had declared that some statement of the Opposition was 'A lie!' and had been told by the Speaker that this was not parliamentary language; so he had amended it.

Actually I was better at maths than literature, disgustingly inept at foreign languages – which would have been so useful in later life – and good at most other things. When it was finally decided I was not strong enough to face the rigours of the journey to and from Manchester Grammar School, my father went to see the headmaster of the Long-sight Grammar School and asked him what he thought I might be likely to do well at. The head replied, 'He'll succeed at anything he sets his mind to.'

I don't know how true that was, but certainly my mother must have had an inordinate belief in the abilities of her ewe lamb. Of course it suited her to have me living at home; and probably she felt if the worst came to the worst she could buy me a bookshop somewhere where I could marry and live out my life comfortably enough. And of course it suited me just as marvellously to live at home and not to be dependent on my earnings for the bare essentials.

In the liverish eye of my relatives I was something of a drip. Since school, when I had appeared so 'clever', I had seemed to go to seed. I sharpened up to play tennis or go on the beach or tramp the cliffs or go to the cinema or in pursuit of a girl, but I did not seem interested in any gainful occupation. I got up very late in the mornings and stayed up very late at night. (Kinder to reverse the description of this routine, one being the outcome of the other.) Since, in the house my parents bought in Cornwall, we had no electricity, this meant reading or studying by 'Aladdin' lamps, or by one candle only in the bedroom, and not infrequently I would read till 3 a.m. My eyes did not have so much demanded of them again until the war, when as a coastguard I would illegally read – usually poetry – by the light of a torch.

I can understand how very irritating it must have been to my father – an intensely practical man who, though with musical leanings, was wholly wedded to the business ethic – to have this tall, thin, frequently jolly, but frail, drooping, sometimes ungracious son, who had no real ambition – no ambition at least that was realizable – and spent most of the day with his nose in a book. And who, through indifferent health and his mother's pampering, was such a disappointment.

Many snide remarks came my way from outside, and my sister-in-law never missed an opportunity to point out to my mother, after my father died, what a useless member of society I was becoming.

In his first two years in Cornwall my father recovered sufficiently to be able to take long walks, to play bridge, to write with his left hand and to do a little gardening. On his last birthday he wrote to his mother: 'My dear Mother, Sixty! I can hardly believe it!' I had had no real idea how old he was, but it so happened that he left the letter open on the writing table, and, going for an envelope, I inadvertently saw it. I had supposed him somewhere in his mid-fifties, and sixty – to an eighteen-year-old – seemed immensely aged.

That same year, on a November afternoon, six years almost to the day after his first stroke, a lady at the door roused me from sleep – I had nodded off to sleep with my head on the page of the novel I was trying to write – to say that my father was ill in the garden. I hurried out, hoping it was just another fit, but it soon became clear that this was a second stroke – this time it had affected the whole of his left side. We got him to bed somehow. He could not speak or move at all, only his weakened right hand endlessly flexed and unflexed, as he had got into the habit of doing to try to strengthen it; that, and a fluttering of one eye.

'Can you hear me, Father?' I would say, and he would wink. It was the only communication left. He died a week later, survived by his eighty-five-year-old mother in Blackburn. Life is not kind – nor is it in any way even-handed. At sixty I was at the peak of my career, though already burdened with a wife crippled in just the same way as my father had been. Happily 'burden' simply does not apply to her; but living with a handicap and living under threat is not conducive to high spirits. She was a miracle. Always optimistic, even when first paralysed, always cheerful, always loving.

At that time, the time of my father's death, and for a long while before and after it, I was appallingly shy of telling anyone I wanted to be a writer, fearing total ridicule – which such a statement would probably have received. The year before he died I had bitterly offended him because he suddenly said to me one day: 'When's your novel going to be finished?' It was the first time he had ever *mentioned* the subject. I replied: 'Oh, this year, next year, sometime, never.' It was a rude and unworthy reply, but I was only just turned eighteen and he spoke with what the French call *pudeur*, as if he were lifting the corner on some distinctly disreputable occupation. I curled up inside *instantly*, like a prodded snail, and those were the only words I could think to say.

The idea that I should ever make a *living* out of such scribblings seemed derisory. And it probably was. I lived a quiet, unadventurous, retired life when, if I really meant to succeed at this strange profession, I should have been plunging into all aspects of living with the gusto and the enterprise of an explorer. Once when Somerset Maugham was asked by an anxious American mother how she could best help her son, who wanted to be a writer, he replied: 'Give him five thousand dollars and tell him to go to the devil.' This advice no doubt would have been appropriate for me.

I did not know a single author, however insignificant, or publisher, however small-time, and I don't think I knew that people called agents existed.

My first full novel, after a long and arduous struggle with an earlier book, got itself written when I was twenty-one. It took me ten weeks – then I retired to bed with complete exhaustion and a stomach complaint. Later I typed the book and sent it to a publisher, who returned it within two weeks with a rejection slip. I then fired it at another, who kept it a month. Then I sent it to Hodder & Stoughton, who kept it five months before sending it back saying the book had distinct promise but wasn't quite strong enough for their list, but if I wrote a second they would like to consider it. Heartened and encouraged, I shoved the first novel away in a drawer and began my second. When this was finally finished I sent it away in great hope, whereupon Hodder & Stoughton returned it with a conventional rejection slip.

I had now been writing for five years and had virtually nothing to show for it. Surely mine was a pipe dream, as everyone else thought and knew and had been trying to tell me for ages? Why didn't I wake up and stir myself and get some regular decent honest work? I was untrained for any profession, but I could surely turn my hand to something practical and realizable.

About this time, having written two unpublishable novels, I found myself involved in amateur theatricals in the village Women's Institute. I acted in one or two small pieces, and at once it struck me how perfectly frightful the dialogue was, and how equally awful the contrived events and denouements. So, while keeping the titles and the general storylines, I began to rewrite the pieces and found the audience most happily responding. The authors got their minute royalties, and we got the laughs.

Just then there was a popular movement to raise money for the unemployed, and someone, interested in what I'd done, said why didn't I write a three-act play and it could be put on at the local cinema for this good cause. So I sat down and wrote a play in six weeks, called it *Seven Suspected*, and this was eventually produced and played to a full and appreciative house for three nights. It was never printed, but copies circulated in typescript, and it was produced in Truro, Camborne, Hayle, Bury, Hendon and elsewhere, always with great success. Looking back, one particular feature strikes me – hardly a line had to be altered from the first draft. When one thinks of authors writing and rewriting scenes endlessly until the moment of first production, this seems preposterous. Of

33

course it was only played by amateurs, who probably didn't know any better, but every line was *speakable*, and when actors found their lines producing laughs they didn't want to change them.

Coincident with this, there appeared on the horizon a Captain and Mrs Craddock, who had taken a house for six months in St Agnes. She was actually a *real, live authoress* and had *published novels* – *many novels* – under her maiden name of Elizabeth Carfrae. A great and important person indeed! She was taken up and lionized by what passed in the district for society, and she heard of my play and helped with its production and was generally very kind and generous to me. When she knew I had written a novel she asked to see it and sent it up with a note to her agent, J. B. Pinker, who had it read and sent it back, saying he did not think he could place it.

At the end of the six months the Craddocks abruptly departed, leaving unpaid bills everywhere, and were never heard of again. It is a characteristic of some authors which I have always determined to avoid. She was published by Mills & Boon, and nowadays we all know about them: 'not lit., my dear, but Romance with a capital R!' I shouldn't have minded. Indeed I should have been delighted to be published by anyone.

I have always valued her kindness in trying to help me.

In all this my mother took little part. She enjoyed her bridge and my company and my chauffeuring her around. She virtually took no sides in the opinion war. I do not know, and now I shall never know, how much she believed in my ability. (Oh, she believed *tremendously* in my ability – was I not her son? – but I mean my ability to make a *living* out of writing.) She was a great one for taking the easy way, for postponing the awkward encounter, for letting things be. She had a son at home – she could just afford to keep him and herself in a pleasant degree of comfort: why should she thrust me out to make a sort of living in some uncongenial job or – even more to be deplored – push me off to live among the vice-ridden streets of London, to sink or swim, as many better men had done?

But although she was unkind enough to pass on the occasional sneer, she never personally interfered nor enquired in a way which would cause embarrassment to me. I was my own man. It was a comfortable life for us both – a million miles too comfortable for me.

I am happy she lived just long enough to see the first explosions of success.

My father's younger sister, Mollie, was unmarried, deeply romantic and intense about everything. She was enraptured to learn that one of her nephews wanted to be a writer. She and my parents must have discussed me at length on many occasions, but I never knew the substance of the talks. Anyway, her approach to me was much more tactful than her brother's, and although I must have been as tight as a crab so far as my own writing was concerned we did have endless talks about literature and about writing in general. She was an aspirant and failed writer of children's stories herself. Whether she believed any more than my father in an ultimate commercial success for me I know not, but she encouraged me in every way she could. In the end I let her read my first novel. I cannot remember whether she said she liked the book when she read it – she was always fiercely candid – but she declared passionately that it was quite wrong to keep it stuffed in a drawer and that it must be tried on other publishers. She persuaded me to retype a few pages that were dog-eared and then lovingly bound it into two volumes, with stitched sheets and cardboard sides so that it opened easily and looked like a book. I sent it off to Messrs. Ward, Lock & Co. Ltd.

Until now I had submitted the typescript to those publishers who published the sort of books I liked to read. This was particularly so of Hodder, who published John Buchan and A. E. W. Mason and Eric Ambler and 'Sapper' and Philip Oppenheim and Dornford Yates, etc., etc. It cannot be said honestly that I liked Ward, Lock books. They were a grade lower down the scale, and, looking them over in a bookshop once, I thought, 'Surely my book is better than some of these!' What I didn't know at the time was that Ward, Lock had started off many famous writers and then, through editorial inadequacy or failure of their publicity department or the meanness of their directors, had allowed them to slip away to more fashionable publishers who proceeded to cash in.

Ward, Lock kept the book seven months, then accepted it. I remember it was the 10th of May and I was in bed with a filthy sore throat. Within two hours of receiving the letter the sore throat had disappeared. I showed the letter to my mother, who looked pleased and startled and ultimately delighted.

The letter from Ward, Lock just said they were sorry for such a long delay but after due consideration they had decided to publish my novel 'on a 10% basis', provided I would agree to toning down one or two scenes in the book, which they said was so exciting that they felt it was not necessary to 'out-Herod Herod in the details'. The letter was signed S. E. Sarcoe. It goes without saying that I agreed to the small amendments. This was the only editing of the typescript that they ever suggested; otherwise it came out exactly as it was put in.

Incidentally, the contract, when it came for me to sign, was only a page and a half in length, and, apart from the fact that it offered me no advance on account of royalties and no increase on the 10% of the published price with increased sales, it was a model of simplicity and generosity. All rights, except for a few small ones, were expressly reserved to the author. No modern publisher would offer such an unworldly contract.

When the news got around in the village it was a sensation. A few still wouldn't quite believe it until they saw the published book – and one relative was frankly doubting that it would ever come out at all. But most people thought my fortune was made. Our local dentist – an educated Londoner – made calculations of the sales the book must have if merely every branch of Boots' Library took one. (He was clearly ignorant that the practice of Boots' Library – like that of most libraries – was to buy a couple of dozen copies and send them around where there was a request for them; so you put your name down and waited until one came free.) It was a bad time for new novelists – I have never known it not – but perhaps it was specially bad with Hitler beginning his long tramp to menace the peace of the world.

The book, *The House with the Stained-Glass Windows*, was accepted in May and published in October. In between I went up to

London and met my new publishers in their substantial building in Salisbury Square, EC4. Ward, Lock was an old-established firm, well known for publishing cook books – including Mrs Beeton – and a vast selection of excellent guides. These were the bread and butter. Fiction was a sideline but a substantial one. They also published the *Windsor Magazine* which, after the *Strand*, was the most important monthly magazine of the day. I met my correspondent, Mr S. E. Sarcoe, who was the editor-in-chief, a cheerful, fast-talking, fast-moving, middle-aged man, whose lips seemed to get in the way of his words, a down-to-earth, no-nonsense, friendly man who knew a very great deal about commercial publishing but whose literary tastes didn't exactly reach the stratosphere. He was delighted to know I had 'almost finished' a second novel (a heart-warming reaction for me) but he startled me by saying that they wanted two novels a year from me. There was 'not much money' in writing, but what there was could chiefly be earned by regular and constant output. They would like the second book by November, ready for next April, and preferably one the following May.

After that I met Wilfred Lock, the chairman of the company and virtually the dictator. He was a strange small man who was never away from the office and had his eye on everything. He had a very disconcerting habit when you met him of falling completely silent and then, when you volunteered something, *immediately* interrupting with a remark of his own. I have never met anyone else with this strange off-putting gift. Was it deliberate, I wondered sometimes? How else could he always have something ready to say within two seconds of your beginning to speak?

He greeted me with agreeable detachment and was pleased to learn that for the moment I did not have to depend on my earnings for every crust. Financially speaking, he said more than once, he always looked on novel-writing as a stick to walk with but never a crutch.

Naturally, from the moment that Ward, Lock decided to publish me, my view of their output drastically changed, and I found out all sorts of new virtues in their list. I felt myself lucky to be taken up by such a substantial and old-established firm. And, by God, I was!

They were London-based, had a fair number of reps (commercial travellers in those days), a high standard of book production, an office in Melbourne and agents in all the 'Colonial' territories. When my book was published it came out with handsome advertisements in the heavy Sunday papers and the best dailies, and it received a fair amount of notice from reviewers.

Even now I'm not sure if I appreciate how extraordinarily fortunate I was – for I now regard this first novel as amateurish, derivative (how could it be anything else?) and sloppily written. The one thing it did have, I suppose, was immense story-telling drive, and if you could believe the story it would grip you to the last page. Had I been a publisher I would certainly have rejected it.

The reviews on the whole were kind, perhaps too kind. Robert Lynd in the *News Chronicle* headed his solus review 'Wicked Uncle' and was mildly amusing at my expense; Torquemada in the *Observer* noticed it, the *Mail* and the *Telegraph* had nice things to say. The review I appreciated most was a thoughtful one in a newspaper called the *Buxton Advertiser*. I wonder if it still exists? It criticized all the things it should have criticized but managed to convey appreciation at the same time. Its last sentence read: 'Nevertheless keep an eye on young Mr Graham, for he has come to stay.'

The reviewer, bless him whoever he was, could hardly have known how truly he was speaking.

The reception locally was flattering. I became known as the local author, and was generally made more of than I had been before. I remember at a bridge drive – a horror I then attended to oblige my mother – a Mr Arthur Mitchell, an elderly retired London chemist who had some pretensions to being the squire of the village, said to me that he had enjoyed my novel, and then, with a half attempt to take a rise out of me, asked, 'When is your next one going to be published?' It gave me exquisite pleasure to tell him and to see his surprise.

Because I had stockpiled by having two novels finished before the first was published, I was able to have a third ready for the following September; but thereafter I fell rapidly behind Ward,

Lock's urgings to produce two books a year. I am not by nature a fast writer, and, although flattered by their requests, I instinctively rejected the idea of becoming a writing machine. In those days I was far less ambitious than I later became. What I really wanted above all was to improve, to learn, to expand, to make each book better than the last, and I thought one whole novel a year was the absolute maximum.

Also I was reading a lot of dangerous books on the technique of writing: Percy Lubbock's *The Craft of Fiction*, John Steeksma's *The Writing Way*, Basil Hogarth's *The Technique of Novel Writing*, and *The Technique of the Novel* by Carl Grabo. These were fascinating but they did me a lot of harm. They grafted self-consciousness on the story-telling stem, and, although they did not throttle it, they doubled the labour without adding much to the quality of the finished product. My fifth book, *The Dangerous Pawn*, was my first attempt at a straight novel. When Wilfred Lock read it he said it was ten years ahead of any of the previous books but 'commercially I could shake you'. How right he was. I was told that Hatchard's had been taking a dozen of my books and occasionally reordering, but when they heard *The Dangerous Pawn* was not a thriller, they would not even look at it.

Not that any of these books had been a commercial success. They had not produced anything like enough for even a single person to live on. (Looking at the figures I am about to quote, I feel as if I am, financially, writing not of the Thirties but of the Middle Ages.) My mother had a more or less guaranteed income from her partnership in Mawdsleys of £360 a year. On this she was able to live in a degree of comfort, with a living-in maid, a small car, and to take at least one holiday at a hotel a year. My first novel earned me £29, my second £33, my third £41, my fourth £35. Occasionally a little extra trickled in from somewhere, but my earnings never exceeded £60 a year. A distinct depression began to settle on me. In the early books on writing I had read, people spoke of the poor returns that might be expected of a first or second novel; they had not alerted me to the fact that a third, a fourth and a fifth might earn no more, or even less. There was no build-up at all. A year's hard work produced £50. To be able to live off my earnings I would have to write six novels a year. Some people did, I knew, using different names. During the Second World War a youngish middle-aged novelist called Maisie Grieg came to live in Perranporth with her husband. She was pregnant for the first time, and this was an area reasonably free from bombs. She also wrote under the name of Jennifer Ames and some other pseudonyms. Her son was born in the July. At the Christmas I went to see her, and someone said, 'How many novels have you written this year, Maisie?' 'Only five,' she said, 'but then I did have Robert.'

That sort of production was beyond me – fortunately, as it turned out. But all through this period Ward, Lock never seemed to hesitate for a moment about publishing each novel as it was finished. And they made no attempt to edit, to suggest, to criticize. Except for the request that I should tone down a few scenes in the first novel, everything was printed exactly as I submitted it to them – to the last comma. It was a very considerable act of faith on their part, and some years later when people told me I had outgrown their list I stayed on with them, feeling they deserved more profit from the association. Perhaps this treatment from my first publisher has bred in me an egotistical belief that when I have finished a book – about which I have never consulted anyone, except my wife – then what I have written is what I wanted to write, and it is said in the way I wanted to say it. Full stop.

After I married, my wife was the one confidante, willing to listen, to talk. Often she was just the listener, so that, in talking it over, I could work out my own problem; sometimes she contributed a vital thought. When writing the *Poldarks* I often went to her for information about country ways, and she drew on memories of her Cornish farmer cousins. Sometimes she seemed to have a sort of folk memory – of things she knew by instinct rather than experience.

Only twice have I had substantial advice from any other outside source, and both with books rewritten from earlier published novels. On *Woman in the Mirror* (formerly *The Giant's Chair*) Carol Brandt's advice was invaluable, and on *Cameo* (formerly *My Turn Next*) Marjory Chapman's equally so.

But if these were years of frustration, there were also years of development, and there were many compensations, not least that of living in Cornwall. Could one choose a better place to be a relative failure? Perranporth has one of the finest beaches in the world – I call it Hendrawna in the *Poldark* novels, Hendrawna being the name of a small area of the hinterland adjacent to that beach.

It was visited frequently by Tennyson, accompanied by his friend Henry Sewell Stokes, in the 1850s, and five years after Tennyson's death in 1892 a poem was published in the *Echo*, for the first time, I believe, and attributed to him. I don't think it has been included in any collected edition of his poems, but Henry Sewell Stokes should have known.

Hast thou ever in a travel
Through the Cornish lands,
Heard the great Atlantic roaring
On the firm, wide tawny flooring
Of the Perran sands?

Sea-rent gully where the billows
Come in great unrest;
Fugitives all white and reeking,
Flying from the vengeful Sea-king,
Striking from the west.

Level broadway, ever ermined
By the ocean verge;
Girt by sandhill, swelling, shoaling,
Down to imitate the rolling
Of the lordly surge.

Nine large files of troubled water
Turbulently come;
From the bosom of his mother,
Each one leaping on his brother,
Scatters lusty foam.

In the sky a wondrous silence,
Cloud-surf, mute and weird;
In the distance, still uplifting,
Ghostly fountains vanish, drifting,
Like a Druid's beard.

Spreading out a cloth of silver,
Moan the broken waves;
Sheet of phosphorescent foaming,
Sweeping up to break the gloaming
Stillness of the caves.

I lived within a mile of this beach, and was free to walk on it whenever the fancy took me, or along the cliffs which rose up between Perranporth and St Agnes. This is Cornwall at its gauntest, at its most iron-bound. For centuries these granite cliffs have withstood mountains of water flung at them by tempestuous seas – literally millions of tons of seawater hurled at them in every gale – and they have lost none of their grandeur, scarcely anything of their shape or form through measurable centuries. The land bordering the cliffs is the habitat of rabbit and gull and errant seabird, mice and stoat and all small things – preying on each other but not yet preyed upon by man. It is rampant with heather and tiny flowers and wind-driven gorse, nothing much being allowed by the gales to grow above three feet in height; uncultivable, empty, wild.

Or should I tire of the sea, there were valleys to walk in – and every valley with a hasty stream. Marlowe's 'By shallow rivers to whose falls Melodious birds sing madrigals' does not apply to the Cornish streams. Birds, yes, in plenty, but the streams are always in a hurry as if they remember their heyday as vital adjuncts for the nearest mine – to provide water for the washing floors and the tin stamps and vital fresh water for the pumping engines which would corrode quickly if the acid minerals in the water they pump up were to be used.

I have no fear of heights when heights are presented by flying in planes, or standing at the top of the Empire State Building or the Eiffel Tower and looking down. But I have a morbid fear of climbing, which I have expressed in scenes in several of my novels: *Night without Stars* and *The Loving Cup*, for example. This stems almost certainly from an early occasion in Cornwall. I used to climb all over the great cliffs, without much thought to the risk, and usually on my own, and one day I decided to explore Sobey's Ladder, which is a narrow mineshaft not far from Wheal Prudence – driven from part way down the black cliffs to the sea below. (Sobey was a miner who used to keep a boat on a ledge down there and use it for fishing.) When I was part way down I slipped and fell about six feet. There I clung on, with jagged rocks licked by the sea a hundred feet below. Slightly concussed, bruised and cut on shoulder and leg, nothing worse, I crawled slowly back to the top, lay there on the sloping grass gasping, and in the confusion of my swimming head it felt as if the grassy floor I had reached was slowly tilting until I was in danger of sliding off over the edge into the sea. There was no one within a mile, and the sun had just set.

I don't remember how long it took to get home, but it was the end of cliff-climbing for me. For years after I had a nightmare of picking my way along a narrow path with cliffs looming above me and the sea licking below, and the pathway gradually narrowing until it petered out.

In the *Poldark* novels Sobey's Ladder has been attributed to a man called Kellow.

Chapter Four

After the publication of my third novel, on one of my visits to London I met a man called Brian Hall. He was a junior partner in the firm of Gordon Harbord, a successful theatrical agency. At a party at their offices where I was excited to meet a number of British actors of the day (does anyone ever remember Isobel Elsom?), Brian Hall told me he was shortly going to Paris, and invited me to go with him. After an anxious counting of my shekels, I agreed. We travelled overnight from Southampton to Le Havre and stayed at a pleasant enough small hotel. Brian had told me that he would be pretty busy every day so I would have to fend for myself. This suited me.

I thought of this first visit a couple of years ago when I was talking to an elderly doctor at the Savile Club, and he told me of his own first visit to Paris many years before, when he was twenty-one.

'It was my first time abroad, y'know. The first time on my own. So, as I had heard so much about the Paris brothels, their luxury, their charm, I decided to try one. So I made enquiries and then went along to a house and rang the bell. I don't mind telling you I was a bit het up. Well, the door opened and Madame stood on the threshold. She smiled at me and welcomed me in. Ever been to a Paris brothel, Graham? Well, it was quite impressive, I tell you. Big room she showed me into – crimson velvet curtains, gold chairs, etc. But standing in this room were a row of girls, various shapes and sizes, in different states of undress. They stood there and looked at me and I looked at them. In a row, like chorus girls about to go on stage. Some not bad-looking either. But a few of 'em were so oddly rigged out that I thought they looked rather silly. They appealed to my sense of humour, d'you know. I smiled and stifled a laugh. They smiled back and one or two tittered in response. Maybe I was a bit strung up but I began to laugh more openly. There was more tittering from the girls, and then in no time we were all laughing together!

'Madame touched my hand. She said: "Monsieur, I think I have something more suitable for you."

'So she took my arm and guided me out of this room and down a passage and opened a door at the other end and gently let me through. It was pretty dark and it took a minute or so to see where I was. D'you know where I was? D'you know where she'd shown me? As the door shut behind me I saw I was standing in the backyard among the dustbins!'

Though long before my marriage, my own intentions in going with Brian Hall to Paris were surprisingly innocent and not at all like the doctor's. I wanted to see the sights and was not specially interested in the seamier side of the city. But the very first day I met a girl who was staying at the hotel; we shared the same sightseeing bus, and from then on ignored the ordinary tourist trips and went everywhere together. We went to restaurants, bistros, up the Eiffel Tower, along the Seine, to Montmartre and Montparnasse, and to the ballet where the language difficulty did not arise.

This, of course, was long before it was fashionable – indeed the done thing – to travel the world in one's youth. Her name had an agreeably Elizabethan ring, Catherine Parr. She was travelling entirely alone and had so far been to Portugal, Spain, Italy and now France. She was an Australian, about my age, slim, elegant and adventurous, and she spoke no single word of any language but her own. She had sufficient confidence in her own not-negligible abilities to go where and get what she wanted. Her lack of languages did not incommode her. She was pretty and she simply smiled and pointed at whatever she wanted. After the second day together she smiled and pointed at me.

Three or four years after this, an elderly retired colonel whom I knew in Cornwall, and who himself knew Paris well, quizzed me about my first visit there, and incautiously I told him of my experiences. I mentioned my Australian friend, and added: 'I must

45

remember to send her a Christmas card.'

As he looked at me, a peculiar expression crossed his face which I found impossible to interpret. He looked surprised, even slightly shocked – or perhaps disappointed. I can only surmise such a reaction might come from the fact that he took the view of a first visit to Paris in the same light as my elderly doctor: eagerness to relish the glitter, the glamour, the wickedness of the world's wickedest city. Of course he would have laughed had I told him of the doctor's fiasco – and told him as if it had happened to me. I had sliced out of bounds on the first hole. Could happen to any feller. But you didn't somehow go to *Paris* to indulge in an *affair* with an *Australian* girl, and, what was more, *keep in touch with her after*. Why, that could have happened in Huddersfield.

About the time of the sixth novel, mindful of the relative success of *Seven Suspected*, I embarked on another play. It was called *Forsaking All Others*. During the late Thirties, a talented young actor called Peter Bull had brought down a company of his friends and colleagues, taken over the Perranporth Women's Institute for about ten weeks each summer, and put on a remarkable repertory of plays, professionally acted, directed and produced. People on holiday came from all over Cornwall to Perranporth to the plays, knowing they could rely on a quality of production rarely seen outside London. Peter Bull was a keen judge of talent, and among the people who came down with him were Frith Banbury, Pauline Letts, Pamela Brown, Joyce Redman, Judith and Roger Furse, and, appearing in the occasional play as 'guest artistes', were Hugh Sinclair, Robert Morley, Valerie Taylor and others. It was all heady and sophisticated stuff and it began to create a national name for itself.

I had come to know a few of them, though not well, and it was with awful trepidation in the late summer of 1938, happening to meet Peter Bull one day, I blurted out the fact that I had written a play and would he be very kind and read it? He said certainly he would, so I sent it to him when he returned to London. After a few weeks he wrote to invite me to supper next time I was in London. I went up the following week in high hopes but accompanying fears. The fears were realized. He saw me backstage of the Robert Morley play he was presenting in London, *Goodness, How Sad!*, and after a cheerful interchange and some complimentary remarks about my own play he added: 'Of course, I wouldn't put it on in London.'

I have no memory of the supper we had afterwards; I hope I was a good enough loser not to show disappointment; but towards the end of the meal he gave me the name of a producer friend of his to whom I might send the play for further consideration and advice. I thanked him and left, already foreseeing that his friend would read the play and return it with an encouraging note. Which is what happened. I felt demeaned by my own incompetence.

I do not think now that *Forsaking All Others* was nearly as good as *Seven Suspected*. It was more self-conscious, more pretentious. In the first play I had written uninhibitedly, bringing in the thrills and the laughs without a second thought. *Forsaking All Others* was full of second thoughts, and more serious, trying to go deeper and, on the whole, failing. Peter Bull was wholly right not to put it on. In the end I rewrote it as a novel and called it *Strangers Meeting*. It was the worst novel I ever wrote.

I returned to Cornwall feeling distinctly fed up. Sitting opposite me in the train was a woman I knew slightly from Perranporth called Ethel Jaggar. For six years she had been running a small private hotel, but was finding the strain too much for her. Her husband, a mining engineer in Nigeria, had recently been appointed to what was an improved and stable position and wanted her to sell the place and join him. She wanted badly to do this but, with war looming, property was a drag on the market. She was hopelessly stuck with it.

Treberran, as it was called, was the best house in the village. It had been built thirteen years before for a Dr T. F. G. Dexter, a well-known philologist whose family had made money out of soap, and he put up this large and handsome house for himself and his wife, with living-in accommodation for a man and wife as servants. When he died the Jaggars bought it, built further bedrooms on and enlarged the dining room and kitchens and ran it during the summer months as a guest house. When I got home I told Jean, my fiancée, and she arranged to go and see it. It was Sunday the 11th of November and I, who had over the years become involved in Toc H, was attending an evening service in the church. Near the end Jean knelt down beside me and said: 'It's *lovely*. I know the house, of course, from when the Dexters were there, but they've enlarged it marvellously.'

'Did they say how much they wanted?'

She breathed a figure that was a monstrous sum for those days, and one that we did not think we could ever raise. But when we saw the house, together with my mother, we thought the opportunity too splendid not to strive for.

Indeed we were so hypnotized by the quality of the place that we never thought to bargain as to the price, but set about raising the money. Obtaining a large mortgage from a bank was in those days only slightly less difficult than tunnelling under the foundations and breaking into the safe, but somehow we persuaded them to put up two-thirds, and by hook, though not by crook, we raised the rest, my mother standing guarantor for much of it.

The period of the late Thirties – from about 1933 to 1939 – was a ghastly time in which to grow up. I was asked the other day how later depressions compared with that of the Thirties. I couldn't answer. I simply didn't remember.

Of course the depression of the Thirties was acute and grim and horrible. Unemployment rotted the cities. The shadow of the means test – whereby the unemployed were forced to sell their few disposable possessions before they could continue to claim the dole – stalked everywhere. I remember two contemporaries of mine who worked in the Manchester Town Hall coming in for a substantial legacy. When this got about, the council sacked them, informing them that in the present economic climate their jobs must be given to two men in greater need.

I was outrageously lucky to be cushioned against this menace. But the other menace to which we were all subjected was infinitely more lethal in every way than a world depression – though that depression was partly responsible for what was to come – being quite overshadowed. By Adolf Hitler.

A lot of wishful thinkers tried in those days to argue that German rearmament was simply a matter of national pride, that a desire to occupy the Rhineland was evidence of a proper wish to be reunited with their own people, that all the other Germans of Central Europe suffering under a foreign yoke should also be properly united with their own kin. *Anschluss* was all they wanted. Then it would be 'peace in our time'.

I remember one sunny Sunday morning in October 1933 going down to the paper shop in Perranporth and seeing the headline: 'Germany Walks Out of the League of Nations'. It was Harvest Festival at Perranzabuloe Parish Church that day. A strange harvest. From that moment I never really believed the end could be anything but war. The black cloud of inevitability hung over the next six years.

For ten years after 1918 people were sick of war and wanted to hear no more of it, but later the mood changed and everyone wrote about it and everyone read it. For a decade the British people, and no doubt people everywhere, had been deluged with accounts of the last war, in autobiographies, in novels, in films, in plays. Films like H. G. Wells's *The Shape of Things to Come* (1936) predicted what would happen when the next war broke out. And everywhere where pictures could be seen we saw the marching Germans, the massed battalions on parade, Hitler screaming his revenge and hate.

Germany had been looked on with great sympathy during the early days of the post-war time. The Versailles Treaty had made her appear the sinned against rather than the sinning, and the reaction against the old wartime propaganda was notable in any company. After the Second World War France was bitterly criticized by later historians, who presumably were in the kindergarten at the time, for not sending French troops into the Rhineland when Hitler unilaterally occupied it. Had they done so, it is argued, Hitler would have fallen and the Second World War possibly been prevented. But had France done this – depriving the poor Germans of land which everyone agreed was their own – whether Hitler had fallen or not,

France would have become a pariah among nations. The howl of execration from the entire British press would have been echoed throughout the world. Hitler, even if he temporarily fell, would have been re-elected by a mass vote of the German people, to whom he would have suddenly become a hero. For France, it was a no-win situation whatever happened.

Opposed to the later Hitler, the more triumphant Hitler, with his 'Strength through Joy' movements, his Youth Corps, his millions of healthy, vigorous, industrious, mindless young men, all pledged to live – or die – for the Führer, what had we to offer? Love on the Dole, hunger marches, Peace Pledge Unions, 'Will-not-fight-for-the-Country' motions, disarmament rallies, grey elderly politicians hesitating and dithering, a general and an understandable hatred of things military. Even the air races which fathered the Spitfire had to be funded privately. I remember a prominent member of the League of Nations Union coming to Cornwall and pleading that the Government should scrap just *one more* cruiser, so that the US and Japan might be softened in their claim for parity. I remember the Baldwin election in which, lying in his teeth that he was devoted to disarmament, he immediately on re-election began a very modest rearmament programme. He said, truly, that if he had not so lied he would never have been re-elected to do even that.

Curiously, the television series which has brought back that nightmare time most vividly to me was *Fortunes of War*, from the Olivia Manning novels. Watching it, one remembered the utter frustrated helplessness of the whole of Europe before the ruthless, disciplined, relentless brutality of the Hitler jackboot.

Many in England as late as 1938 wished to make peace, at almost any price. The Munich Agreement, denounced as a sell-out – as indeed it was – united the British people as they had never been before it, and gave them a priceless year in which to rearm.

It can of course be argued that a later generation grew up under a worse shadow, that of a nuclear war. The difference lay in the inevitability. And to some extent in one's assessment of the Russian character. I had far more to lose in the Fifties than in the Thirties, but

I never felt a tenth of the same oppressive, apprehensive conviction of doom.

My first meeting with my future wife had been when I was eighteen and she was fourteen. It was soon after our arrival in Cornwall and we were in church, she with her parents, I with mine. I think they spoke first, we being the newcomers. The meeting made no special impression on me; apparently it did on her. I just remember a stocky little girl with straight blonde hair, bobbed, under a school hat. We met again as families do in a small village. I saw her here and there over the next few years during school holidays; then slowly we became firm friends. This friendship was greatly fostered by her mother, who seemed to like me as much as her daughter did. Happily, unlike some mothers-in-law, she never changed her mind.

I spent the Christmas of 1936 in London; I can't now remember why; but on January the 3rd 1937 I was home again and decided to go to a dance at the Droskyn Castle Hotel (then the foremost hotel in the district, now long since fallen from its high estate to become flats).

It was quite a smart dance and the hotel was gayly lit. I remember coming into the ballroom and seeing Jean Williamson sitting with some friends at a table across the floor. She had changed greatly from our first meeting. I looked at her carefully and then said to myself: 'She's the girl I'm going to marry.'

It was not so much a moment of enlightenment as one of recognition of what I should have known before. It was recognition that my life would be unacceptably arid without her. I can't remember whether she was the best-looking girl in the room, but I vividly remember that she had so much more *character* than anyone else there, male or female. Again, this was not so much distinguished by any special behaviour on her part – it just lit her up.

Later in the evening when I was dancing with her I said: 'I can't afford to marry yet, but when I can, will you marry me?'

Her smiling bright eyes met mine for a few seconds, then she said: 'I think I just might.'

Chapter Five

Jean Williamson's father had been in the navy all his life. He had been a gunnery officer on board the *Royal Oak* at the Battle of Jutland, and among his other medals was that of the Order of St John, awarded by the Russians; though this must have been given him for some earlier adventure. Gunfire damaged his eardrums, and when I first met him he was already deaf.

At the end of the First World War he was sent as a gunnery expert to superintend the dismantling and blowing up of all the explosives at Nobel's Dynamite Works, which had been situated on the Cornish cliffs about two miles outside the tiny village of Perranporth. Thinking his task might run for a couple of years at least, he bought a pleasant, largeish square-built house on the hill above the village and brought his wife and two children from Devonport to live there. But after six months he was transferred to Portland. As his next appointment was also likely to be temporary, his wife and family remained at Perranporth, and that is where his children grew up.

It must have been an unspoiled Cornish village then – some years before even we arrived. Jean remembered the mine opening on the cliffs a quarter of a mile out of the village, and the difficulty they had in hauling the huge cylinder for the engine up the steep hill, with eight horses straining at the traces and the wheels of the wagon inches deep in sticky mud. They failed to get it up the cliff road and so had to go up St George's Hill – almost as bad – and round the corner into Tywarnhayle Road and then to the cliff and the mine.

Unknown to any of the happy Williamson family at this time, the Geddes Axe was pending, whereby the navy was savagely truncated in a post-war retrenchment, and Commander Williamson, at the age of just fifty, found himself redundant. The navy had been his life from the age of eighteen, and without it he had no life at all. He lived another twenty-one years, and took on a variety of paid and unpaid jobs, but fundamentally – although he could be jolly enough on occasion – he remained a moody and an embittered man. I remember when the Second World War broke out he immediately packed his bag, waiting to be called up, although by then he was sixty-eight.

Among Samuel Williamson's earliest friends in the navy was a sturdy, cheerful, devil-may-care young man called Charles Alexander. Charles was a good bit the older, had run away to sea when a boy, had served before the mast in the clipper ship *Thermopylae*, sister to the *Cutty Sark*, and had finally joined the navy as an AB in 1873. When he married Emma Mitchell, a Cornish girl living in Plymouth, he sailed away to the Antipodes almost immediately after and did not see his eldest daughter until she was three and a half years old. The navy had little regard for the family life of its sailors in those days.

In the fullness of time Charles brought his friend Sam back to his home in Devonport, and Sam, now thirty-nine, proposed to Charles's eldest daughter, who was twenty-six. Two children came of this marriage, Reginald, who eventually went into the banking world, and Jean, who married me.

When Charles Alexander eventually retired, first from the navy and then from the dockyard, they moved to Camelford and lived there for the rest of their lives. My wife, though born in Devonport, had a lot of Cornish cousins and was herself a quarter of Cornish blood. (The other quarters being London, Derbyshire and Scottish.) When her father was prematurely axed they were still living in Perranporth, and her mother, called to subsist on the miserly pension of a commander in the Royal Navy, had begun to 'take guests' at their home in the village, so my future wife was not without some experience in her new profession. But ours was of course an altogether bigger venture.

It was agreed – I'm not now quite sure why, possibly on the reasoning that married life and a new and exacting occupation shouldn't be attempted at the same time – that she should run Trebarran herself – with such suitable help as she could muster – during the summer of 1939, and that we should be married in the October. And so she took on the new enterprise. Let down by the abysmal professional types whom she first engaged, she quickly reverted to friends of her own class and one or two good working types in the village, and somehow made an outstanding success of her first summer. I continued to live at home and go up daily, chiefly to supervise the ordering and to do the accounts, paying bills and making them out, at all of which, following my mercantile ancestry, I was good. Having been spoon-fed all my life, I knew nothing of the rolled-up-sleeves side of the enterprise. And to do my beloved wife justice, she never expected it of me.

Jean and I had come to look on this new venture as a challenge: exciting, exacting but of limited duration each year. To be together, married, owners of a handsome house within sight of the sea, independent, one hoped; for the first time able to look on my personal earnings as a supplement to what came in, instead of the only source of income. (I remembered wryly Wilfred Lock's remark when I first met him, that one should regard the writing of novels as a financial stick, never as a crutch.) We could be a team: it was no novelty even then for both husband and wife to work to maintain the household.

Privately I sometimes ground my teeth just the same. I was a *published* novelist, for God's sake, with a collection of handsome volumes on my shelf, with my name on every one, and admirably favourable notices on the back covers. I was an established novelist, whose books were reviewed in the *Observer, The Times*, the *Financial Times*, and in places as far away as Otago and Kuala Lumpur. When I wrote I needed to have no qualms about whether the next book would be published: it was taken for granted.

Looking back on those days I realize now that what I grossly omitted to read were enough biographies and autobiographies of famous and best-selling authors who had written maybe six or even a dozen unsuccessful books, being forced to support themselves by other work – often uncongenial work – until one day they struck oil.

Anyway, there it was at that time, my new wife was wonderfully gifted, and such a dynamo of energy that the project was bound to be a success.

And it surely *was* a success – so far as it lasted, it could not have been more successful. But as we had all expected, Hitler was not to be satisfied with Austria and the Sudetenland. One August day I heard on the BBC that he had concluded a non-aggression pact with his lowering, suspicious neighbour to the east. A thunderstorm broke over the village that day, and in the middle of it I rushed down to Treberran and found Jean making her wedding cake in the company of Barbara Bryan-Haynes, her contemporary and friend who was helping to cook for her that summer. I came on their glowing happy faces with a look as thunderous as the weather and told them that war could now only be a matter of weeks. The wedding was fixed for the 18th of October, by which time the house would be blissfully empty. It has to be brought forward, I insisted. With a house booked to be full of people until mid-September, Jean said there was no way in which she could abandon her new commitment. We parted in mild dissension.

In the event, with war breaking out on September 3rd, I insisted on the wedding being not later than the 18th, so the paradox emerged that we, who had wanted to marry for several years, had in the event to be married by licence, with the sanction of the bishop. Coming back from Truro in my mother's car, I picked up a young man I knew in Toc H called Joe Stephens and gave him a lift home. On the way I explained about having just been in for the licence and the haste of the wedding.

Before I could get any further he broke into an embarrassed laugh and said: 'Oh, I didn't know you was in the same sort of trouble as me!'

After a rush to Plymouth to buy the wedding dress – the one ordered wouldn't be ready in time – and the choice of a single bridesmaid instead of three (my cousin's daughters heartbroken at not being able to get there) came the day, a Monday, sun and cloud with a fresh breeze; sixty guests, a wedding cake on which the icing had not sufficiently hardened, so that, towards the end of the breakfast, there was the risk that the lowest tier would not stand the strain (it was like the Leaning Tower of Pisa); an officiating vicar, Sir John Charles William Herschel, Bart. (great-grandson of the discoverer of Uranus), who either from the decrepitude of age or the stresses of the new war tried hard throughout the service to marry me to a girl called Christine; tea in Truro afterwards with my dearest friend, Fred Harris, and Jean'ssolitary bridesmaid Barbara, and then off to Mousehole for the beginning of our honeymoon.

Through the summer of 1939, on the fairly rare occasions when we had been able to get to the sea together, we had walked through the smaller surf, arms linked, planning a holiday in Scotland and singing or humming 'Over the Sea to Skye'. This was now out of the question, with petrol rationing newly instituted, the blackout in force, evacuee children, air-raids expected. So we spent ten days at the Old Coastguard's Hotel in Mousehole and the Godolphin Arms in Marazion.

I will not pretend that I greatly enjoyed our honeymoon. (It didn't matter in the end, for we had so many marvellous ones later.) But at the time the war was too imminent (or do I mean immanent?). On our first morning we heard that the battleship the *Royal Oak* had been torpedoed and had sunk with few survivors. We took a fishing boat out to the Manacles, and the fisherman in charge of it congratulated us for being able to eat ham sandwiches in such a heaving sea. In the evening the blackout was so complete that going out of the hotel one could see nothing, only hear the hum of voices as people all round the horseshoe of the harbour came out of doors to talk neighbour to neighbour. One man, coming out of a pub, stumbled over a coil of rope and complained: 'Tis dark as a bloody sack.'

That was more or less the outlook for us all. The evil war news of the over-running and destruction of Poland, the home news of the introduction of rationing, of the prospective call-up into the services of all men between the ages of eighteen and forty-five, the evacuation of millions of children, the endless decrees; these hardly made a favourable background for a peaceful, happy honeymoon.

We also knew that the house we had left was not empty. Some people had stayed on because of the outbreak of war, others wanted to remain till Christmas; and there was the risk that such a large house would be commandeered either for troops or evacuees.

I saw a film a few years ago called *Hope and Glory*, which was set in London at the outbreak of war and during the Blitz. This showed men hurrying to recruiting stations as soon as war was declared and emerging a few weeks later khaki-clad and ready for the fray. Where this was dreamed up I don't know; probably from memories of the First World War. It was not true of the Second. Notices were issued that men should *not* flock to recruiting stations but wait to be called up in an orderly fashion so that total chaos could be avoided. Towards the end of 1939 there was a cartoon in *Punch* depicting one man in civilian clothes talking to a man in khaki. The first man says: 'In the Army, I see? You must have influence!'

When it came time for me to register I chose what I thought the least uncivilized of the three services, which was the navy. I won't catalogue all the ailments I had suffered in my teens and twenties; and when I was eventually called for a medical in the early summer of 1940 it obviously crossed my mind that I might be found partially unfit. However, on the day I sailed through everything and, but for one doctor, I would have passed A1. But the one doctor's little tick meant that I was out of the navy altogether – they would take only the best – and I must be turned over to the army. This occurred, but another medical followed, and at it I was downgraded from B to C.

I am reminded of Bob Hope's experience when, in the early days of the war, he was living in Hollywood and feeling that he should return to England and help in the war effort. Knowing that some of his friends had volunteered for the Canadian Air Force he asked one of them who had been accepted how he had got on.

'I suppose,' he said, 'you have to go through a strict physical test?'

The other man growled at him: 'They'll take you if you're war-rm.'

Well, my downgrading meant that at least for the time being, I wasn't warm enough. It didn't matter that I had a fair skill with words, persuasive or abusive – or that in maths I was ahead of most people – or that I was bursting with a desire to do Hitler down. Because I wasn't up to square bashing I was totally out.

Had I had influence in London something would of course have been fixed for me. (One reads in autobiographies of a dozen such instances.) As I had not, nothing was. Being newly married, very much in love, and with a hefty bank overdraft to sustain, it was not difficult to reconcile myself, at least for the time being, to the thought that a non-combatant's lot was not an unhappy one. When volunteers were invited for the Coastguard Service I applied.

At the first interview for this service a selected but not select group of volunteers was examined by a crusty elderly naval lieutenant. We gave our names and such other details as were asked for, and then after a bit of discussion he looked crossly round the room and said:

'Well, there are twenty or more of you here and we only want seven. How am I going to select you?'

There was a pause, then he said: 'No suggestions? Maybe you'd like to fight it out between you.'

I looked at my neighbours, summed them up and said: 'I'll take my chance.'

'Right,' he said instantly, 'you're in.' And I was. Later he made me station officer.

Such acts of braggadocio, I may say, don't occur frequently in my life.

The Auxiliary Coastguard Service, as it was properly called, was distinctly combatant, and under semi-naval discipline, but it was largely recruited from those too old or unfit to serve, and some of the patrols and the night watches were so local that one could sleep at home.

So I had a very, very 'lucky' war. (One of my friends who was called up at the same time as me went down in the *Repulse*.) Apart from occasional bombings at Penhale three miles away, and the drifting in of corpses or unexploded mines, our duties were boring rather than dangerous. The constant regular – or rather irregular – hours on watch and patrolling the cliffs and beaches in all weathers, from the crystalline sunshine of a June day to the blinding force-10 night gale, when one clutched at anything to stay on one's feet, gave me the sort of health I had never had before. It was a prolonged sea voyage without often being afloat. And though I had little time to write I had immense areas of time to think, to meditate, and to dream, so that, when the war ended, ideas and scenes and stories came out, much matured from what they had been before. Also, more than ever previously, I came to watch and understand the sea and to love Cornwall in a new way. When I began to write *Poldark* I drew on this part of my life as in another dimension.

When the newly recruited coastguards assembled in July 1940 we were a motley crew of seven, under a regular officer from St Agnes, called Sparrock, and a senior commander from Plymouth, called Coombes. Coombes was a fatherly old chap, Sparrock a martinet. We had no uniform of any sort and our total defence equipment was one Ross rifle. These rifles were relics of the First World War and had been kept in store in Canada for twenty-odd years before being shipped across to supply the Home Guard and people like ourselves with the object of resisting the parachutists and landing craft of a professional German invasion army. I sometimes pictured myself taking it in turns with my compatriots to aim a single potshot at Nazi invaders equipped with automatic weapons and hand grenades. Fortunately for the survival of these reminiscences, it never happened.

Our watches were of six hours a day, plus a one-week-in-six of patrols. The day watches were always on one's own. But in the hours of darkness one worked in pairs. I loved the solitariness, the isolation, but six hours sitting with another man who would perhaps talk for two hours nonstop and then snore for an hour – though he was not supposed to – could be boring to desperation. One of the men I double-banked with was a Protestant Irishman – one of the landed gentry whose house had been burned down during the 'Troubles' and had fallen on, relatively, hard times. Early on, a cask of some liquid was washed ashore and appropriated by him (since he had found it). Our local chemist, confronted with a sample, pronounced it to be pure spirit. Waller, the Irishman, used it in his motor cycle with some success, but then discovered it was *drinkable*. He was scandalized that he should have wasted any of it on his motorcycle. Thereafter, until it was all drunk, he was an awkward customer to share six hours of darkness with. Every twenty minutes or so he would make an excuse and go out to see if his motor bicycle was safe and come back with breath that was ignitable. As time went on each night, he would become steadily more quarrelsome; so there were occasions when one was not far from a private war of one's own.

Another man, Sampson, an old sailor, had the sort of blinkered, one-track mind which was interesting to study but indescribably boring to be with. He had a restricted number of views on a restricted number of subjects. One only had to mention the relevant word, and it was like putting a penny in a slot: the reaction was instant and utterly predictable. The dangers of having such a mind were sometimes fascinatingly demonstrated. Once at the beginning of a watch we were visited by Sparrock, and Sampson was sharply reprimanded. I heard the interchange. Sampson was so indignant that he talked about it without a stop for the whole six hours. At the beginning of that time his memory faithfully reproduced the interchange. But over the hours it gradually altered with each telling, so that by the end of the watch it was Sampson who was putting the officer in his place.

I used him as one of three models for Jud Paynter.

Laced with the deadly dull routine were the occasional emergencies: the mines drifting in on the beach, the corpses wedged among the rocks, the stray German raider, the bombed convoys, the Spitfire diving into the sea, the invasion scares; but in the main it was watching the horizon, an occasional practice with Sten guns – when they eventually came – and the telephoning of the passage of ships along the coast.

As always short of stamina, I used to find the six-mile walk to the end of the beach and back, usually over soft sand and carrying our one precious but very heavy Ross rifle, a physical trial, so I bought a Smith & Wesson .45 from an officer just back from France, and was given permission to carry that instead. When well out of earshot of the general public, with illimitable stretches of empty beach on all sides of me, I would take pot shots at pieces of flotsam brought up on the tide.

The thing I disliked most to discover – after decomposed corpses – was a mine. We were forbidden, of course, to tamper with them, so it meant trudging back to the village, telephoning Plymouth and then, when the bomb disposal man arrived two hours later, walking back to where the mine had been seen and watching the operation from a safe distance.

On one occasion rather more than halfway along the beach I found a crate. It was undamaged, had open slats, and through the openings you could see an eighteen-inch-long, four-inch-wide object wrapped in waterproof sacking, and suspended, to protect it from damage or jolting within the three-foot-square crate, by steel springs tautly secured to the bars of the crate. I approached it with caution, but there were only numbers on the crate and no indication whether it was British or German. I debated what to do. The enormous trek back, with the long wait and the trek out and back again? It looked like no bomb I'd ever seen – nor in fact like anything else I had ever seen. Clearly it was of value, and was either explosive or, more probably, delicate and must not be jolted for that reason. I found one or two stones on that enormously unstony beach and threw them at the crate, but they only shook it slightly. The sensible thing was to shoot at it and make sure it was safe, but I did not like to destroy what might be some valuable item of equipment.

I went up to it again and saw that the springs were simply hooked by tension to the sides of the crate and so could be unhooked. With a good deal of care I gently unlatched it until only one hook remained. This was more difficult but it eventually yielded and I slid the object out of the crate and began my trek home, the thing dangling from my hand like a spring-heeled puppet.

When, having wended my way through the sparse holiday-makers and climbed the steep hill, I reached the coastguard look-out I found myself the most unpopular man in Great Britain. Compared to me, Hitler was a friend. Although I hung the object on a wire fence some twenty feet from the little station, every one of my fellow coastguards joined in condemning my foolish and dangerous action, an action which not only endangered my life but, more importantly, their own. I rang Coombes in Plymouth, and spoke to him and then to a bomb disposal officer and answered a number of questions. The officer didn't think it was explosive, so Coombes, who was coming for one of his inspections the following day, said he would look at it when he came.

For these inspections all seven of us had to be present, and they all stood around with the greatest alarm and annoyance while he examined my find. The top of the waterproof covering was secured by a metal ring. As he removed it he suddenly shouted: '*Ph-izz!*' Six of the coastguards jumped a foot in the air. Coombes had a great sense of humour.

My curiosity as to the identity of my find was never entirely satisfied. I was told it was a newly introduced type of radio valve, but accepted that with a pinch of salt.

On another occasion, in mid-June, when I was double banking, an alarm came through that two soldiers from Penhale Camp – three miles along the beach – had been cut off by the tide and were on the cliffs and in danger of drowning. Lifesaving apparatus was sent for from St Agnes and a group of us, headed by the irascible Mr Sparrock, made for the cliffs beyond Flat Rocks. In mid-June in fine weather there is no real darkness in Cornwall. At two in the morning the sun has long sunk but the sky over the sea is a luminous cobalt already promising a dawn two hours off. It was such a night when we set out to rescue the soldiers, windless, more gloaming than dark, the tide coming to the full, hissing over the sand; rock pools and shadowed cliffs, faint stars in the distant sky, shaded lanterns, splashing feet. It was wonderful to be alive on such a night.

The upshot of our rescue operation was that we climbed the cliffs and after a while located the soldiers. But, by the time we got the rope ladders in place and clambered down over the precipice, the soldiers, helped by the tide which had now begun to ebb, had fled. In spite of strenuous enquiries, they were never identified. They had been breaking camp and somehow got back undiscovered.

The fury of the rescue team knew no bounds. 'If I got near them,' fumed Sparrock, 'I'd help them up the frigging cliffs with the toe of me frigging boot.' He was particularly mad because on the way to the rescue he had stumbled and fallen flat on his face in a foot-deep sandy pool. For me that was the high spot of a thoroughly delightful night.

The next day, bleary from lack of sleep, I had to attend the funeral of an old friend at St Agnes, a fine Belgian violinist called Dupont who at one time had been leader of King Edward VII's private orchestra. In the warm, glittering midday, scented with the roses flowering in the churchyard, my stomach kept giving convulsive jerks. If anyone saw it I hope they thought I was weeping. In fact I was trying helplessly to control the laughter brought on by memories of the night.

In the meantime my personal life was not without vicissitudes. With the constant risk of evacuees being billeted on us, the house could not be allowed to remain empty except for our small family; so, as a protection from worse things, paying guests – of whom there were a few around – must be taken all winter and through the next summer and the winter after that, etc., etc., etc. It meant no rest for my young wife, and, beset by staff problems, rationing, blackout precautions in a house with an excessive number of windows, and every other sort of wartime restriction, it was not the sort of early married life we had pictured.

But we were together a lot, which was far more than I had ever dreamed possible, once war had broken out. And so far as one could see, unless some better use were found for my unimaginable talents in London, or the war casualties became so high that the barrel had to be scraped clean, I was likely to remain in Cornwall.

Sometimes I made unpatriotic use of the meagre allowance of petrol we were permitted, and drove around in search of food to feed our guests. There was a farm in Roseland, owned by the friend of a friend, where a few discreet eggs could be bought. Driving home we reached Truro. It was market day and busy, and just as I entered the town I touched my horn at a pedestrian and the damned thing stuck and would not stop. It is not a large town, but it seemed large that day. I drove right down the hill, through the crowded streets and up the other side with the horn relentlessly blaring. Everyone stood and stared. It was as well I was not picked up because in addition to a wife and baby son in the car I had eight dozen black-market eggs in the boot.

To complicate things a little more in our home life, my mother, always a difficult person to satisfy where maids were concerned, had by early 1940 run through a succession of them and been left frequently adrift and untended; so in the end we said she must come and live with us, at least for the duration of the war; though I think we all knew it meant for the duration of her life. We were able to give her a private sitting room, and the arrangement worked fairly well.

By 1943 the airfield at Trevellas, two miles away, was fully operational, and one day a flight lieutenant called and told us we must provide accommodation for six pilot officers. For this the Government would pay us 6d a night.

Of course we welcomed the young men – all younger than I was – and we made many warm friendships, none of which, alas, endured. Our young men were constantly changing; and not many survived the war. We lost two while they were staying with us – not from enemy action but from hideously ordinary flying accidents. They were the cream of youth: supremely fit, intelligent, high-spirited, zestful, courageous but fatalistic. There were some Poles among them too – equally splendid men. I have written about two of them in my novel *Cameo*.

A further complication in our lives, though a happy one, was the birth of our first child, a son, Andrew, in June 1942 – about the time of the Battle of Stalingrad. But while Jean was carrying him – clearly as a result of the tension and overwork of the last three years – she developed asthma, a complaint which was almost to kill her in the next half decade. She began to have savage monthly attacks, from which after two days in bed she would begin to crawl about, thin and wasted but with the tremendous stamina that she had, rapidly becoming her old self again. Then she would have about three weeks before the next attack. This, plus half a hotel to run, six young airmen to be seen to on occasion, a delicate mother-in-law who could do nothing in the house, and now a young baby to tend, was more than enough for one young woman.

Of course we got away from time to time, thanks to my mother-in-law and one or two other people who could temporarily take the load; and these short holidays – in spite of everything much more high-spirited than our honeymoon, because now the dangers were out in the open and could be faced and some of them already defeated – quickly made up for anything lacklustre in the first. Several times we went to London and ignored the air-raids with theatre-and concert-going. Once at the ballet at Sadler's Wells we saw a young girl dancing one of her first key roles. When we came out, the sky was ablaze with searchlights. We hoped they were out to welcome the arrival of Margot Fonteyn.

During my time as a coastguard I spent many long hours looking down at the remains of a wreck. Only the weed-grown timbers showed, a skeleton of a French ship called *La Seine* which had been driven ashore in a January gale in 1900. Waller, the Irishman, a vividly vigorous sixty-year-old, as soon as he saw it wanted to put the wreck to good use and, standing in water sometimes up to his shoulders, since wrecks always create pools around themselves, he rigged up a very long rope between the coastguard station and the wreck and erected an endless whip, whereby a thinner line with baited hooks upon it could be rotated out to sea at full tide and back again. It was a Heath Robinson contrivance, but after a few false starts it suddenly worked in abundance, and one night we found ourselves with two dozen mackerel and two huge skate. Food was so short that I telephoned my wife and, pregnant though she was, she walked the mile from our house and traversed the single-file precipitous cliff path to the station. It was nine o'clock on a wild black winter's night, and when I heard a rattle of stones I went out with the Ross rifle and challenged her.

A faint voice came through the windy darkness. 'It's your *wife!*'

Unfortunately the large canvas bag she had brought wasn't big enough to take the skate lying down, so to speak, and when she came to cut it up next morning rigor mortis had set in, and she was confronted with a huge crescent-shaped fish covered with sharp abrasive scales. We ate it in due time. But presently news of Waller's enterprise reached headquarters and it was put a stop to.

After the war, when the little coastguard station was converted into a sophisticated, instrument-crammed building concerned to measure the height of waves (waves, it seems, diminish on their long journey from the Mexican Gulf, but they do not alter their relative size, one to another), the remains of the wreck were blown up so as not to disturb the pattern of the sea. But from 1940 onwards I stared at it and thought long about it: it seemed a wonderful relic of an age long past – although in fact it was then only forty years gone. Indeed one of the seven of us on watch, a man called Tom Mitchell – Farmer Tom, to distinguish him from all the other Mitchells in the village – had seen the vessel actually come in and the following day, as a boy of nine, had clambered over the ship. He was able to tell me all the details of the wreck, and I pondered over the lives of the people who had been drowned and those – the majority – who had been saved.

On one of my infrequent days off I took my wife to Falmouth and found a rather disreputable cafe–restaurant where the proprietor did not send round to take your orders but bargained fiercely with you as you came in as to which joint you should have some slices of, these being arrayed on the counter at his side. As sometimes happens with an author, two fairly disparate scenes come together to make a novel, and from these scenes – the shipwreck and the cafe – emerged *The Forgotten Story*.

It was published in the spring of 1945 while the war was still at a crucial stage. It seemed to me at the time that it was written too hastily and too casually and had been scribbled down in the spare moments of a broken and traumatic few years. I have never written a novel I thought less well of at the time. The previous book, *The Merciless Ladies*, most of it written before the war, had come out in 1944 and was now beginning to sell. I was sufficiently clear-sighted to be aware that this was largely due to the times: shortage of newsprint, shortage of new novels, and a public which, deprived of many other outlets, was reading more than ever before. All the same I thought well of this book and feared that the publication of what seemed to me to be a relatively trivial novel like *The Forgotten Story* would do my growing reputation no good at all. As publication date drew near I became more and more anxious and worried, so that at the end if someone had offered me £50 to withdraw the book I should have done so.

In the event *The Forgotten Story*, simple though it was, drew a new critical attention and soon began to sell on its own merits apart from any popularity born of a newsprint shortage. *The Merciless Ladies*, in my view now, was a rather pretentious, 'literary' novel, which, if I had ambitions to suppress anything, should have been the better target. In later years I rewrote it entirely and, I hope, ironed out some of the worst bugs. But there seems no doubt that, judging as objectively as possible, *The Forgotten Story* is far the better of the two. So can one totally deceive oneself at the time.

I remember walking up to the coastguard station one day just before the end of the war with the glowing – dizzying – knowledge in my heart that the recently published *The Forgotten Story* was earning me around £50 a week. Fifty pounds a week! Today's equivalent is about £1,000. At this rate I would shortly be rich and independent.

After that a lot of things happened more or less together. Just before we were married I had told Jean one evening that I had an idea to write an historical novel about Cornwall. For a young woman who had a sublime faith in my abilities, she – for once – looked doubtful. I think it crossed her mind that I was really attempting too much.

I had in fact over the previous ten years been 'taking in the air' – the ambience – of the county in which I now lived. Like all my family, I had fallen in love with it, but unlike them, being more imaginative and of an impressionable age, I took in more – and eventually gave out more. Being quite unaware of the sublime superiority of the Anglo-Saxon race, I got on well with the Celts, indeed found some affinity between them and my own North Country breed and upbringing.

I met them and liked them and laughed with them and talked to them, and listened, of course – to old miners and young rugby players, old fishermen, young laywers, middle-aged butcher boys, clerics and farmers, doctors and dentists and dustmen. And their wives and sisters and daughters. From many old men I heard about the mines and the county's strange history. Romantic, of course, with its stories of smuggling and wrecking, but equally interesting in its political and social life, the gambles of mining, the forty-four Members of Parliament, returned mostly through 'rotten boroughs', the social life of Truro, the rich families and the poor. All this went along with my special appreciation of the tetchy, beautiful, unreliable weather, the great seas, the massive cliffs, the crying of the sea birds, the smell of heather and gorse, the tantrums of the wind.

I had read, of course, the 'Cornish' novelists, and found them on the whole a disappointing lot. Some of them wrote good novels, but these could just as easily have happened in Devon or in Norfolk. The writers used the county because it was romantic, but never even tried to understand it. From these strictures I naturally excepted the real Cornish writers like Baring-Gould, Quiller-Couch, and Crosbie Garstin.

There had been growing in my mind a story which was unoriginal in its inception but which fortunately broke the mould as it went along. Before the war I had sketched out a few characters, then while I was waiting for call-up I used to walk to my mother's bungalow – furnished but empty since her coming to live with us – and there I began to write the first few chapters of *Ross Poldark*. It was a strange contrast for me between the formidable war news and the many complexities of modern life and the total isolation of an empty bungalow – a mile from my house – with a long lawn, a flowing stream and pastoral silences.

Sometimes late at night in bed I would read aloud a part of what I had written, while Jean's blue-grey eyes would mist over with the sleepiness she indignantly denied.

Necessarily all this was broken; and I did not begin to rewrite what I had written or to continue the story until the war was near its end. But while on watch in the daylight – and during the long nights – I would think and dream and consider the characters and allow them to grow. So that when the war was near its end and when to everyone's inexpressible joy it did end, the story was there for the writing.

I had no thought when I began *Ross Poldark* of a continuing series of books. It was just to be a story of eighteenth-century Cornwall, with a gloomy beginning and a happy ending, and that was that. In the course of it I rewrote and rewrote and rewrote, polishing and pruning, adding and subtracting, trying to get the perfect balance in each chapter between emotion and restraint. Some chapters I wrote nine times: each time I went to them they responded to something different in my own mood and had to be done again. In some ways I was very young – younger than my years – in spite of having been a professional writer so long; and I was too romantic. My approach to women was too romantic – it still is – but it was by then a part of my nature and was too inbred to be changed.

This novel, although preceded by a sort of 'trailer' in the form of *The Forgotten Story*, was in fact a big departure from anything else I had written, being slower moving, concerned with mood and scene rather than action – though there was plenty of that too – and it took some imaginative stress to build up the historical background behind the characters. When my publishers saw it they liked it very much but suggested I should cut 20,000 words from the first half. It was the first time they had ever suggested any amendment since my very first novel. It was, I am sure, a genuine criticism on their part, but also it was activated by the extreme shortage of paper and their knowledge that an economy of forty pages would be a handsome saving of their short supply. I just said no. I said I regretted I wasn't willing to cut anything, so they took it as it was. Whether they were in any way justified I don't know, but no one ever since has said that the beginning was drawn-out or slow.

When the book came out it was a terrific success in Cornwall. W. H. Smith in Truro sold 700 copies in the month of December. It did not receive as many favourable reviews as *The Forgotten Story*, possibly because critics, a disillusioned race, don't care for romance. But it continued to sell moderately well all through the succeeding year – and it has never stopped selling in all the years since.

Before this I was well on with the second *Poldark* novel, *Demelza*.

Towards the end of *Ross Poldark* it became clear that I had far more to say and to tell than could be contained within a single book. There had to be another, and perhaps even one after that. Not only did Ross and Demelza grip my thoughts but all the lesser characters: the Martins, the Carters, Dwight Enys and Karen Smith, the Bodrugans, the Chynoweths, and of course the Warleggans. These people had come alive and clamoured for attention.

So *Demelza* came into being. All through the time I was in the Coastguard Service I had come particularly to appreciate being alone. I remembered the strange stimulating isolation of those few months in 1940 when, awaiting call-up, I had written the first chapters of *Ross Poldark*. In the final few weeks before being demobilized – since there was little now we could constructively do – I had shamelessly carried my books up to the coastguard station and spent the time writing. When the station was closed I looked for somewhere else. On the opposite side of the beach was a wooden bungalow, nearly always uninhabited except for a few weeks in high summer. It belonged to a Mr Harry Tremewan. I went to see him and hired it.

I have had a lot of happiness in my life, but those next few months rank high among the high spots. Each day about ten I left our house, with a few books under my arm and a haversack on my back containing perhaps potatoes, boiled ham, a tomato, lettuce, a few slices of bread and some butter, and walked through the village and out onto the sandy beach – sometimes with the tide miles out, sometimes with it thundering and hissing at my feet, sometimes having to wade through sputtering surf up to my knees – and at the other side climb the Flat Rocks and go into the bungalow where, collecting dust even from yesterday, would be the pile of reference books and old papers that had already accumulated. Sitting in my deckchair in the immense silences, I would pick up the book in which I had been writing yesterday and continue with the story.

It was a remarkable experience. Sometimes in moments of critical self-examination I had asked myself if I was really a novelist or just a craftsman with a story-telling ability. In writing *Demelza* I knew myself with conviction to be a novelist. What I was writing was not a planned thing, it was organic, with the characters working out their own destiny. Sitting there in the grey old empty bungalow, I felt like a man driving a coach and four, roughly knowing the direction in which the coach would travel, but being pulled along by forces only just under his control. It was physically and mentally both exhausting and exhilarating. Every now and then after a long passage the coach, as it were, would lurch to a stop with a half-dozen possible roads opening ahead and no signposts. A day or two of agonizing indecision; then the road would be chosen and we would be off again. Occasionally during the day I would go out and stroll around the bungalow and watch the gulls and the translucent tides, feel the wind on my face: it was a mile or so from the old coastguard station but with a different, gentler view. At about five I would pack the haversack, take up the written work, and begin the walk back in the glimmering twilight with the sea far out and the waves glinting like mirages on the wet sand. I was going back each evening to the real world, waiting to welcome me at home; but it is doubtful which to me just then was the more real. All I knew was that I was writing something out of my very guts, and that I was content.

New-found prosperity was also offering a new perspective. We had had fun and a deal of anxiety and responsibility in running our private hotel. It was good while it lasted, but we now had a family, and Jean had become asthmatic. Our first intention was to put it up as a going concern and move to some comfortable small house; but this was superseded by an even more agreeable prospect. We could shut the doors of Trebarran with a bang and then just go on living in it as a private residence. Before it was enlarged it had been one of the most attractive houses in the district; let it revert to its original purpose, and if we had far too many bedrooms we could shut them up or spread ourselves to occupy more of them. My wife was pregnant again, and in March 1946 we had a daughter, whom we called Rosamund.

In the years when we ran Treberran as a small hotel, only one – the summer of 1939 – had in any way been a normal one. After that it was always wartime. But through it we met many charming and delightful people, some of whom were to have a strong influence on my future.

In late 1940, a fellow writer called Max Murray, who had come to Cornwall to escape the Blitz with his wife Maisie Grieg – the enormously prolific author – who was having a baby, told me that his friend, Benno Moiseiwitsch, the famous pianist, needed a holiday away from the bombs; could I put him up? I was overwhelmed at the thought, for I had heard Moiseiwitsch a number of times giving recitals in London before the war, and I had a tremendous admiration for his playing. Except for two Dutchmen (bulb growers, very nice men, who had been crossing the Atlantic when Germany invaded Holland and found themselves stranded in England) our house was just then empty. If it had not been, I would have emptied it for Moiseiwitsch.

My mother had sold her piano when she came to live with us, but we had my mother-in-law's upright Bechstein, which was a pretty good instrument. We had this put in his bedroom so that he could use it when he had the mind. So he arrived with his wife and his small son, Boris; and it was an enchanting three weeks. All of them, Benno, Annie and Boris, were unpretentious and delightful. God knows what we must have seemed like: certainly young and eager but so desperately short of food and fuel and staff. Their life in London was the height of sophistication (I was to sample it later) but they never complained or showed any dissatisfaction with anything in the house. Within a week we were friends, laughing together at the war's deprivations.

He practised three to five hours a day. It was like a separate spirit in the house, singing, intoning, inhabiting every corner of one's existence. He would take a light breakfast in his room and then practise for the rest of the morning, smoking incessantly. An hour of scales and wonderful arpeggios, then more complicated finger exercises written by one or other of the great teachers of the past. After lunch he would rest for a while and begin again about four, this time playing pieces that he would soon be giving at a concert. Particularly he played the more difficult parts – and they are infinitely difficult – of Rachmaninov's Piano Concerto No. 3 in D Minor, which he was to perform shortly in Liverpool. And he learned, for the first time, Beethoven's Concerto No. 3 in D Minor at our house; the whole thing from beginning to end. He had no objection to my sitting with him while he played, when I had time, sometimes giving running commentaries on the object of a particular passage or what he was trying to do with it. At six he would stop and very often walk down to the Perranporth Hotel for a drink with Max Murray and me. After dinner he would play bridge, usually with the two Dutchmen and my mother. He was an infinitely witty man, sometimes destructively so, but never to or about his friends. I may be prejudiced but I have always thought he played Rachmaninov better than the composer himself; without sentimentality but with more true emotion. (I have very recently discovered, to my surprise and pleasure, that this was also Rachmaninov's view.)

One day when we were walking down to the Perranporth Hotel together we passed two friends of my mother's, a Mrs Retallack and a Mrs Trevithick. They were both in their seventies, dressed in the height of bourgeois fashion, gloved, jewelled, austere, prim. After they had passed, Benno said to me: 'Ah, I see the ladies of the town are back on their evening beat.'

He had a dog called Rach, named after his old friend Rachmaninov. Benno's comment when I met the dog was: 'One word from me and he does exactly as he likes.'

At Christmas we went up to see the Murrays, and Maisie gave Benno a gift wrapped in expensive glittery paper. Before he opened it he said: 'Oh, Maisie, thank you. It's just what I've always wanted.'

Once, later on in the war, we saw that Moiseiwitsch was giving a concert in Plymouth. I was on duty but Jean contrived to take the time off and made the two-hour journey by train. When she got there all seats were sold. So she went round to the stage door and Benno immediately commanded that she be given a special seat by herself on the platform.

We remained friends until his death, and when Andrew was christened, Annie Moiseiwitsch was his godmother. Benno stayed with us twice more, as our true guest, and I stayed with him at his home in Berkhamsted and helped to time his playing of Chopin's thirty-two preludes, which he was shortly to record. I went with him often as his guest to the Savage Club, where I met Mark Hamburg, James Agate, and others of that set and played an occasional game of bridge but never poker, which was Benno's favourite. I remember on one occasion sitting behind him while he was at the poker table; he was on a winning streak and a club servant came to tell him that his taxi had arrived to take him to Paddington, where he was to catch the overnight train for Swansea for a concert on the morrow. He told the servant to cancel the taxi, he would catch a later train. I said to him: 'But you've got a sleeper booked. If you catch a later train it will mean sitting up all night.' 'It doesn't matter,' he said, 'I'm only playing the Rachmaninov No. 2.'

It was my misfortune to be with him on the morning that he received word from the surgeon that his beautiful forty-five-year-old second wife, Annie, had inoperable cancer.

A second meeting was even more formative for me, and again it was with a musician. I cannot remember at all how it came about that a Lieutenant Peter Latham, stationed at Penhale, wanted his wife and daughter to spend a few weeks in Perranporth so that he could see more of them. I suppose someone recommended us, and presently I met this tall, thin, gangling middle-aged man who had the utmost charm in the world.

He worked at the Royal Academy, teaching and examining, and was later to become Gresham Professor of Music. He had served in the First World War, and had been severely wounded, with the result that he shambled as he walked, and had a deformed shoulder. Being intensely patriotic, he had at once applied to rejoin his regiment when the Second World War broke out, and the War Office, with its usual perception, appointed him to be a gunnery instructor, a subject about which he knew virtually nothing. So he had been sent to Penhale Camp where morning gunnery practice took place, shooting at a target being towed at a (fairly) safe distance by a slow-moving biplane.

This was the beginning of another friendship, which lasted until Peter's death, and then Angela's death many years later. They became close friends – even closer than Benno and Annie. We again had the piano moved into the bedroom, and Peter, when off duty, would come along and play there. Though clearly he could not begin to match Moiseiwitsch's brilliance, he was a fine pianist and an immense musicologist, with a fund of reminiscence and anecdote and funny stories and limericks, many of them scabrous – the jolliest and most lovable of men. His wife, a pretty, eccentric, intellectual, sparkling woman, was by profession a fresco artist, and when *The Last Supper* in Milan was showing uncheckable signs of deterioration she was invited by the Italian government to go to see it and advise on its preservation and restoration. After the war we saw them many times at their home in Hampstead, and they came, like Benno, to stay with us as our non-paying guests in Cornwall when Treberran had become a private house again.

Peter and Benno opened up to me a world that before I had only been groping to find – a world in which conversation was no longer chatter, in which anecdote was not gossip, in which wit and fun and intellectual debate were all.

But the strongest influence Peter Latham had on my life was to put me up for membership of the Savile Club – of which much more later.

I remember another guest at Treberran, a Dr Dancy – whose elder son later became headmaster of Marlborough – saying to me one day towards the end of the war: 'When this war is over it will be the beginning of a new life for you.' He spoke even more truly than he knew.

Chapter Six

During the war I had become friendly with the actress Valerie Taylor, who was then married to Hugh Sinclair. They owned a bungalow in Perranporth, and between intervals of work we visited each other's houses and had suppers together. She was a highly strung, highly articulate, highly intelligent, beautiful but rather overpowering young woman, who was full of ideas, and one evening she told me what she thought was a brilliant opening for a film. I in my down-to-earth style agreed that it was an interesting idea. Of course it was no more than an idea at this stage: it lacked a story, as almost all ideas do (people often confuse the two), but a month or so later I said to her: 'I've been thinking of your opening, Valerie, and it's certainly an interesting one. If I were writing it, I would, I think, tend to develop it this way ...' She immediately lit up, and henceforward rang me up persistently, full of suggestions and wanting to know if I was making progress.

In short, in between finishing *Ross Poldark* and beginning *Demelza* and celebrating the end of the war and completing our last 'season' at Treberran and getting demobilized from the Coastguard Service and looking after my mother, who was ill, and Jean's mother, who was ill, and Jean, who was intermittently ill but most of the time doing her usual ball-of-fire act, and awaiting the birth of our second child, I was working on a screenplay with Valerie Taylor which eventually became *Take My Life*. When it was finished – finally, finally finished – she took it up to London and tried to interest various film friends in it. Some of them liked it but all said it was far too expensive to be put on.

The screenplay as it finally evolved concerned a young British opera singer, Phillipa, who comes with an Italian company to

Covent Garden. On the first night, on which she plays the lead, her husband, Nicholas, an ex-army officer, is there and encounters Elizabeth, an old lover of his who is playing in the orchestra, and Phillipa sees them together. In their flat after the opera her tension after a night's success causes her to challenge him about his old affair, and in the quarrel which follows she throws a scent bottle, which hits him on the forehead. He walks angrily out.

In the meantime Elizabeth returns to her flat and is followed by a man who knows her and forces his way into her flat and murders her, but not before he has sustained a wound on his forehead similar to Nick's.

Nick is accused of her murder. He claims that he has never been near the murdered woman's flat, until a witness identifies him.

It was too expensive to produce, everyone said, until Valerie asked the advice of Clive Brook, and he recommended his agent, Christopher Mann Ltd.

The Mann office was then at the height of its prestige; the most powerful agent in London. If it took you up, you were on the ladder. It succeeded in selling *Take My Life* to the Rank Organisation, and the film was eventually made by Cineguild, one of its most distinguished subsidiaries, the company which had made the then famous film *Brief Encounter*.

At the time we were writing this script Valerie was engaged in a passionate love affair with a mining engineer called William Saunders, whom, after divorcing Hugh, she eventually married. As she was always quite incapable of getting names right, William often became Winston, and Winston, William. As a result the rumour spread around that *I* was having an affair with the lady. Indeed perhaps her husband was himself not too sure, for when a couple of years later I wrote the film as a novel and sent him a copy he replied to thank me and to say that perhaps the book should have been called 'Take My Wife'.

My daughter, Rosamund, was born during a brief and significant snowstorm on the 1st of March 1946, just after the film had been bought and when I was about halfway through *Demelza*.

She brought us extra luck. Only a few weeks after this the Rank Organisation, in the guise of Cineguild, decided that *Take My Life* was just the sort of film that the burgeoning British film industry wanted and that Valerie and I must be encouraged – indeed drawn into the industry full-time as a special pair of writers capable of turning out more films of the same kind and quality. After a few brief interviews with Valerie on her own, she being in London, they decided that I must be the guiding, inspiring light in the partnership, so they telephoned me, inviting me to London to consult on the making of *Take My Life* and other possible films. I said I was sorry but I was just finishing a novel but I'd be glad to come up in two or three months' time. This shocked them and they telephoned back that if I would come up in two days' time they would pay me £80 a week (for today's equivalent, multiply by at least twenty) and provide me with a free flat in Hallam Street and a secretary to take down my lightest word. This, when I accepted, they did; also I had a chauffeur-driven Rolls-Royce to take me down to Denham every day. I must say, although a new boy, that I was treated with the utmost respect and kindness by everyone in the industry.

Rosamund was only six weeks old when I went to London, but Jean came with me, leaving our two children in the fairly safe hands of a nurse called Christine and two grandmothers.

I knew London moderately well from regular if impecunious visits before the war and hectic short feverish breaks during the war to brave the bombs and see the latest plays; but I knew nothing of the opulent vistas of the film world. Encouraged by the government, Rank was pouring in his millions and trying to double the output of the British film industry. It was a time of a sudden wild prosperity, when the films being made seemed to justify the expansion. Productions like *Great Expectations, The Seventh Veil, The Wicked Lady, This Happy Breed* were pouring out, showing both quality and popular appeal. Mr Rank's Young Ladies were being brought in and groomed for stardom. (Some achieved it, most are long forgotten.) But what apparently was not foreseen was that you cannot suddenly quadruple the production of an artistic industry and rely on the talent to be there instantly in ample supply.

The Mann office in those days had three partners: Christopher Mann himself was a small, dapper, seemingly modest and insignificant figure, who would slip unobtrusively in and out of the office, with a stub of cigarette endlessly between his lips, and who wielded great power in the industry by packaging films, i.e. bringing together a subject, a star, a producer, a director and a writer and arranging the finance. (He did none of these things for *Take My Life*, but much for me later.) Chris had a passion for Madeleine Carrol and had been responsible for putting her into most of her starring roles; when she went to America their affair (apparently always unconsummated) fell through and he married Eileen Joyce, the fine Australian pianist.

The second partner was his brother-in-law, Alan Grogan, who had married Winifred Mann, Chris's sister. Alan was a much more imposing character, 6ft 3ins tall, well-built, dark, good-looking, humorous, a man with a very astute sense of values and a keen musician. Winifred Grogan was a small delicate woman, as inscrutable, until you got to know her, as her brother. She and Alan were devoted to each other. She had borne one child, a son, but had shortly afterwards contracted tuberculosis and given it to her son. She survived but the child died, and she was too delicate to have more. I used to reckon that the ultimate in marital accord was achieved by them when they took a passenger into their two-seater E-type Jaguar. Winifred, a slight woman, would sit over the gear box and change gear for Alan, while he declutched. They even double-declutched successfully.

The third partner was Aubrey Blackburn, a charming, good-looking middle-aged man who dealt chiefly with the acting side of the business and whom I saw quite rarely.

Jean and I travelled up that cold day in April by the Cornish Riviera Express, and went to the palatial offices of Christopher Mann Ltd. in Park Lane. It was on the seventh floor, lushly furnished, and commanded a fine view over the Park and Marble Arch. I cannot imagine any agent today being able to afford such grandeur.

I met Alan Grogan and Christopher Mann, and Jean was left in Winifred's charge while Alan took me off at once to meet the group who were going to make *Take My Life*: Anthony Havelock-Allan, heir to a baronetcy he later inherited, Ronald Neame, Gordon Wellesley, who was a story editor for Rank, and one or two others. They did not, however, want me immediately for *Take My Life* but to work for a couple of weeks on a film, already scripted, called *Pleasure Beach*, by Frank Tylsley. They were not happy with the script and wanted me to produce some new ideas. For this two weeks' work they offered me £150 over and above what they were offering me to come to London. (Remember, please, the discrepancy with today's figures. You could get a good single bedroom at a respectable Bloomsbury hotel for 8/6 a night, bed and breakfast. The Cumberland was 12/6. Claridges was £3. (Now it is £300.) You could buy a brand-new car for £125.) Ever willing to have a go at a new idea, I accepted, not knowing what on earth they were really looking for. I had never seen a film script before, except the one Valerie Taylor had produced as an example on which to model the technical side of our own story.

Right at the end of the war was a strange time to be suddenly rocketed into such an exotic and glamorous world. With clothing coupons limiting one's ideas, I hadn't bought a suit for eight years, and that was not a very good one at the outset. That first week, before she returned to our burgeoning family, Jean jetted off to Petticoat Lane and there was able not only to buy clothes for herself 'off the ration' but also to buy clothing coupons for me so that within a week I had been able to get a reasonable jacket and trousers – from, I think, Jaeger – and also to go to a good tailor in Cork Street, who in the fullness of time and after numerous fittings produced the most beautiful suit I have ever had.

Left alone in the Hallam Street flat when Jean went home, I struggled with the script of *Pleasure Beach*, going down to Denham every other day. But eventually nothing came of it. I had had one or two original cinematic ideas in *Take My Life*, but neither I nor anyone else seemed able to get our creative teeth into the Frank Tylsley story.

After the non-event of this film I was directed to the development of the script of *Take My Life*, a much happier field. Valerie Taylor had accepted an invitation to play two key Shakespearian roles at Stratford, so I was left to do this on my own.

These were all essentially young men I was working with – or young in my terms. I was the youngest, but all three directors of the Mann office were under forty, and so was almost everyone connected with the film. It was an exciting, nerve-straining, exacting, stimulating, exhausting summer. I met a lot of stars and had a lot of fun, but have always been glad that I had a hard North Country head which wasn't easily turned.

The heroine of our film was a concert artist. Mainly because I have always loved piano concertos, I made her a pianist. But Cineguild felt that because of the recent success of *Brief Encounter*, where the background music is piano music by Rachmaninov, they should change the instrument. So after long discussion they made Phillipa an opera singer. We spent a whole day (or it may have been two) at Denham with a pianist, specially engaged from Covent Garden, sitting at the piano, going through the operas with us, trying to choose which would be most suitable. One opera after another did not suit because the clothes were unbecoming or unsuitable, or for a variety of other reasons. In despair at the end I suggested sarcastically that the best thing would be to write our own opera. This they seized on as a brilliant idea and William Alwyn, who had been commissioned to write the music, was commissioned to write an opera called *Take My Life*, or as much of it as was necessary for the purposes of the story.

In the meantime *Demelza* was finished lovingly in May and June, and was published in December 1946, with acclaim and sales similar to its predecessor. Also the Rank Organisation had been going through my backlist and through its daughter company, Gainsborough Pictures, bought the rights of *The Forgotten Story* and another novel, *The Merciless Ladies*. Neither of these films was eventually made because as they were being set up the economic blizzard hit the industry.

The government was a good deal responsible for this blizzard – at least it was responsible, if one may vary the metaphor, for the spectacular boom and the catastrophic fall. The Chancellor of the

Exchequer, Hugh Dalton, in order to aid the British film industry, had clapped a quota on American films being shown in this country and had relied on British films to fill the gap. It was an impossible task suddenly to make sixty films a year instead of twenty; quality suffered badly in those that were made, and the distributors had the prospect of offering the exhibitors repeats of old films to keep their cinemas open. Also, the Americans threatened retaliatory action by refusing even to fill the quota. Thereupon Mr Harold Wilson, by now President of the Board of Trade, without even consulting the British film industry, rescinded the whole quota system and allowed the Americans free and full access as before. The result was that the British industry, producing a few good but many inferior films, was squeezed to death. Nor would the Americans in any way reciprocate by allowing the few good British films access to their markets.

Tommy Trinder starred in a film called *The Foreman Went to France*. A friend congratulated him on the fact that it had been released in America. Trinder said: 'It wasn't released, it escaped.'

The Rank Organisation lost millions during this period, and subsidiary companies like Gainsborough Pictures closed down altogether. Great numbers of technicians and tradesmen were thrown out of work for ever.

But when *Take My Life* was made, all this fortunately was in the unforeseeable future. During long periods while the film was in production I stayed in London and so saw a lot of the filming from the studio floor and came to know everyone concerned with the production very well. Tony Havelock-Allan, who produced the film, badly wanted his then wife, Valerie Hobson, to play the lead, but Ronald Neame, whose first picture this was as director, was much against this, and I was in the invidious position of being in the middle. I would certainly have greatly preferred Valerie Hobson, whom by this time I knew and admired very much, to the girl who was eventually chosen, Greta Gynt. But in fact, carefully dressed and well directed, she was very good in the part.

The premiere was on the 24th of May at the Empire, Leicester Square. In those days, a premiere was like a charity premiere today, merely lacking the royalty. Police held back the sightseers who crowded to see all the celebrities. Reporters dodged in and out, flashbulbs flickered, a thirty-strong band played us to our seats. My wife, looking marvellous in a new white Grecian dress, took her seat beside me and the lights went down.

We saw the film again. Gordon Wellesley, when he saw me in the foyer beforehand, said I looked 'very cher-u-bic'. If I did, I didn't feel it. I just felt sick.

After it was all over we drove back to Hallam Street and fell into bed in a happy stupor, for all the auguries were now good.

But still we were not prepared for the rest of the reviews. On the Sunday we drove home together to Cornwall, stopped in Mere to buy all the Sunday papers, which echoed the opinion of the dailies. 'How I enjoyed it!' one wrote. And another: 'Nobody had told me how *good* it was going to be.' Even C. A. Lejeune, the doyenne among the more austere critics, headed her article in the *Observer* 'Ice on theSpine' and said she wouldn't swap *Take My Life* 'and a couple of marbles' for the two expensively advertised American films released that week. Jimpson Harman of the *Evening News* said it bucked him up for the rest of the day. The *Spectator* and the *New Statesman* carried long columns about the film.

It was a wonderful time for me, for along with this success had gone the recent publication of *The Forgotten Story, Ross Poldark* and *Demelza*, which made my name known throughout the West Country.

During 1947 I kept my flat in Hallam Street, working intermittently on one film and another; then I wrote the script for the film of *The Forgotten Story*. But I was growing disillusioned. I have never had a very strong literary ego, and to spend a week writing something to order and then going to a script conference to hear your work discussed, and most often pulled to pieces, was destructive to my creative confidence. In the light of other people's stronger opinions I found myself doubting my own judgement. I also felt I was beginning to think in the form of visual scenes. (I have always written very visually, but not in bits of boiled-down action and dialogue.) So I decided it was time to make a move. I gave up my flat in London, ended my flirtation with the film industry, and returned to Cornwall absolutely determined that now I would sit down and write a novel that no one would *ever* film. I succeeded.

Wandering through the local parish churchyard of Perranzabuloe a few years before, I had seen a weather-beaten tombstone, on which one could only discern the name and the date. 'Cordelia, 1869.' The name was in large letters, which stretched from one side of the stone to the other, and standing there in the misty afternoon light I began to wonder what sort of a person this woman had been, how old she was when she died, how she had come by this attractive but romantic name, what her life story was, if only she could have told it to me.

During the last years of my mother's life, I listened, as with a sense of something soon to be lost, to her reminiscences as a young girl in the Manchester of the 80s and 90s. She had a brilliant memory, and through them I can trace my own family – *her* family anyway – in endless ramifications back to 1800. It was not just the main stems she remembered, but all the branches. Among them was an uncle, a rich dyer, who built Acacia Hall in Burnage, and something of his life story is reflected in the life of Mr Ferguson in the novel (*Cordelia*) I then wrote. Some of the characters and much of the background reflected things that my mother had told me, including the character of Mr Slaney-Smith, the atheist, who was based on Jack Slaney, whom I have referred to before, and who was a great friend of my grandfather.

So most of 1948 was taken with writing this long book, peering into my own and my mother's past. It was published in 1949, which meant that apart from a novelized version of *Take My Life*, which in my view was not nearly as good as the film, I hadn't published a book for nearly three years. Nor for the last two had I earned anything at all from the film industry, so that, with exceptionally high earnings in 1946, I found myself in 1948 paying more tax than my total earnings for that year.

In 1949 my mother died. She had been able to read and appreciate *Cordelia* in typescript. During the explosive success that hit me from 1945 onwards, she had seen her ewe lamb make good in a way she probably never quite expected. She had enjoyed all the successes at one remove but had been too frail to go to London to see any of the excitements for herself. However, such was the acclaim for *Take My Life* that the Odeon Cinema, Falmouth decided to put on their own premiere, at which Valerie Taylor and I were presented on the stage, and my mother was able to go to that. She said it was only then, observing the deference with which we were treated, that she realized what a success the film had been.

When my six-year-old son heard she was dead he put his head down on the dining-room table and cried. My daughter was perhaps too young to understand; but in the three years of their time together a tremendous rapport had grown up between the old woman and the little girl. Only when I saw my mother with Rosamund did I begin to understand how much, when I was born, she had wanted a daughter; how in early years she would have loved to dress me as a girl if she had dared; perhaps it explains some of the otherwise inexcusable pampering.

My mother's and my daughter's hair was identical, and even smelt the same. The last words my mother said to me about Rosamund were: 'Take care of my little love.'

In my new notoriety I was re-approached by Hodder & Stoughton, who offered me a handsome contract if I would write more books in the general style of *Take My Life* and *The Forgotten Story*. They promised to publish me with the greatest possible enthusiasm, and put their whole publicity and sales force behind the books. On the other hand they did not appear too keen on long family novels of eighteenth-century Cornwall. They thought the two I had done were quite enough.

Until now I had remained with Ward, Lock, whose chairman, since Wilfred Lock had retired, was a Colonel Shipton, an ex-soldier with much greater charm and address than his uncle, but not a man in the literary swim; and a personal friendship had sprung up which made the move, together with my in-built loyalty, much more difficult. Also the *Poldarks*, though latent for three years, remained active in my subconscious mind. The deep, almost passionate involvement in these books remained as a stirring memory. I was certainly going to write one more, if not two. I put it to Hodder that they should contract for my next three modern novels and that any *Poldark* novel or historical novel I wrote in the foreseeable future should still go to Ward, Lock. They willingly agreed. This meant that I might get the best of both worlds: a modern aggressive publisher for my modern books, my old colleagues for two more *Poldarks*.

The arrangement worked pretty well. During the next few years I had *Night Without Stars, Fortune is a Woman*, and *The Little Walls* with Hodder (two of them filmed) and *Jeremy Poldark* and *Warleggan* with Ward, Lock.

Something else was happening in the meantime. In 1949 an American publisher, Ken McCormick, chief editor of Doubleday, was in London on one of his scouting trips and my newly acquired agent Audrey Heath gave him *Cordelia* to read; he bought it for publication in the United States, where it came out in 1950.

American publication, though it promises much, may produce little. In my case it kept its promise. Before the book was published Doubleday sold it to the Literary Guild, who printed half a million copies in hardback and sold considerably more. The trade edition did well – and it was well reviewed.

In the same year Hodder published the first of my new modern novels, *Night Without Stars*, and it was filmed the same year. In 1947 an emerging new French publishing firm, Éditions Begh, had bought *The Forgotten Story*, and they published it in 1949. They also bought the first two *Poldark* novels but by the time these were translated the firm was running into financial trouble; it went into liquidation, and the *Poldark* books did not come out until many years later, under another imprint. The partners of Éditions Begh were three: Marie-Louise Deschamps-Eyme (Ma Lou); Basil Holroyd, an Englishman, and father of the now well-known Michael Holroyd; and Marcel Brandin, a fifty-year-old, dissolute, pale-faced, sophisticated, charming Frenchman with whom I maintained a fond friendship until he died. Basil was madly in love with the truly beautiful Ma Lou, who was herself mistress of the millionaire newspaper proprietor who financed the firm. How it all fell apart I never quite knew, but Marcel, who had been high in the ranks of the Maquis as a resistance fighter, and who was much disillusioned by the return of the old squabbling political parties to post-war France, deeply interested me, and I used him as the chief French character in *Night Without Stars*. In 1948 I met all three partners for the first time, then took the Train Bleu to the South of France.

Shortly before I left England I had met a man who, after a lifetime of partial blindness, had had an operation which enabled him to see everything properly for the first time. His account of his *annus mirabilis* made a great impression on me; and I felt I wanted in some way to write about it.

Then while in the South of France a number of minor experiences occurred and began to adhere to the story just growing in my mind. One day in a shoe shop in Nice I was served by a stunningly pretty French girl. I stood up and walked across the shop, trying out a new pair of shoes. Half-blinded by the sunlight flooding in from the street, I stumbled and fell over another box of shoes lying on the floor. Following this, two days later, there came a hair-raising trip by car over worm-narrow mountain roads beyond Grasse, when, as we were trying to squeeze past a workman's lorry, one wheel of our car slipped into a shallow gully on the edge of a precipice and nearly overturned. Then I discovered that the street beside the Hôtel Bristol at Beaulieu, where we were staying, was about to be ceremoniouslyrenamed after a *Résistance* fighter who had been shot by the Germans. I could now see the novel very well. This was published as *Night Without Stars*.

When the book was filmed later that year Hugh Stewart was assigned as producer, and the director was to be Anthony Pelissier, the son of Fay Compton and the nephew of Compton Mackenzie. Naturally, with my reputation inflated over *Take My Life*, I was chosen to write the script.

In July 1950 Hugh Stewart and Anthony Pelissier went to Paris to try to find an actress to play the French girl heroine of the novel, so I went along. With a degree of austerity imposed by the now impoverished Rank Organisation, they stayed at the Scribe. I stayed at the Continentale, which had not then been bought by the Intercontinental Group. In the Scribe we spent a whole day interviewing French actresses for the part, among them a delightful young girl called Nadine Alari, whom Marcel Brandin had recommended. But I fear that, assuming all the recommended girls to be actresses of some degree of competence, Anthony Pelissier's standard of judgement was not so much which girl would appeal to an audience as which girl appealed to him. His eye settled on an actress called Maria Mauban who, although watched over by a hawk-faced duenna of a mother, clearly returned some of his glances, and so it was settled – or so we all thought. Contracts between agents were about to be exchanged.

But when we got back to England Earl St John, chief executive director of Rank, under John Davis, would have none of it. Who was this Maria Mauban? Never heard of her. All very well for Tony to fancy her, but a 'name' was what was needed. In the end, after a lot of bitter argument, Nadia Gray was chosen, who was later to make a hit in *La Dolce Vita*. I remember a month or two later joining Anthony in Claridges where we were to meet Nadia Gray for the first time. We sat in the hall and she, disdaining the lift, which would have given her no 'entry', came lightly but slowly down the curved marble staircase, her skirt billowing round her matchless legs. I personally was disappointed – she was too sophisticated for my Alix – much better Nadine Alari – also she had freckled arms, which I have never cared for. However, I could see Anthony was prepared to make the best of it; and before the end of the film make the best of her he certainly did.

There were many suggestions as to who should play the half-blind Giles Gordon. Hugh Stewart's suggestion was David Niven, but this was vetoed by Earl St John. Niven was finished, he said. 'Box office poison.' (This in 1950, on the eve of the greatest successes of his career!) Then I made a daring suggestion. While *Take My Life* was being filmed I had gone up to Stratford to see Valerie Taylor play the lead in *Cymbeline* and to tell her how things were going in the studio, and I had been absolutely mesmerized by the performance – in quite a small role – of an unknown young actor. When he was on stage there was, to me, simply no one else there. His name was Paul Scofield.

This suggestion was not greeted with any enthusiasm at all by the Rank studios. They knew *of* him, of course, but he had done *nothing* in the film world, and in any case was a crazy mixed-up kid. No, they had to look elsewhere. In the end they chose David Farrar, who had made a fair success in a number of English films and wasn't bad in the part. But he had not a tenth of the elfin appeal of David Niven, and as an actor was simply not to be spoken of in the same breath as Paul Scofield.

Well, I wrote the script, and producer and director both said they were very happy with it. Pleased at this, I did not stay to watch the film being made but went to America with Jean, our first of many trips, to meet the rest of the Double-day board, who entertained us most royally and yet most tactfully, for three weeks, so that we enjoyed everything but were never pressurized. After this we took off for New Orleans, Jamaica and the Bahamas for another three weeks. During this wonderful trip my stomach, conditioned as it was to wartime rationing, gave out with a bad attack of gastritis in New Orleans, and for the rest of the trip and for a year afterwards I would get repeat performances. In the Bahamas Jean had her worst attack of asthma ever and looked as if she was going to die. One doctor who was called in gave her some pills which made the asthma worse. We told him this and he said: 'They can't do. Look at what it says on the bottle.' Eventually another doctor with the splendid name of Quackenbush was called; he came, very unsteady, from a cocktail party and broke the needle in her arm.

It was a pretty grim time, with constant visits from the doctor, great heat, no air conditioning in the hotel and only a lazy fan stirring the air, me with a bad stomach and damaged eardrums from flying from New Orleans to Miami in an unpressurized plane, the intense darkness of the nights and the hum of the mosquitoes. The doctor told me not to fly again for a year, so while we waited for a ship – they were scarce even in those days – we took a trip to Eleuthera. How it has been developed since those days I don't know, but it was then primitive in the extreme. The only vessel on which we could travel was the coastguard cutter because of the narrowness of the harbour. Jungle almost overgrew the few bumpy tracks, giant waves broke on white sandy beaches, with land crabs scuttering everywhere and, of course, the ubiquitous mosquito. We stayed at the solitary hotel, called French Leave, which – an innovation, I thought, in those days – had a central reception hall, lounge and dining room, and accommodation in small bungalows separate from the hotel. When we stepped out of our bungalow after dark to go to the main building, or vice versa, the mosquitoes fell on us like a cloud of MiGs. The hotel was run by a middle-aged well-educated Englishman and his wife. He had been a gunrunner for the Mexicans until a few years before.

One isolated modern colonial-style house belonged to a Colonel McGrath and his wife, the writer Rosita Forbes. They had been permanently settled there for years, but she told me that in early 1940 she felt she must return to England to do what work she could to help in the war effort. She arrived at Liverpool just after Dunkirk and the collapse of France.

While the customs officer was examining her baggage she said to him, 'Isn't it awful! Could it possibly be worse?'

He looked up and said: 'What? Oh, well, yes. It's been raining like this for days.'

While in Nassau we were able to attend a famous trial in which a man was accused of blackmail, following the murder of Sir Harry Oakes. We also got to know a fortune teller called Madame Grenadine who for some reason not made explicit had had to leave her rooms in Half Moon Street, Mayfair, in a hurry, and came to live in a distant British colony, where she had established a thriving practice. She told us that both the prosecuting and the defending barristers in this notorious court case had come to her for advice and for her to prophesy the outcome.

Leaving her rooms one day, where we had been to take tea with her, not advice, I spotted a peculiar thing like a little wrapped mummy hanging on a tree. I pointed it out. She said casually, 'Oh, someone has put an obeah on me.'

In retrospect it may seem nothing; but seen in the brief twilight before the sudden fall of night, with palms rustling and the over-sweet smell of dying blossoms, it was ominous and nasty.

On another occasion when we called in, a white man and woman were leaving with their son of about sixteen. When they had gone Madame Grenadine said: 'They came to see if I could help their son. But I can't. He's got leprosy.'

I always intended to write a novel – but never did – about the Bahamas, which seemed to me in those days to combine the worst features of British Colonialism and American Big Business. They also had the fascinating problem of the 'poor whites', the original white settlers who kept strictly to themselves over the generations and interbred so constantly that all sorts of lovely complaints seemed to be endemic, such as mental deficiency and susceptibility to leprosy. I was advised by my crystal-gazing lady friend to read a book called *Pink Pearl, A Study of Bahamanian Degeneracy*, but, again, never did.

We returned to England on the *Reina del Pacifico*, a fine ship but returning in ballast; and a force-8 gale made the eight-day crossing very uncomfortable. Particularly for Jean with her recurrent asthma.

After a few days at home to re-meet our children and to recuperate, and with Jean due for her next visit to Harley Street, we went up to London together and I took a look at the finished movie, made during my absence, of *Night Without Stars*. I could not follow the story.

It seemed that after I had gone Tony Pelissier had decided he didn't like my screenplay and had rewritten it as he thought best.

In fact the whole film was an example of the road to hell being paved with good intentions. Everybody had worked very hard to make it a success, and neither the producer, the director nor the writer was without talent, but it turned out a disaster. These things, as we know, can happen so easily either on stage or screen, and it is virtually impossible to point a finger at the cause.

Of my six films made, four are constantly repeated on TV. The two which are seldom shown are *Night Without Stars* and *The Sleeping Partner* – which was another even damper squib, though since this was taken wholly out of my hands and made in America I feel no responsibility for it. (The novel was also later made into a successful one-hour TV film by John Jacobs for Anglia.)

Although *Night Without Stars* was such a failure, my friendship

91

with Hugh Stewart and Anthony Pelissier was unimpaired. I never, of course, in all my life ever had any friction with Hugh, but it is probably a testimony to us both that Anthony and I used to enjoy each other's company until he died.

The other formative influence in 1950, one that I have already briefly mentioned, was that I became a member of the Savile Club. In early 1945 Peter Latham had suggested it, and when I was in London invited me to dine there to see how it appealed to me. In fact, having always been so much a loner, club life did not appeal at all; and at that first dinner I sat with the eminent zoologist Sir Peter Chalmers Mitchell on my right and H. G. Wells opposite me. Wells must have been about eighty at the time. I remember he wore a grey herringbone suit with a dark red tie and shirt with the wings of the collar in disarray. He was polite but uncommunicative. He had just published his last book, called *Mind at the End of its Tether*. Neither he nor Chalmers Mitchell at that late time in their lives were exactly apostles of lightness and joy, and I thanked Peter very much and asked to be excused. At about the same time I had also seen a fair amount of the Savage Club as Benno Moiseiwitsch's guest, and he had similarly put the suggestion that he would like to propose me for membership of the Savage. Again, I thanked him and pleaded the excuse that I lived in Cornwall and wasn't really the clubbable type.

Now, in 1950, I was invited to spend a night or two with Hugh Stewart and his wife Frances in order to discuss the film of *Night Without Stars*, and almost immediately Hugh asked me why I didn't become a member of the Savile Club. By then I was a little more inured to the prospect, and I told him that a chap called Peter Latham had suggested this five years ago, that I had said no, but now, having seen so much more of London in the interim, I might think of it more seriously.

'I'll see Peter,' he said. 'You must come to lunch there with him and we'll talk it over.'

I did. We did. My name went down in the book, and in the July I was elected a member. And shortly, within a year, I began to feel that, in addition to Cornwall, I had another home.

Chapter Seven

The Savile Club in those days was an extraordinary institution, like no other club, I believe, in the world. It is not now quite what it was but is still very good.

When William Golding was made a Nobel Prize winner a few years ago, the Savile put up a small notice on the board congratulating him, and listing the seven previous Nobel Prize winners who had been members of the club. (In fact it is seventeen, as the historian of the Savile Club, Anthony Garrett Anderson, has established.) The other literary names were W. B. Yeats and Rudyard Kipling, the rest being scientists, astronomists, physicists. The club coruscated with great names: Hardy, Stevenson, Elgar, Priestley, Wells, Walton, Vaughan Williams, Cockcroft, Rutherford, Chadwick, J. J. Thompson. It was a place where the great went to relax; it could be as unceremonious as a public school, as intellectual as the best university, as Bohemian as a Soho restaurant.

When I first joined, the place seemed to be full of eccentrics and intellectuals, of raconteurs, wits and half-wits. Looking back, I suppose most of the members of the club were fairly ordinary chaps by temperament who had distinguished themselves in some walk of life. But the men I met and came to know by staying in the club, not just using it for occasional meals, were the nucleus, the hard core of regular attenders who got the most out of the club by putting the most in; and it was these men whose ranks I intermittently joined and by whom I was accepted. I remember Sir David Milne, the then head of the Scottish Office, saying to me in the billiard room one night: 'You'll do. I thought you were too quiet, but I see you're going to be one of us.'

When Benno Moiseiwitsch heard I was thinking of joining the

Savile he said it was 'the snob's club'. He could hardly have been more wrong, unless one included intellectual snobbery, of which there was a reasonable amount. So far as class was concerned the sign over every Toc H meeting place, 'All Rank Abandon Ye Who Enter Here', would equally have applied to the Savile.

I came to look forward to my visits: they were a tremendous mental stimulus. While remaining dedicated to Cornwall, I found this the first break in the total commitment of earlier years.

One thing that concerned me a little about my evenings at the club was the amount of hard drinking that went on. By some extraordinary piece of good fortune, excessive drink never appealed to me – though I could always take a modest amount and love it – but it startled me to see how much some of my new friends put away. Many of them were very famous men – and all were pretty well at the top of whatever particular tree they had chosen to climb – it seemed wasteful of talent and good health to pour so much down their throats. God knows, I was not censorious, or they would soon have detected it; and I was able to get along on my limited intake without its being noticeable. But I couldn't help but think, 'If you become President of this or Chairman of that, or the leading authority on some aspect of astronomy or architecture or disease or whatever, there must have been a lot of dedicated striving – whatever the talent – to reach such eminence; is this excess really the best way to celebrate it?'

As a committed heterosexual I have never paid much attention to homosexuality. I have never felt strongly on the subject at all – except some resentment at the purloining of that lovely old three-letter word of twelfth-century French, used to describe a happy condition, now turned into a word to describe a sexual preference. But aside from that …

Two of my closest friends when I first went to live in Cornwall were (a) a bachelor Scout master and (b) a widowed curate. As a schoolboy I knew the facts of life, but little more, but I knew precisely where my own instincts lay.

When the curate was moved to another living, he invited me to spend a weekend with him. I accepted, and we slept together two nights in a double bed. There was no thought in my mind that there was anything untoward in this, but if anything *had* happened I should have been as scandalized and angry as a Somerset Maugham spinster – not shocked out of prudery, but out of a total savage disgust.

As for the scoutmaster, I never saw him with other boys, but I would bet my bottom dollar he was one of those men to whom sex means almost nothing at all. There are some such men, and women, though it is unfashionable to suppose so.

I mention these matters here because when I joined the Savile in 1950 I believe it was the only one of the great London clubs who would accept 'gays'. I never heard any such hint dropped in the election committee at the Savile, but let some hint of it be dropped in any other committee and the man would be quietly dropped too. In the Savile, it was not a factor in the equation. It was of no more relevance than if a candidate was married, single, or divorced. It was his behaviour in the club, and of course his intellect and his achievements, which were all that mattered. So long as he didn't, in Mrs Patrick Campbell's famous words, 'frighten the horses', what he did outside the club was his own damned business. (I remember at one such committee a member saying, 'The only trouble with this chap is that he looks like a Borstal boy.' A man opposite said, 'He'd be more interesting if he'd been one.')

At a time when all the taboos were still up one might have thought this tolerant attitude on the part of the Savile would have resulted in there being a large number of homosexual members. It did not seem so. Some perhaps I never noticed, for I never thought about it. A few were obviously gay, and as the moral climate relaxed, they became a little more overt.

This led to one of the best bits of repartee, at one of the round tables at the Savile, when a couple of members started teasing Humphrey Hare about his sex life. He bore this with his usual good temper, but eventually with a great laugh, for which he was famous, shouted: 'What d'you expect me to do – go to bed with a horse?'

A little man at the other side of the table immediately remarked:

'I thought the age of cavalry was past.'

Humphrey Hare was the son of a general, an old Etonian, an ex-Guardsman, a great friend of Compton Mackenzie, to whom he offered much candid advice on the subject of Monty's writing. Hare was completely bilingual and supplemented his private means by translating French books into English for various publishers. So good was he that he did not need to write anything down. As he read the French he would dictate the translation into a dictaphone and post it off when done.

Hare was a very handsome man, tall, erect, noisy, amiable. For some reason, Frank, our valet at the club, did not like him. He would come into my room with a cup of tea at 8 a.m. and say, 'Mornin', sir. Nice cup of tea. Just eight o'clock,' and as he left the room he would add venomously: 'Hare's asleep.' Fifteen minutes later he would return with my shoes duly polished and say, 'Quarter after eight, sir. Plenty of time. Shall I run yir bath?' And then, as an angry postscript as he left: 'Hare's asleep.'

I took these interchanges back to Cornwall, and it became a family saying, 'Hare's asleep.'

Then one day in Venice when Jean and I were walking down the Merceria we met Humphrey Hare and his mother, who were holidaying like us. Jean was astounded to meet this tall broad-shouldered Adonis, when she had thought from my stories that he was a small wizened man.

In view of his military background one would have expected Hare to be right wing in politics; in fact the very reverse. He fought in the Spanish Civil War on behalf of the government against Franco, and teamed up with two others of similar lineage and persuasion: Nancy Mitford and her then husband, Prod, as he was known in the Savile, that is the Hon. Peter Rennell Rodd.

As Franco began to gain the upper hand they were involved in the bitter rearguard action before Barcelona. One of the three then perpetrated one of the best puns of the decade. As they hastily chartered a ship to convey many of the government's most prominent supporters out of reach of Franco's vengeance, he – or she – said:

'Well, I've heard of people having all their eggs in one basket. I have never before heard of anyone having all their Basques in one exit.'

Chapter Eight

Meanwhile events moved well for me in the United States, and it can be said that from 1950 until 1970 three-quarters of my affluence came from across the Atlantic. One after another of the books I wrote were Book Club choices, and paperback sales abounded. In England sales were steady but unexciting by comparison. When *Marnie* hit the headlines in 1962 I remarked in a press interview at the time that I was 'the most successful unknown novelist in England', and the phrase stuck and has often been repeated. Now that the great flush of the *Poldark* television series is long past, perhaps there is a chance that it may become true again.

The strange imbalances in the public awareness of my prosperity may also be partly the reason why so many innocent souls thought the TV series had 'made' me. One dear lady from Cornwall wrote to me saying I must think it strange achieving success at last after 'writing away all these years'. Cornish and West Country newspapers sometimes still contribute to this myth.

Though fond of animals – particularly cats, of which for many years we had two Siamese – I never until my middle life owned a dog.

But walking across the beach at Perranporth one day we saw a huge white dog with great floppy paws, ponderous but gentle movements, a tail like one of the Prince of Wales's feathers, and a dignified but friendly manner. The two children, aged about ten and six, fell in love at first sight. We approached the owners, who said it was a Pyrenean mountain dog, and they had got him from a breeder in Leicester. The outcome, after much discussion, was that I wrote to the breeder and asked if they had a puppy for sale. They replied that they had not, but one of their bitches was expected to give birth in September. By Christmas we could have the puppy. With considerable excitement we agreed. We all decided that he should be called Garrick. What more suitable?

In November we heard from the breeder. A male puppy had duly arrived, sound in wind and limb, soon would be fully house-trained and was lively and intelligent. There was one slight hitch. Due to some breeding quirk, he had a slightly defective tail. It would probably, the dealer said, grow naturally as the dog developed; but if we felt this slight imperfection was not acceptable another of their bitches was expecting in April, and we could instead put in an order for this puppy for next June. If we preferred to go ahead with our present order they would reduce the price by X guineas (I forget what).

I was doubtful, thought at first of trying some other breeder; but the children were adamant. The dog was to be their *Christmas present*! And as for a defective tail, how utterly appropriate could that be? Garrick, Demelza's dog, whose tail was part cut off at Redruth Fair! Daddy, it had to be!

The delivery date was fixed for mid-December. The puppy would be sent by train from Leicester and would arrive at Truro station at 5.30 a.m., where we were to collect him. The night before Jean and I were going to a hunt ball at Newquay (not that we hunted, but a few of our friends did). Newquay is about ten miles from Perranporth, and Truro from Perranporth is about the same. We arrived back from the ball about 3.30 a.m., changed, lay in bed for an hour and then set off to meet our new friend.

It was pitch black, of course, and Truro station was almost deserted; three old men, on a seat, a porter pushing an empty trolley, the long station dim lit. The train came in on time (as they often did on the old Great Western Railway) and at first only four people got off. Then we saw the luggage van at the other end and hastened towards it. Two boxes of books, a sheaf of newspapers, then something larger was carefully lowered down. It was our new puppy, already three times the size we had expected, who had made the journey from Leicester in a large laundry basket.

Garrick grew, and he grew, and he grew, like some monster in a fairy tale. The only part that did not grow, which remained stunted and misshapen, was his tail. What did that matter? Indeed it had its special significances. Well … but …

Did the breeding quirk that deformed the tail also imbue him with his outrageous amount of energy? Would this bounding, bouncing ever-enlarging bundle of vitality ever grow into a ponderous, dignified, warmly stately animal such as the one we had seen on the beach? Could a year or two's ageing make all the difference?

Our house had two long halls meeting at an L turn. Indoors Garrick was as well behaved as a good-tempered child, settling into our ways and, it seemed, totally happy in them. We gave him his own bedroom, the last on the ground floor and near the back door. In the evenings he would lie stretched out in front of the fire in our drawing room, which was at the extreme end of the other arm of the L. At about 10 p.m. I would kneel down beside him and whisper in one great floppy ear, 'Time for bed, Garrick.' I never had to say it twice. He would cock a bloodshot eye at me and after a moment heave his great bulk onto its feet and proceed entirely on his own down the two long passages and slump into his own comfy bed to pass the night. Later Jean or I would go along and say good night to him.

As soon as he was free in the morning he would come lolloping up into our bedroom and salivate over my sheets until I gave him the digestive biscuit I had had waiting. In spite of his bulk and his great energies I never remember a solitary thing he broke in the house, not a plate, not a cup, not a glass. The perfect animal.

In the garden he was well behaved. I have a movie picture of him chasing Jean round the garden, grabbing at her skirt, but never, never tearing it.

As he grew we took him on increasingly long walks, and when we could we would let him off the lead. That was where the trouble began. He would charge about fascinated in finding new dogs to smell, birds to chase, motor bikes to pursue. Suddenly he would be deaf, or not choose to hear his name. Panting after a long run, we would eventually catch up with him, grab him by the double ruff and get the lead on him again. But even this was not much of a solution, for he would at once want to go ahead at twice our speed and drag one of us – or sometimes both – lurching after him. As he got larger he got more uncontrollable, and we had to resort to the chain collar which was supposed to tighten about his neck the more he pulled. This is a resort frowned on by some dog lovers because it is supposed to hurt the dog. With his great ruff it seemed to make no difference at all.

Jean took him many times to a training school for dogs in Camborne. Every time he behaved impeccably while he was there, even, Jean said, showing himself more intelligent than most of the rest, but reverting immediately when he got home.

The children thought much of him and made much of him, but were often away at school. He made much of us all; but he had no control over his roaming instincts. We could not spend all day superintending him. We would leave him snoozing comfortably on the back lawn and half an hour later the telephone would ring, sometimes from as far as three miles away, and a voice would say: 'Mr Winston Graham, we have a big white dog walking around in our vegetable garden … No, I don't think he has done much damage. He let me read his collar. Could you come and collect him?'

Jean or I would go and collect him. It was amusing enough to begin, but repetition became wearisome. Garrick would react appropriately to harsh words or honeyed ones. There was no harm in him, never an ill intent.

Two factors weighed heavily against him. He had a passionate dislike of two-stroke motorbikes, and the local policeman rode a two-stroke motorbike. The policeman could, perhaps, be placated. Perhaps once only. The worse and much more dangerous prospect was that once or twice we had just succeeded in restraining him from chasing sheep. That in a district where sheep was the commonest form of farming was an amber light turning to red.

We began to think of selling our beloved dog, or even giving him away. Who would buy him, who would take him? Indeed, who would love him, as we did? We hung on for a while, hoping for the best. The climax came when one day we locked him in the house. He galloped up the stairs to the first floor, found the landing window ajar, pushed it open, squeezed his bulk through the narrow aperture and slid down the tiled roof and leapt or fell the remaining twelve feet to land on an escallonia hedge, and, hurrah, he was free! We returned to hear the phone ringing and were told that Garrick was up at a farm in Trevollas four miles away, playing with a half dozen other dogs.

After a fitful further six months we parted from our warmhearted, loving, rollicking split personality of a dog with grief and kisses all round.

We gave him to a professional footballer living near Newquay, who took a five-mile run every morning and needed a companion. I have always hoped he had found the companion to suit him.

In the twenty years following the publication of the fourth *Poldark* – *Warleggan* – I wrote (with only one exception, *The Grove of Eagles*) all modern novels, ten in total, five of which were filmed on the big screen and five – not always the same – were major book club choices in the US. In addition the huge Bertelsmann book club in Germany took two of those books and the Club degli Editori of Italy two. The cumulative effect was considerable. So was the oppressiveness of the tax situation. In those days so much was confiscated by the Inland Revenue that while one could live in fine style it was virtually impossible to accumulate money, and with the two children at expensive schools and a wife with a taste for good living at least the equal of my own, I was aware of the possible impermanence of prosperity. I was writing – as always – what I wanted to write and not what I thought the public wanted. Three of the ten books were not a particular success, but that was an acceptable proportion. Public taste is fickle. And tastes can change. It would be a good and timely precaution to retain a bit more of one's earnings.

So towards the end of this period I began to look around. Our house, which we had occupied for thirteen years since the end of its commercial activities, badly lacked a garden. The house was built on rising ground overlooking the village, but it was made ground, from the stone and mineral refuse, the 'attle', of a long extinct mine, and a six–inch veneer of soil had been spread to cover the rock. There was never a trace of subsidence in the building, but gardening was not rewarding work. During the war we tried to plant potatoes, with ludicrous results. I wanted a garden, and preferably one with soil that rhododendrons and camellias would tolerate. Over the spine of Cornwall where the soil, though still fairly shallow, was superbly acid, and watered by the soft rains, these exotic plants luxuriated. Also, although the winds on the south coast were still savage, they were almost zephyr-like compared to the tempests which fell upon us on the north coast. In Perranporth scarcely a tree flourished. To encourage a sycamore to grow a dozen feet high was a major achievement. On the other hand, lime-tolerant shrubs, bulbs, roses, low-growing bedding plants, gorse and heather and foxgloves and poppies brought a blaze of colour in the spring and early summer. At Treberran in favourable, specially created, pockets we had lovely flowers. I even made a rhododendron bed by bringing back soil in dustbins in the back of my Alvis from the other side of the county. The bed prospered. In spite of prophecies that the lime would get into the bed and eventually kill the plants, they were still flowering freely twenty years after we left.

But it was makeshift. Why should I go on tinkering with gardening, making do with the third rate, when I could have the best? If we moved, then clearly somewhere near Falmouth or St Austell were the areas to look in. It was a different, softer Cornwall, but it would still be within easy reach of the beaches we loved.

Yet southern Cornwall did not attract us so much to live in. Most of the small villages and towns by the sea had even in those days been invaded by the retired, from up county or locally, by genuine and would-be yachtsmen, by a certain social stuffiness that did not attract us. Perranporth, for all its gimcrack attempts to attract the tourist, was robustly alive and many of the families remained stubbornly Cornish. The very violence of the winds was a challenge and a stimulus.

And such a move would do nothing to solve the tax problem.

Go abroad? Live abroad? Become a tax exile? Ever since the end of the war my wife and I, sun and sea worshippers and revelling as we did in the beaches of Cornwall, had taken our holidays further south where there was a hotter sun and a warmer sea: Italy, Greece, Spain, France, Yugoslavia, etc. Of these countries France was the most accessible, the one whose language we moderately understood, the most civilized and certainly the land where we had the most friends. If we left Treberran we ought to leave England, at least for an experimental period. We put Treberran up for sale with that in mind.

Again it was in a trough in house prices, and it took over a year to sell. But it happened in the end.

Two incidents I specially recall. One was soon after the sale when my son was home from school and we were out somewhere together and decided to have a bottle of champagne to celebrate the sale. He said quietly: 'What is there to celebrate?' So much for the opinion of both our children.

Being lumbered with a specially vivid imagination and being apparently able to see all sides of every question, I had agonized long about the decision to move, knowing that I was not deciding the future of one but of four. No one will ever know whether my decision was the right one.

The other incident occurred the night before we left. Half the furniture had gone into store and we were sleeping in our usual bedroom on the ground floor. In the later part of the night there was a loud crash, and when we went into the uncarpeted hall we found that a picture had fallen and smashed the glass. It was a John Speed map of Cornwall, dated 1614, a prized possession. The cord had broken. I still have the map, but sometimes wonder if it was an omen that we should never live in Cornwall again.

Having given – or lent – our cat to a friend, we left for London, and after six weeks in a furnished house there, drove off to the South of France in two cars, a Mini and a three-litre Alvis, laden with books, a few personal belongings and two children. Andrew, my son, being now seventeen, had passed his driving test, so we shared the driving between the three of us – though I think at that time I did not let Andrew drive the Alvis. Wherever we stopped we were surrounded by people staring at the Mini. It had come out in 1959 and this was the spring of 1960. Even in England it was a rarity (I had only been able to buy one because of a pull I had with a garage owner) and in France *nothing* like it, nothing so small, had ever been seen before. We should have been presented with a free Mini for the publicity we gave it in France.

For the previous two years we had driven down to the Côte d'Azur, and after a preliminary holiday in Italy, had ended up at Cap Ferrat and stayed at the Hôtel Voile d'Or. Michael Powell, the director of so many prestigious movies like *The Red Shoes* and *The Life and Death of Colonel Blimp*, owned it, having inherited it from his father, whose mistress, Madame Alice, ran it – together with Michael's own wife, Frankie, who deserves a book to herself. Irish, pretty, fey, vague, extravagant of gesture and emotion, warm, throwaway, impulsive, generous, feckless and devil-may-care, Frankie knew everybody. The hotel was not well run but it was jolly, and whom might one not meet there? Not only did she know everyone in the film industry, she seemed to be on terms with half the artists and intellectuals of France.

Having got to know her pretty well in the two previous visits, I told her that we were coming to live in France and would like to rent a villa somewhere along the coast. She instantly discovered the Villa Caprice and took it on our behalf.

We therefore went down in March, halting on the high ground above Dijon to hear, on the fading long-wave BBC channel, the details of the latest British Budget, and then plunged onwards towards our Mediterranean summer.

The Villa Caprice was a four-bedroomed house, pleasant but small, perched directly above the road leading round the harbour. It could hardly have been more central: when we opened champagne, the corks would fly over the road and into the harbour. We settled there for the Easter holidays, and at the end of them the children went back to England until the summer break. We had brought a motor-powered Kleppermaster with us for sailing round the coast and for waterskiing. We also for a time hired my friend Max

Reinhardt's cabin cruiser with its two 40 h.p. Johnson engines. In late July our children came back, and over the summer holidays we had a succession of their friends to stay, as well as our niece Jacqui Williamson, who had a wonderful time.

In effect it was a wonderful time for us all. We picnicked nearly every day, either on Passable Beach or on Paloma, or at sea. Most Fridays we drove to the market at Ventimiglia, where every week we found something new to splash our money on. Shoes, gloves, shirts, blouses, beach equipment, sheets, food, fruits, cakes – then further on into Italy where we usually managed to reach San Remo for a late bathe before lunch and then endless bathes after; beach football and tea and then the longish drive home along the Lower Corniche, stopping at some little hotel or restaurant for supper and reaching Cap Ferrat about 11 p.m. A fourteen-hour day of incomparable pleasure.

In the evenings there were parties or the local cinema or – rarely – we went to the Casino at Beaulieu, or to grand opera out of doors in Les Arènes in nearby Nice, or orchestral concerts given before Prince Rainier and Princess Grace in the Palace in Monaco.

I say 'rarely' to the Casino for I have never had any interest in gambling. In 1950, on our first trip to the United States aboard the first *Queen Elizabeth*, we had a little trouble when disembarking in finding a customs officer to mark our luggage.

We eventually found one, who in friendly fashion said: 'Where are you staying, Mr Graham?'

I replied, the New Weston.

'Aw,' he said, 'that's real good. That's a real good bar. D'ye know during the war it was one of the few places in New York where you could squander money economically.'

I shook him by the hand and said: 'My friend, this is something I have enjoyed doing all my life, but I have never been able to describe it before.'

I was doing just that in the South of France. To go to the Casino would have been in my view to squander money uneconomically. Besides being a bore.

We made a lot of interesting and entertaining friends: Graham and Kathleen Sutherland, Gregory and Veronique Peck, Princess Starraba; and others, like Jack and Doreen Hawkins and Prince and Princess Chula of Thailand, we had known in England. My daughter, being a natural blonde and very pretty though only fourteen-and-a-half, was besieged by handsome young French boys, who could not resist her. Among her other suitors were Steven Peck, Gregory's second son by his first wife, and his second wife's brother, Joe Passani, who was also her age.

Gregory Peck had been married to his second wife only five years at this time, and had two young children by her. They had taken a large villa with a huge swimming pool just behind the Voile d'Or, and Madame Passani, his new mother-in-law, was with them. She was a distinguished Russian woman, still in her forties, an intellectual of great charm and force of character, with formidable good looks that appeared and disappeared with her moods. Gregory was not present much at first, being still bound up in the making of *The Guns of Navarone*, which was running months over schedule, but Madame Passani – or Shoshone – took a great fancy to us, and our friendships blossomed and lasted for years. Her charm of character and personality made a great impression on me, and generations later she surfaced as Shona in *The Green Flash*.

I think her husband, who had some time ago disappeared from the scene, was half-French, half-Italian, and Veronique must have resembled him more than her mother, being a dark, attractive Latin. Joe, her much younger brother, who is now a successful surgeon in California, always looked the Russian to me.

After we had returned to England, Gregory and Veronique Peck also moved to England on a new film he was making, and the friendship ripened. We went as a foursome to theatres and restaurants; also we spent a day with them at the house they had rented in Denham, where Veronique showed her comic abilities by mimicking some elderly earl they knew playing croquet. Once when staying in Cornwall a maid came to the table where we were dining and said in a trembling voice: 'You're wanted on the phone, Mr Graham. It's – it's Greg – Gregory Peck.'

Later, when we went to Hollywood we dined with them and

were on the best of terms. Some years then passed when our only exchange was of Christmas cards.

Then one year I heard that Gregory was going to Venice for the Film Festival, so I wrote to him and suggested we should meet there. There was no reply. I asked my agent to get in touch with his agent, which he did. No response. When we reached Venice I sent him round by hand a note from the Danieli to the Gritti, but it brought no reply, and we never met thereafter.

He always seemed such a normal, charming, courteous man that this lack of response has long puzzled me. It could, I suppose, have had something to do with the tragic loss of his son.

During that summer in France we bathed and sunbathed and boated and socialized and drove up and down the coast in our big open Alvis, and went to the Festival of Flowers in Nice, and an August fiesta there with fireworks of extravagant variety, and to the Monte Carlo Grand Prix, and to other events wherever and whenever the fancy took us.

A girl called Penny, who was at school with Rosamund in England, and of an age, arrived to stay for a couple of weeks. Compared to Rosamund's piquant good looks, she was quite awful. Her black hair was lank, she walked with a limp, her eyes were lacklustre, her skin pasty, she didn't have much to say for herself. Jean looked her over for a couple of days and then took her in hand. She found the shuffling limp was due to ill-fitting shoes; she bought her new ones – with high heels. Penny was taken to a hairdresser, and came out with her straight dull black hair shining like a sword and draping attractively over one side of her face. A new dress, a bit of tactful make-up and she was transformed. The lacklustre in her eyes disappeared overnight. She was killing. For the first few days of Penny's stay, Rosamund found her friend a drag on her cheerful activities. After that she was slightly chagrined to find gazes straying from her to this sultry dark-eyed girl with the brilliant eyes and the fresh complexion and the elegant walk. No filmic transformation was greater. It was *Roman Holiday* over again.

A big American aircraft carrier came in to Villefranche Bay.

Rosamund decided to take a pedalo, along with Penny, from Passable Beach to reconnoitre. Only when they came back did we discover that Penny could not swim. Thereafter they had two American sailors who came over to see them whenever they were free. We nicknamed them Mutt and Jeff. But in imagination I began to compose a letter to Penny's parents: 'It is with the deepest regret that I have to inform you that in a drowning accident in Villefranche Bay …'

At the end of the summer holidays our two children went back to England to school, and, a bit later, when our lease of Villa Caprice expired, we followed. We could have renewed the lease but did not.

We had had a wonderful time. A few years later Philip Larkin, writing of expatriate authors, speaks of:

> … the shit in the shuttered chateâu
> Who does his five hundred words
> Then parts out the rest of the day
> Between bathing and booze and birds.

I didn't have a shuttered chateau but a pleasant small villa and the possibility of buying some property nearby. I was never a boozer, but wine was plentiful and cheap. I was happily married but that was not exactly a liability. But I was ready to go home.

For one thing I had perversely chosen to write my one historical novel of those twenty years, *The Grove of Eagles*, at this juncture, and although I had weighted down the cars with reference books I still needed more. For a second I don't think I was averaging anything near five hundred words a day, little though that seems. If one puts on bathing trunks for breakfast and goes down to a beach with a picnic lunch and a beach ball and returns at five, satisfactorily drunk with sea and sun – and then settles down to work – it just doesn't come off. Elleston Trevor, who lived high in Monte Carlo and used to drive down to the beach before breakfast in his ancient Rolls, bathe and then return to spend the morning writing, had established a routine that I would have to have adopted if I had made the decision to stay.

A third objection was that the Villa Caprice, being right down by the harbour, was an enervating place to live. Used to the Cornish sun, which is always welcome in such light air – or to shorter dosages of the Mediterranean heat – I had always been a sun worshipper. (Many of our friends used to look with envy on Jean because she had a husband who loved to spend all day on a beach.) But perhaps it's not altogether surprising that the Druids lived in Britain where the sun is errant and therefore always welcome. The Mediterranean sun, after some months, and enclosed as we were by rising ground about us, became oppressive. Sometimes we would drive up and picnic on the Moyen Corniche where the lighter air made the sun more enjoyable.

Much of this could, of course, have been corrected by a change of residence. You needed a place three or four hundred feet up. Elleston Trevor had the right idea, though I wouldn't have wanted to live in a flat in Monte Carlo. We priced the cost of one or two small villas for sale and – by English standards then – they were exorbitant. So far as I can remember, the cost of living in France was not muchdifferent from England, but I did not fancy buying a small, ill-built villa, after living all my married life in a big house. (No doubt Cap Ferrat and its neighbourhood was one of the worst places to try: we were surrounded by millionaires.)

Although we had plenty of friends in Cap Ferrat, notably those I have mentioned, I lacked the stimulus of my London friends. I missed the theatre and the cinema. I missed the Savile, I missed the availability of endless books to read. There were cinemas in the neighbourhood, but they never started until nine and were distinctly smelly, and there was always a sudden break in the middle of the feature film when everyone loped out for ice-cream or a fruit drink, and usually the programme did not finish until nearly 1 a.m., so that one arrived home feeling bleary. And there were, of course, the bits of officialdom common to all countries, such as re-registering as an alien at regular intervals; the cars were still insured in England; our furniture was in store there; did we go back and sell it or have some of it shipped over?

Another influence was my own physical well-being. In July I had a bad attack of stomach pain, vomiting and diarrhoea. The local doctor gave me morphia for the pain and antibiotics to effect the cure, saying it was probably caused by the local wine. I was soon about again but thereafter subject to fortnightly or so attacks of a sort of colitis, which was weakening and horribly uncomfortable. These symptoms were faithfully driven away by antibiotics, and as faithfully returned when the antibiotics stopped. The sequence continued despite all dietary and other changes until several months after our return to England. Also my wife's asthma, which had been enormously improved as a result of two courses of injections from Harley Street, but which always threatened and which needed pills and inhalers handy to ward it off, had shown no sign of improvement in the warm Mediterranean air. It was if anything slightly more troublesome than it had been in Cornwall. (I was still not entirely attuned to the idea of climate and environment having a drastic effect on her asthma, but I had hoped for some improvement. It used to frustrate me sometimes when we would leave Cornwall on a beautiful light and airy and sunny November day and her breathing would be so tight she could hardly go a dozen steps without using an inhaler, and we would arrive in London in dirty fog, and she would immediately begin to breathe freely. Such, I would say, is the cussedness of human nature.)

A few other straws in the wind drew us home, among them a feeling that, however delicious and funny and stimulating a time they had had when they were on the Côte d'Azur, my children felt the need of a root in England. I remember particularly my son's delight when he heard we had bought a house, even if it was not in his beloved Cornwall.

Chapter Nine

But where was home? If it had to be England in spite of the tax, then should it again be Cornwall? I had grown increasingly fond of London (or, at least, a small area in the centre) and although we had taken houses and flats in London four times for shortish periods in the last few years, we had never actually lived near enough to feel it within easy reach. It was a stimulating idea and I felt that while we were footloose we should experiment. To return to Cornwall so soon – though that was in our eventual sights – would be defeatist.

Several times in earlier days we had driven to London and thence to Glyndebourne and by stages home. Often also we had passed through Sussex on the way to and from the Channel ports. We both thought it a lovely county, one of the only ones I thought I could bear to live in after Cornwall. It was convenient, it had a long sea coast with easy access to France – which we still wanted to visit – it was wooded and undulating. It was a great cricketing county (though abysmal at rugby). It was near London and a lot of my friends.

I answered a number of advertisements in *The Times*; furnished houses to let. We had replies from five, so, regretful at the end, we packed up our two cars and our Kleppermaster – which was to go by rail – and made our affectionate farewells and started for home.

Having a choice of houses as far separated as Midhurst, Partridge Green and Uckfield, we chose Uckfield, because the house was eighteenth century and handsome and roomy and because it was immediately available. Hotel life with two cars overflowing with personal possessions did not attract. We moved in as quickly as we could, drove down at the earliest opportunity and recovered our Siamese cat, and settled to another world, another experience.

I shall not forget that first winter in Sussex. The weather was gentle, mild and sunny – I remember driving to Brighton one January day and seeing people sitting on the promenade in the sun. I thought: Good Lord, so this is winter in the south-east, how infinitely preferable to a Cornish winter with its cold rain and its ranting, bitter winds! The next summer, looking for a house to buy (we saw about forty), I was struck by the dishonesty of estate agents and the semi-squalor in which so many apparently respectable people lived. When we visited the house we eventually bought I observed an attractively distorted Japanese cherry in the garden and thought to myself, If this were in Cornwall I would think that tree had been so shaped by the wind – of course not in this balmy climate! We moved in in the following February, and the night after our arrival we were struck by a massive gale that shook the house to its foundations and nearly uprooted the cherry. It then proceeded to blow from every direction for the next twelve months.

But one strange thing was emerging: my wife's asthma was going away. For years, almost from the time my son was born – and he was then eighteen – I had never seen her lie in bed without at least three non-feather pillows to prop her up. Now she was beginning to lie flat, relaxed, sprawled, on her back, on her side, on her stomach, the way most people sleep. One doctor in Cornwall, who loved to think himself a psychiatrist, had tried to find some linkage between her comparative freedom when she was away from home and her immediate tightness when she came back. He perceived that there was some deeply buried and unhappy connotation between his patient when she was away from home ties and when she returned to the domestic round. He even began to query whether most of it was my fault. Was I in some way too demanding, too critical, too expectant of perfection, and, knowing this, did her subconscious react, putting up a barrier of illness and disability?

It seemed in fact that all that happened when she went back home was that she returned to the sea. (Buxted is rather more than fifteen miles from the sea.)

When I first looked over the house in the village of Buxted, near Uckfield, which became our new home I said as we came out: 'If anyone expects me to purchase that broken-down Victorian ruin, they're very much mistaken.' But having seen thirty-nine others, much more hideous and equally expensive, I consulted an architect to see what he thought of 'the Gossage house'. Being an architect, he was enthusiastic (shouldn't I have guessed?). He then produced plans for a possible renovation, which we disliked on sight; but more importantly he introduced me to a rich builder called Clarence Preston, who, although spoken ill of by many of his contemporaries, apparently took a liking to us and proceeded to offer his practical help. Liking him, I accepted it, and that was the greatest piece of luck.

The previous owner, Lady Gossage (widow of Sir Frederick Gossage, who during the war had been in charge of the barrage balloons of London's air defences and who inevitably had become known as Sir Frederick Sausage), had lived alone in the big house and had allowed it to fall into disrepair. The twelve acres that went with it included two cottages which were in pretty good trim, but the main house was in a state of ghastly neglect. The alterations to be undertaken were enormous (the builder first suggested putting a charge of gelignite under the house and starting afresh) and would need major structural changes involving the knocking down of inner walls to make small rooms into large, virtually turning part of the house round to face the other way, more than half reroofing, and complete rewiring, replumbing, redecoration and new central heating. When the local doctor came to see it when it was nearing completion there seemed to be no room on the ground floor that he recognized.

'No, don't recognize that. No, completely different. No, don't recognize that.' Only when I took him into the room which I had chosen to be my study did he say: 'Ah, I know this! This is where General O'Brien lived and died.'

Very wisely we did not take up the architect's suggestion that we should go and spend six months in the West Indies while the major work was done. Instead, precipitately, we moved in while everything was in chaos. With half the roof off, rainwater frequently ran down the stairs; our big dining room gaped at the end like a memory of

114

the Blitz, and was full of cement bags and piles of long planks; and in order to move from the kitchen to the morning room – the only two habitable rooms downstairs – I would regularly put on a hat and coat. Our son came home from Oxford on one occasion and found us both in bed upstairs, his mother in her fur coat and me in my overcoat and fur hat, while the bitter east wind blowing through exposed rafters below lifted the carpet on the bedroom floor as if we were on an Atlantic swell.

In the summer before this, while we were still in our furnished house, we went down to Cornwall for a holiday: all my friends urged us to come back; and one said to me, 'There's a charming house just come free above Polkerris in St Austell Bay. It belonged to a Dr Charles Singer, but he has just died and it is now up to rent – or maybe to buy. Why don't you look it over?'

I said: 'I can hardly do that as I've just paid the deposit on a house in Sussex.'

I did not realize then that in the present ridiculous law of purchase one can simply withdraw from such an agreement and demand one's deposit back and walk away without even an apology. Had I done so I might – just – have gone to see the house. And if I had seen it I might – just – have decided to buy it and come back to live in Cornwall after all. It was the house, Kilmarth, which later Daphne du Maurier, dispossessed of Menabilly by the return of the Rashleighs, was to take from them and where she spent the remainder of her life.

In the meantime my work had not, it seemed, materially suffered by the disturbances. Perhaps the long historical novel about sixteenth-century Cornwall, *The Grove of Eagles*, would have taken a bit less than the three years it actually did take to finish; but, looking back on the amount of research that had to be done, one can't be sure. The book was begun in the South of France looking out over a blue bay somewhat different from the wind-flecked blue of Falmouth Bay that the narrator of the book, Maugan Killigrew, looked out on from the great house of Arwenack where he was born. The book was continued for eighteen months in the furnished house we took, where the room I used as my study looked out on a beech hedge, some birch trees and a road; and it was finished in the room in my present house which has been my study ever since, where the view is of green fields and copses of woodland, with the Sussex Downs in the distance.

Just after we moved into our new house my agent rang to say an anonymous Hollywood buyer had made an offer for the film rights of another novel, called *Marnie*, which had been published before we left England. My three previous films had been British, though the third, *Fortune is a Woman*, had been financed by Columbia. This was the first direct Hollywood bite. The offer was for X thousand dollars, which seemed a big one to me. I talked it over with my agent, who said the anonymity was suspicious and he thought one of the leading women stars of the day fancied playing the lead and was buying it anonymously to keep the price down. He said we should ask double. We asked double. The reply came, accepting, but stipulating that we must agree within a fortnight or the deal fell through. We agreed.

It was a month after that that the news came: the buyer was Alfred Hitchcock. I was wholly delighted. I had admired his wonderful films since I was a boy. After the film was made he told me with satisfaction over lunch one day that he had bought the book anonymously for exactly the reason my agent suspected, to keep the price down. I did not tell him that such was my admiration for his work, if I had known he was the buyer I would gladly have sold it him for his original offer. The information would have spoiled his lunch.

Some months after the sale of the rights the news burst upon the world that Hitchcock had persuaded the former Grace Kelly, now Princess Grace of Monaco, to play the lead. All hell broke over my head. Newshounds from the five continents sought me out. The telephone never stopped ringing, nor the doorbell. One morning I had a telephone call from Sydney, another from Montreal, a third from New York, while a girl interviewing me for the *Daily Mail* was in the house and two more reporters were waiting. Very, very few people, it seemed, had ever heard of the novel and now everyone wanted to read it. There were no copies to be found. The book had just gone out of print, and my then publishers refused to reprint it, announcing a huge paperback issue for the autumn. An assistant at Harrods was heard to remark: 'If anyone else asks me for a copy of *Marnie* I shall go out of my mind.' I was dragged into a bitter legal battle between Amalgamated Press, who had bought the serial rights, and Express Newspapers, who, having been outbid, decided to pinch the story anyway. Writs and ad-interim injunctions flew about. My American publisher said the whole thing was a million dollars' worth of free publicity.

After some months, Grace Kelly decided to withdraw. It seems that when the Monegasques discovered that their princess had agreed to play the part – not of the Madonna or some stately queen of history, but of a girl thief who cheated and lied all through the film and who was sexually frigid – there was a sort of palace revolution. Reluctantly, having regard to the enormous sum Hitchcock had offered to pay her, she announced she must back down.

Although disappointing, life became normal for me again. The legal battle between the two newspaper groups (with me involved on one side) was finally settled out of court. The following year the film was made, with Sean Connery, and Tippi Hedren playing the title role.

I did not see any of the filming of this novel because I was having an operation in Hove at the time. Although agreeable and complimentary over the telephone, Hitchcock could not have regretted this. A man of many estimable qualities, he was, as far as film-making was concerned, the complete egoist. Writers, actors, musicians, editors, they were all disagreeable necessities in the making of a film; only one person was important. Everyone else and everything else ministered to him.

Two scriptwriters worked on the novel: only one, Jay Presson Allen, appeared on the credits. The scene of the film was switched from Plymouth in England to Baltimore in the United States, but that didn't matter so much as the many nuances of the story missed and the drastic oversimplifications which took place. Of course the screen is the medium of broad brush strokes, and Hitchcock's films are noted for their emphatic structure.

Bernard Herrmann, who wrote the music for the film, said to me when we met: 'Of course the real conflict of the film was not about Marnie's frigidity – it was about Hitchcock's sexual frustrations.'

Hitch had always had this fixation on ice-cool blondes, and after losing Grace Kelly to Prince Rainier, he had picked Tippi Hedren out from a TV advertisment to play in *The Birds*. When Kelly backed out of *Marnie* he cast Tippi in the lead. During the film his fascination with Tippi had overflowed, and one day he followed her into her caravan and made advances to her. Tippi rejected them – not too tactfully, Herrmann said – so that throughout the rest of the film they were not on speaking terms. When he was on he set Hitchcock would say to the Assistant Director: 'Tell that woman to do So-and-so.'

Not perhaps the best environment for the making of a successful movie.

When the film was shown in England it got a fairly cool reception from the critics; but within ten years it was being hailed as one of the most important movies Hitchcock had ever made. Significances were discovered. I never quite know how the minds of critics work, either constructively or destructively. When the film was shown on BBC television on Boxing Day, 1992, their reviewer wrote: 'Your heart goes out to the utterly believable Tippi Hedren, who is a combination of ice-cool sinner and vulnerable victim, in this gripping, subversive, jagged-edged emotional powerhouse of a thriller.'

The last time I saw Hitchcock was when we lunched with him in his caravan on the set in Hollywood. It was a hot, sunny day but all the blinds were drawn. He sat there like a large boiled egg, round, tough – part cockney, part ad-man, part genius – eating a fillet steak and nothing else at all, and drinking mineral water; talking with a hint of cynical amusement of the book François Truffaut had just written about him.

'He asked me what the special significance was of that very bad backdrop of Baltimore harbour, when Marnie visits her mother. I didn't tell him but in fact it had no significance, it was just a very bad backdrop.'

Since writing this I have received a copy of *The Making of Marnie*, a book published in January 2003 by the Manchester University Press. It is by Lee Moral and is a well-written, academic study which devotes the whole of its 211 pages to the one film, from its inception as a novel, and extensively tells the exact details of the purchase of the novel by Hitchcock, the Princess Grace involvement, the problems of the scriptwriters, details of the shooting, of the distribution, the showing, the reviews, the financial outcome, and the story of its later special significance in the eyes of the intellectual French film makers.

Hitchcock, as I have implied, did not take the highly intellectual Frenchmen's analyses too seriously – nor do I – but neither should they be disregarded. Lee describes me in his book as an instinctive feminist. Maybe that is right. Maybe the Frenchmen's analyses of my writing reveal more in the work than I knew of. Maybe the analyses of the filmmaking reveal more than Hitchcock himself was aware of. Artists, creative people, that is, often work by instinct. Possibly I did; possibly Hitchcock did. It remains for others to perceive what they may.

One point in this book which I find surprising is its reiteration that the film was a financial failure. I'm sure it did not live up to expectations. But when I met Hitch at Claridge's when the film had been running three weeks in London and had had mixed reviews, he did not seem at all downcast. He complained bitterly about the amount Sean Connery had cost him, but then after a few more comments, added: 'Anyway we're already in profit.' I can see no possible reason for him to say that if it had not been true.

But of course there had been the high expectations.

Proof, however, exists – for instance in the quote from the *Radio Times* – that opinions of a film can change radically even without the weighty influence of the French nouvelle vague.

Hitchcock was making a big event of the premiere in Rome, so I decided to go along. They said they would be delighted to arrange accommodation. When I arrived I at once had to give a couple of interviews and a bit of other publicity. It was only at about six o'clock, when I asked them where I was staying, that they suddenly were shocked to find that they had forgotten about my accommodation. Rome was bursting, every hotel full, but after some frantic telephoning they were able to twist somebody's arm and found me a room at the Bernini-Bristol in the Piazza Barberini.

It was a very hot day, and at seven I got a cab and dragged myself into the portals of the hotel. I was expected and was allotted room 342. I went up: the room was large, with a big double bed and a deliciously spacious and cool bathroom. Hopefully I ran cool water to the brim of the bath, stripped off everything and plunged in. Five minutes later I climbed out, gorgeously refreshed, and came out of the bathroom, wrapped in a small towel, to look for something in my bag. As I crossed the room a key grated in the lock, it rattled, and the door opened to display a stout middle-aged American lady with blue-rinsed hair. What it revealed of me, I'm not sure, but I hastily retreated behind a blue velvet curtain.

'What,' I said, 'what the devil are you doing here?'

'This is room 342, isn't it?' she said. 'I was given the key to room 342.'

'Well, 342 is taken,' I said angrily. 'This is my room!'

'So it seems,' she said, and retreated.

As soon as the door closed, I padded to the telephone.

'Look!' I said. 'I have just been given room 342, and almost on my heels, almost, almost on my very heels, you have sent up some blue-rinsed old girl claiming it's hers. What in hell's going on?'

There was a pause. Then the receptionist said: 'I'm very sorry, sir, that we could not find anybody younger and better-looking.'

I slammed down the telephone and collapsed on the bed, choking with laughter.

In what other country in the world would you, in a five-star luxury hotel, get such a reply from a receptionist? *Vivat Italia*!

I have mentioned Christine, who came as nursemaid for our daughter. She was a tall, good-looking girl of about twenty, slim, well educated and well mannered, but she had one or two foibles.

She took at least three baths a day, and her passion for horses far exceeded the norm for a girl of her age. She spent all her spare time at the riding school. Then one day Jean went into her bedroom when she was out, and there was a letter from her mother lying open on the dressing table. It was so peculiar that she brought it down for me to see.

It was full of hate – and the hatred was for men. Christine must learn to keep them at a distance, never encourage them, never allow them to *touch* her, they were filthy and any contact with them would contaminate her. She must be careful how she dressed, not ever to attract their lascivious glances, etc., etc., etc.

I am told that a few years later the girl committed suicide. But to all intents and purposes she was reliable and intelligent and a good nursemaid. It is only certain notorious cases that have made the headlines of the press since then that have made me realize the risk taken in putting one's beloved child into the care of a comparative stranger, however normal and nice she may seem.

Just before that, during World War II, Perranporth received many scores of evacuees. A family was put up in a cottage near us. It consisted of a mother and three children, the father being in the navy and therefore usually absent. There were also in the village a large number of soldiers, some English, but later many American. Mrs A., the evacuee mother, was highly respectable, and the three children fairly well behaved. Andrew quickly began to talk with an East End accent.

One could see Mrs A. in the morning, out for her walk to the shops, trailing two children and walking with an entirely affected knock-kneed walk, almost as if in reaction to the thought that she would ever open her legs to anybody. In fact she took it upon herself that it was her patriotic duty to offer comfort to the poor boys who were so far from home. It was kept very discreet, but it got about that if a man she fancied came to her cottage late at night and tapped on her window, Mrs A. would pick up her youngest little girl, who normally slept with her, take her into the next room, and then gently slide open the window.

This went on for many months. Then Mrs A. found herself to be pregnant. Her husband was far from home, and no one – but no one – was to be told. Of course the village, like most villages, eventually got to know the truth. But she still denied it. Being very slim, she was able to wear disguising clothing until near the end. When the pains came on, she got the old charlady next door to help her, and she was delivered of a fine healthy boy. Her determination still to keep it a secret was eventually thwarted by a persistent haemorrhaging, so her helper went to call the doctor. While the other woman was away, Mrs A. stranged the child and wrapped it in a newspaper and hid the body under the bed in the spare room, where it was later discovered.

The mother was found not guilty because of 'puerperal insanity'.

Two years later, the little daughter who was accustomed to being turned out of her mother's warm bed at nights, and who probably witnessed some of the scenes of the new baby's birth, began to steal, and the last I heard of her she had acquired a criminal record.

I do not know how I came to meet Sandy Mackendrick – it could have been at the Savile – but it was after the two splendid comedies, *Whisky Galore* and *The Ladykillers*, he had made for Ealing Studios, and before he left for Hollywood, where he made the big hit, *Sweet Smell of Success*, with Burt Lancaster and Tony Curtis. I had had three of my novels made into films by then, and he was interested in me and my work. Anyway, he invited me to have dinner with him one night at the Ecu de France in Jermyn Street.

We had a very pleasant meal and talk, and towards the end of it conversation turned to my books. He suggested I might write a book that he could film.

Then he said: 'D'you know, Winston, your women characters are always particularly good, attractive, intelligent, they are *real* people, real women, with real emotion. But they are all what I might call *white* ladies, people who embody the right side of life. Have you ever thought of writing a book about a *grey* lady, one who is maybe a transgressor of some sort?'

I replied that I had not. I am not, as may have become clear, an easily suggestible man so far as my novels go. Whatever the quality they may have, or lack, they are homegrown. We did not pursue the subject, but I was flattered that he should take so much interest, and I said so. The evening ended agreeably, and we parted, to meet only once more before he left for his triumph in Hollywood.

So far as I know, I entirely forgot his suggestion, but it has occurred to me more recently to wonder if it had lodged itself in my subconscious and had itself contributed to the genesis of *Marnie*.

Chapter Ten

When *The Grove of Eagles* was published it was a Book Society Choice.

About fifteen years before this, at one of my meetings with Somerset Maugham, he had said to me: 'Take my advice, young man, n-n-never read reviews.'

I had taken it. I had cancelled the press-cutting agency subscription and bullied eager young ladies in my publishers' offices not to send anything *at all* – good or bad. I found it a tremendous help. But for *The Grove of Eagles* research had been so extensive that I was ready to jump on anybody who dared to query it on historical grounds, so I relaxed the prohibition. As it happened, nobody did; but the barrier has not gone up so completely since. I wish it had.

The origin of this long and detailed historical novel about Cornwall and religion and Spain and the later Armadas derived from a day when I was reading some eighteenth-century papers while writing the third or fourth *Poldark* novel. The entry referred to one 'John Killigrew of Arwenack, governor of Pendennis Castle in Cornwall, who in 1596 sold his castle to the King of Spain.' This seemed such an outrageous and outlandish statement that I felt I must some day find out the truth about it. The time was not then, or it would divert me from the Poldarks. The time came, many years later, when, in the middle of a spate of modern novels, I decided this had to be the next assignment.

Obviously a more suitable subject could have been chosen for the only period in my life when I have been footloose and without a settled home. But one doesn't always choose subjects. They may come partly from conscious decision, partly from outside pressures, but usually and mainly from a subconscious urge from within. I know that, at least for myself, once a subject has been chosen there is no going back. Never in my writing life have I begun a novel and not finished it. Nor have I ever been able to break it off for another novel and finish the first one later. Often in the direst trouble, I have tried to jettison a story – or at least put it aside for the time being – but to no avail. I can't begin to create something different while a book is in the process of creation.

Three times in my life it has taken three years to write a novel – and in all cases I have done nothing whatever else in those years: no articles, no short stories, no reviews of other people's work, nothing for radio or television. In the case of *The Grove of Eagles* an itinerant life may have caused some of the delay, even though the volume of research was chiefly responsible. In *The Green Flash* there were all sorts of obstacles which I recount later in this book. The third of these novels was *Angell, Pearl and Little God*, and after its success in the United States, I was invited to write an article for an American literary magazine about the way the book came to be written. I hope I shall not be thought pretentious if I reproduce this article, since it sheds some light on the difficulty faced in this book, and also refers to the inception of *Marnie*.

It is likely that the problems which made my last novel, *Angell, Pearl and Little God*, so difficult to write would not have affected a young writer at all. At least, they would not have affected *me* as a young writer because when I was young the overmastering need to tell the story would have ridden roughshod over the manner of its telling. But with the years and with experience one becomes more selective, more self-conscious, and one has more desire for perfection of technique.

(At this stage it will be better to advise all who despise 'a story' in the novel that they may safely pass on to the next article. For although I have always had more to say in a novel than the telling of a story, the story itself has always been the framework on which the rest has depended for its form and shape. I have never been clever enough – or egotistical enough ... to spend 300 pages dipping experimental buckets into the sludge of my own subconscious. I have always been more interested in other people than myself – though there has to be something of myself in every character created, or he will not come alive. I have always been more interested in people than in events; but it is only through events that I have ever been able to illuminate people.)

It is a commonplace of the suspense novelist to use the first person singular in presenting his story. It brings an immediacy to events, to danger, to crisis, to the smallest detail of the central character's life. It concentrates the narrative wonderfully by preventing the writer from wandering off down byways of irrelevance. By limiting the point of view it helps mystification (on any level – from Proust or Henry James to Raymond Chandler or the latest paperback writer) and the very limitations are a challenge and a stimulus to both author and reader.

But the personally told story has a number of drawbacks, and one which is frequently overlooked is that the narrative character usually remains something of a negative personality – a sort of multiple mirror reflecting other people's images but never his own. Things happen to him, events occur, he feels heat and cold and pleasure and pain, he may have endless narrow escapes and struggle among the enveloping sheets of a dozen lecherous beds; or he may spend the book's lifetime trying to unravel the mystery surrounding two haunted children. In either or any case, it is the villains who beset him, the women who seduce him or, even, the ghosts who haunt him, who come to have personality and remain in the reader's mind. Not 'I'. Not the mirror person.

How does one retain the first person and overcome the obstacle? Or can one?

Various authors have tried to do so in the past. *Marnie* was my first attempt. It seemed to succeed. But whether it succeeded or not, the process fascinated me and made the novel doubly worth writing.

The fault with the average narrator is that he is too normal. His very normality is the plain mirror reflecting the oddities of others. But let the narrator be a psychological case, like Marnie, a compulsive thief and sexually frigid. *Her* mirror is not plain, it is flawed and distorts what it reflects. All the other characters therefore are at first slightly out of true because of it – that is until the reader adjusts himself. Then you have the intriguing situation of the narrator betraying her character, her slightly twisted reasoning, unselfconsciously, so that the reader gradually perceives what she is, while she does not know she is so revealing herself …

The first character to present himself to me in *Angell, Pearl and Little God* was the first one named: a stout, greedy, middle-aged lawyer. For years I had had the idea of such a man marrying a pretty shop girl or factory girl less than half his age and then allowing the events to move forward, the tragi-comedy to work its way out, from there. Not an unusual situation in life. Not an unusual situation in a novel. But here again I wanted to see it through the eyes of this mean and unattractive man. The narrating mirror was not going to be quite clear. One would not see Pearl exactly as she was but as Angell saw her. One would also see the rival – as yet a shadowy figure but weekly growing in substance – through Angell's eyes. The tragi-comedy of Angell's betrayal would take on another dimension precisely because he was telling it himself. One would see only a third of the picture, and the light cast upon that third would be brighter for the shadow covering the rest.

But at this stage, not only was I becoming more interested in Pearl, but Godfrey Brown – or Little God – was emerging from the mists and was threatening to monopolize my attention absolutely. At first, just a tough little rowdy on the make, ready to turn any sort of mildly dishonest penny, he shortly changed in my mind to a mechanic respraying stolen cars and handy with his fists, earning a few pounds here and there sparring in the London East End gyms; and from there he gradually developed into a chauffeur and suddenly into a man with a career in boxing and the ability and the ambition to get to the top.

At this juncture I knew virtually nothing about boxing, but constant visits to the East End of London quickened my interest. Several times I borrowed a seedy raincoat from the Secretary of the Savile Club, wore my oldest trilby, and slouched down to the Thomas à Becket pub in the Old Kent Road, where with a stub of cigarette in my mouth I would prop up the bar; and presently, when folk had got used to me, I would saunter up to the gym upstairs and watch Henry Cooper sparring.

Then by chance I got an introduction to one of the big fight promoters, Mike Barrett, and he generously opened every door. By this time fascination with the subject itself had taken over from any mere matter of duty-research, and it seemed abundantly clear that I could write a book entirely about the boxing career of Little God. I attended meetings between the various promoters when their protégés were being matched. I went to weigh-ins, sparring bouts, sat behind the scenes in the dressing rooms before and after they went up to fight. I even attended the pay-outs. The world of prizefighting had become much more interesting to me than the world of law offices or even of a pretty girl on the perfumery counter of a big store.

Yet, since I generally find it a mistake to be diverted from original intentions, I began to write the novel in the first person of Wilfred Angell, middle-aged Bachelor of Law.

At first it went well. To begin, it is all Angell's adventures: his consultation with the doctor, his visit to Switzerland, his meeting with and courtship of Pearl. It is fascinating and right to see all this through the slightly distorting eyes of a stout, selfish, greedy man. But very soon I began to appreciate how much I should lose. The drawback as well as the stimulus of the first-person singular narrative is, of course, that the adventures of only one person and the workings of only one mind can be revealed. In this book, one would have had to see Pearl's adventures with Godfrey only insofar as she told Angell of them. One would have had to see only the boxing matches that Angell went to or such as he might have had related to him by Pearl or Lady Vosper or Vincent Birman, two other characters in the story. After about 25,000 words I stopped for reassessment.

Now something like this had happened to me once before – in the writing of *Marnie*. That time I was halfway through the book; it was the first time I had written in the person of a woman; and I found myself gagging at the love scenes in which the narrator was made love to by a man. So I stopped and began again at page one, writing

128

it entirely afresh in the third person and from an omniscient point of view. And, although one can begin cheerfully enough writing 'she came down the steps' instead of 'I came down the steps', it doesn't go on like that. Whole areas of the book take on an entirely different complexion. So I persevered in this revision, and having rewritten (in longhand, as I do everything) about 45,000 words of *Marnie*, I stopped and left it alone for a month, and then went back to read it through. And quite clearly the new version was losing enormously in the change. Not merely was the distorting mirror removed but the language lacked the colloquial immediacy of the original. The whole book seemed prosaic where before it had been dynamic.

So back I went to the original version, reading it, rewriting it here and there until I came again to the troublesome love scenes. But this time I had somehow sunk deeper into the character of the girl, and they went through without let or hindrance. When the book was finished I was convinced – and still am – that the first person narrative was a tremendous gain upon any other possible way of presenting *that* novel.

A reluctance, therefore, to change from this method of narrative in *Angell, Pearl and Little God* is understandable, and it was only after an agony of indecision that I eventually sat down and laboriously rewrote the first 25,000 words in the omniscient third person.

Again a month's wait, again a careful reading, again a tremendous sense of loss. Angell's predicament cried out to be told in the biased first person. Also, even though so differently told from *Marnie*, [there was in *Angell*] a loss of colloquial immediacy in the telling.

So one came to an impasse. Neither way would work. Either way meant giving up so much. After about a further month's horrible indecision, I decided to leave the first chapters, as told by Angell, in *his* skin; and then began to tell the next part in *Pearl's* skin. This way one still got the urgency of first-person narrative, and still it could be told through the mirror of another personality; it was only that the person changed part way.

After this it was quite a simple matter several chapters later to switch the personal narrative a third time to Little God. In this way the novel even seemed to gain something, because each time one saw the other characters through a different flawed mirror, thus helping to create them in all three physical dimensions …

Thus I reached about the halfway mark of the book. After Little God's piece it was natural to turn to a new long piece by Angell. After Angell, Pearl. This way one could gradually work right through to the climax of the novel and so finish it. It was almost a new idea!

Again a gap of a month, and I read through what I had written. A new idea? Surely not. It had been used by other novelists before, and never, as far as I could remember, with complete success. What begins as a brilliant device ends as a gimmick. To change the narrator once or twice is perhaps permissible. After that the wheels begin to creak. The author labours to bring it off, and both he and the reader are conscious of the effort.

After this rejection – and it was ultimate and absolute on my part – I was left once again with the alternatives of either choosing one of the three principal characters and restricting the knowledge and the illumination of character to what he could perceive, thus gaining a little but losing a lot. Or accepting the fact that as this novel had developed, the challenge of the first-person singular could not be taken up, and returning to the omniscient third person, with its loss of idiosyncrasy and immediacy but its enormous scope, its complete lack of blinkered vision.

So I now scrapped what I had written – all but the 25,000 words in which I had experimented in this style six months before – and from then on wrote the book as it later appeared.

Although I cannot judge this objectively, the success of the book, and particularly the success of the characters, does give me the impression that possibly this preliminary experimentation, this lighting up of the characters, so to speak, from different angles, helped to give them extra solidity and shape.

It was an interesting experiment, but I commend it only to those with ample time and endurance.

In between *The Grove of Eagles* and *Angell, Pearl and Little God* I had written two other novels. One, *After the Act*, based a good bit on my own experiences in France, got marvellous reviews but failed to attract the mass market except in Italy, where it was the choice of Club degli Editore. It did get a specially good press reception in the United States, which attracted an American film-maker called George W. George, who took an option on the film rights, and then a second and then a third but could not get it off the ground. Later a French film company took up two expensive options. When George W. George heard he said, 'Perhaps only the French can make it.' But in the end they too gave it up. The other book was *The Walking Stick*, which was, if one judges solely by financial criteria, the most successful novel I have ever written.

Long before I was married, a family came to live in Cornwall with a polio-crippled daughter who had the most beautiful face and such a charming manner that I half fell in love with her. Thereafter, as if purging my feelings, lame girls have repeatedly appeared in my novels; Holly in *The Merciless Ladies*, Rosina Hoblyn in the *Poldark* books. *The Walking Stick* finally channelled this vein to its limits, and possibly for that reason had a poignancy that moved readers too. Apart from the two book club choices it got in America and one in Germany, Hollywood took a great fancy to it. When more than one producer wants a novel there is competitive bidding, to the author's great advantage. Eventually Metro-Goldwyn-Mayer went off with it in triumph. The film they made of it was a failure, but in retrospect this may have been because the way the film was made was ahead of its time. It is now repeatedly shown on television and seems to please viewers. When the book was first published, someone described it as 'a love story with a "Rififi" middle', referring to a widely successful French film about a jewel robbery. Eric Till, the director, was, I believe, much more influenced by a Swedish film called *Elvira Madigan*, and when it came to the robbery in the middle of the film he chose to use the robbery scenes as an explosion of noise and violence instead of the silent and nail-biting tension of the scenes in the novel.

David Hemmings played the lead and played it very well. In the all-important part of the girl with the walking stick, Till wanted

Judi Dench. MGM, typically, insisted on an international name and chose Samantha Eggar. She too did very well, but Judi Dench would have given it an extra dimension.

A sad postscript here is that when the novel was nearly finished I could not find a title for it. My wife suggested *The Walking Stick*. Within six months of its publication she needed one herself.

After the film had been made, MGM gave Jean the walking stick that Samantha Eggar had used. It was a handsome ebony-black stick, but after six months it broke, being made of some composition and varnished over. Like so much in the film world, it was not as real as it seemed.

BOOK TWO

Chapter One

The Walking Stick is the novel with which I again changed publishers.

I had become somewhat disillusioned with Hodder, partly because of their failure to market *Marnie* while the Grace Kelly sensation was at its height, but there were other reasons too. When it became known in the publishing world that I was thinking of making a move, four publishers were quick to make approaches. I ended up by moving to Collins, who were not the highest bidder but had a great reputation. I had known Billy (later Sir William) Collins, though casually, for twenty years, and liked him and felt he liked me. I had met him once in New York on the dance floor of a hotel, with one of the new young women writers he was promoting, and he had said to me: 'I see you've moved publishers. If you ever think of doing it again, why not get in touch with me?' Also I had become friendly with Lord Hardinge, who was then working editorially for Collins, and George, who greatly liked the Poldark novels, took one of them to Billy to read, with the remark that they were, in the popular phrase of those days, 'a licence to print money'. Even so, I was on terms of closer friendship with Charles Pick, the head of Heinemann, who had put in the highest bid, and I was far more deeply committed to the thirdbidder, the Bodley Head, whose owner was my closest friend, Max Reinhardt.

There was no question in the minds of my wife and our two children: 'Oh, you must go to Max.'

I was in those days doing very well out of my writing, able to live well and to maintain my family in the style to which I felt they had become accustomed; but I was often ailing, and who was to know if some illness should put me off working for a year or two?

So I consulted three people: Cyrus Brooks, my agent, Arthur

Coleridge, the head of *Reader's Digest* in England, and Edmond Segrave, the editor of the *Bookseller*. At least two of these were totally unbiased. All three were unequivocal: I *must* go to Collins.

When I told my children of my decision, they would hardly speak to me for a couple of days. It was in their eyes morally obligatory to go to Max. I agreed with them, which made it worse. I could only tell them I was doing it for their sake as well as my own.

The move paid off – financially and in other ways. Max took my decision like a true friend, as did Charles. (I was able to offer some other books to Max later.)

I remained on good terms with Billy and Pier Collins until they died, and similarly with George Hardinge. But in the next twenty years I never got to know Billy any better. He was cheerful, jolly, enthusiastic, just as when I had met him on the dance floor of the New York hotel. Very likeable but slightly unknowable. And soon after I joined Collins, George Hardinge moved to Macmillan.

But there was an unexpected bonus. I met the Managing Director of Collins, one Ian Chapman, who was among the most distinguished publishers of his generation, and, a few months later, Marjory, his charming wife. We became personal friends and have remained so ever since. I look on them now as my most valued and loving of friends.

Companioning Jean and me on about three-quarters of our trips to Europe were our two children. Living where we did in a small Cornish village with a cinema, nine excellent tennis courts and a golf course, and limitless cliffs and bathing beaches nearby, to say nothing of their friends, it might have seemed to them that what they left behind could hardly be bettered by what we were taking them to see, but they usually seemed ready for adventure. (Surprise, surprise, they might have taken after their mother.) True, Rosamund looked on foreign food with grave suspicion, and I learned to be able to ask for ham omelette in five languages. So off we went in our big open Alvis, in search of better weather and warmer seas than what we were leaving behind.

For some reason I cannot now explain to myself, I had a fixation on mountain passes, and up and down and round endless hairpin bends we went, ears cracking, to this col or that in the French and Italian and Austrian Alps or in the Pyrenees. Pleasure was gulped at, culture was more slowly and haphazardly imbibed. Our way of life in Venice must seem vulgar in the extreme: year after year we stayed at the Danieli, and in the morning the children would dash out to buy the ingredients for a picnic, then we would all take the CIGA launch to the Lido, where we had a cabin booked on the Excelsior Palace beach. We would return to Venice about four and take tea in St Mark's Square. By the time that was finished, most of the museums and churches would be closed or closing. In the fifteen times we visited Venice, its beauties were only partly explored. What is more deplorable is that because Jean and I had been to Venice before the children came, we had ourselves done much of the sightseeing that should have been reserved for them. However, they have seen most of the indoor treasures of the city in their own time. And I have never heard a word of complaint from either of them about the routine we followed when we were all there together.

The timing of our visit each year to coincide with the Venice Film Festival was not without a serious purpose, and I met a fair number of film stars and producers on the beach of the Lido, and we attended various film premieres. I remember one day on the Lido meeting Dustin Hoffman, and his being very enthusiastic about my novel *Angell, Pearl and Little God*, which had just been bought by Paramount. 'I really *want* to play Little God,' he said. 'I've never done any boxing, but I'll gladly learn enough of it to play the part. I don't know any cockney dialect, but I'll mug up on that too. But I won't play with a lousy script.'

At great expense, Paramount got three scripts, all equally lousy, so the film was never made. It still lies as an asset (so called) in the books of Paramount Pictures.

One of the scripts was sent to Marlon Brando, with the offer of a million dollars if he would play Angell. He did not bother to reply.

Travelling abroad with Jean after her stroke (of which more later) was often an anxious business. For long I could not forget the suddenness with which the illness had struck her down in Crete. Who was to say it would not happen again? If she went down to our greenhouse to pick some tomatoes for supper and was five minutes late returning, I would keep an over-keen ear open for the sound of a footstep or a walking stick. If we were deep in the wilds of Brazil surrounded by forest and in downpours of rain, I could not help but keep fingers crossed.

At times she had an appalling cough – like someone tipping coals, I would say – remnant of her asthmatic days but, according to the best medical opinion, not significant of any illness. I told her that she would earn a fine lot of money dubbing for anyone in a film or TV drama who was supposed to be dying of TB. (Their thin affected little coughs were entirely unconvincing.)

I remember taking her to Madras and then on to Mahabalipuram. It was pitch dark when we arrived at Madras, and Jean was hustled from the plane in an unsprung wooden wheelchair, pushed by a cheerful careless child who thought that bumping along at speed over a broken roadway was fun. When we got in the old taxi and began to push our way through the ill-lit suburbs of Madras and started on the Stygian twenty-mile trip to our hotel, I said to myself, 'Are you *mad*, bringing this ailing, delicate woman *all* this way to an unknown hotel in an unknown village in the depths of night, *miles* away from anything but the most unsophisticated medical treatment?'

(As it happened the hotel had forgotten our booking, and we could only be offered a boxroom for the first night, and the whole place was dirty, with fingerprints everywhere. That is by the way.)

But the answer to the question I asked myself in the taxi was answered in the next two weeks. She lost her cough. And the dynamics began to work. In two weeks we were in Kathmandu, and she was eager to take the two-day trip to Bokhara to see the sunrise over Annapurna. And when we got safely back, she jogged my arm until I took her on the dawn flight round Everest.

I have sometimes wondered how she brought herself to do so much. It was as if she would not *allow* herself to believe herself ill. She never *had* been. She never *would* be. Her favourite phrase, when I ventured to mention some new symptom or the recurrence of an old one, was: 'Oh, it's nothing. *I'm* not worried.'

She was perhaps a little like her grandfather, Charles Alexander, the sailor. He lived well on into our married life, and whenever I met him and asked him how he was, his invariable reply was: 'Capital, Winston, capital.' The difference is that he *was* 'capital' almost to the day of his death. She was not.

Whatever resources of optimism she drew on, it was a blessing for her, a blessing for me, and a blessing for the children.

As for the two children, this is my autobiography, not theirs, and it is quite possible that they will one day publish memoirs of their own.

It might be wrong to suppose that the four Poldark children and their relationship with Ross and Demelza bear a passing similarity to that in our household. I suppose I could claim a passing resemblance.

There has been a companionate friendship between us which has seldom been disturbed. They both seem to have been born at least partly civilized. A few standards which were not transgressed, otherwise an easygoing lack of any stern discipline, along with mutual respect.

What discipline existed most often came from Jean. She was loving but firm of purpose. I was loving but too easily persuaded. Unlike most fathers, I was often about the house, though not a little absent-minded. She built me up in their eyes. I sometimes think that perhaps she reflected to them her own opinion of me. (Largely unmerited, I fear.)

In the first half of our married life she 'looked after' me in every possible way she could. It was a source of sad satisfaction that in the second half I was able to do everything possible to repay the debt.

Chapter Two

One autumn long ago The Most Noble the Marquess of Donegall (as he was called in his passport) bought a new Bentley Continental and invited me and Nigel Tangye, an old friend of us both, to join him on a trip round Europe to run the car in.

Don, the sixth Marquess, was then in his fifties. He had succeeded to the title when he was rather less than one year old. He never got along with his young widowed mother, who disapproved of his lifestyle and who when she died left all the disposable money to Canadian religious charities and none to her only son. Don, even when his mother was alive, was poor (by his standards) and for many years before the Second World War had written a weekly column – almost a page – for the *Sunday Dispatch* and had made his name as a first-rate gossip columnist and at times serious commentator on world affairs.

Nigel Tangye, a Cornishman, descendant of the Tangyes who moved from Cornwall to Birmingham to establish their engineering works and make their fortunes, had inherited the family home of Glendorgal, near Newquay, but very little else. After a fine war career he had become Air Correspondent for the *London Evening News*, but soon afterwards he married the film actress Ann Todd and became her manager. This marriage fell apart when Ronnie Neame, director of my first film, *Take My Life*, had for his next assignment been appointed director of *The Passionate Friends*, from the Wells novel, with Ann Todd in the leading role, and had found himself unable to work out any understanding with or cooperation from her. David Lean was called in to take over and at once fell in love with his star, and she with him. So the Tangye–Todd marriage ended in divorce, and Ann married David.

Before this the tremendous smash hit of *The Seventh Veil*, starring Ann Todd and James Mason, had made her an international star, and Nigel, managing her affairs, had prospered mightily with her. (I remember when I was first going to America in 1950 Nigel said to me that the only possible way for a young British author to go to New York was *en prince*. I repeated this to Alan Grogan, my agent – and hers – and he replied, with a cynical glint in his eye, 'He means, on Ann's.')

But the divorce, apart from the very genuine distress it caused Nigel, literally did leave him without a meal ticket, and it occurred to him that one way of making a living was to convert the handsome family house, Glendorgal, into a hotel. Its position was ideal, being built on a promontory between two sandy beaches, and it required only a few extra bedrooms to turn it into a profitable concern. This he had done, and to my admiration he had made a great success of it. Of course it appealed to the snobbery in us all. No one was better connected than Nigel, or knew more famous people, and he was able to get many of his friends to come as paying guests. Prices were high and food rather pretentious, but the service and ambience were excellent. Nigel himself played the piano to his guests every evening (among his many talents was an ability both to compose light music and to play it), and who knew what famous film star or member of the aristocracy – particularly the sort of aristocracy that got itself in the news – one might meet at this small and select hotel?

By the time of our European trip things had moved on, and Nigel had married again. Baron, the then famous society photographer, while staying at Glendorgal, had said to Nigel, 'Would you like me to introduce you to the most dangerous woman in England? Her name's Lady Marguerite Hayward. She's divorced, with two children, and she's living in Cornwall at present, modelling in St Ives.' It was too great a temptation for the handsome Nigel Tangye to resist.

Throughout that winter he would drive over to St Ives twice a week, usually on his great motorcycle, and usually he would call on us on the way, since our house was medially situated. In the cold weather he would come in so wrapped up, his long hair straggling, looking like a great bear. Sometimes he carried a hot-water bottle and we would refill it for him.

Eventually they married and Marguerite came to help at the hotel, receiving and looking after guests. She was in fact one of the most beautiful women in England, certainly one of the most darkly fascinating I have ever seen. But after a few years she tired of the hotel and wanted to separate herself from it. So Nigel bought her a small house on the other side of the cove, and she came over to help or didn't come over, as she thought fit. Then she began to refuse to allow Nigel even to touch her, and he had to take sedatives to subdue his natural instincts.

It was at this stage in his life that I joined him and Don for the trip in Europe. Alan Grogan, my agent and a sophisticated man of the world, expressed himself slightly shocked ('surprised' was the word he used) that I should go on such a holiday with two such randy playboys.

For Donegall too, of course, had had and was having a varied love life. He had married a Combe (of the brewery family) and had considered that he and his wife-to-be had achieved a good, sexually matter-of-fact relationship before they married. But right at the beginning it turned out all wrong because she took great exception on their wedding day to his keeping a golfing engagement in the afternoon; and their semi-companionate marriage never really worked out. They were now long separated but she refused to divorce him, being determined that there should be only one Marchioness of Donegall so long as she was alive. For our present trip Don had made a date to meet a new girlfriend in Paris for the weekend which was to terminate our trip. Thereafter we were to make our several ways home.

On the drive round Europe, which in fact confined itself to Belgium, Germany, Switzerland and France, I was heavily outgunned, so far as knowledge of women was concerned, by the experiences and reminiscences of my two formidable friends. I was the ingenuous one. But by pure chance I was able to make a much better showing than they did on this particular holiday.

On the way home we spent a couple of nights in Geneva, where

Nigel wanted to interview potential staff to engage for his hotel next summer, so I telephoned my dear friend Vreni Wittmann, who came over in her car, a pretty blonde in a smart Alfa, and bore me away with her to spend a most entertaining afternoon and evening. Our next stop was Dijon, where I discovered that my friend Nadine Alari – my failed protégée from *Night Without Stars* five years before – was playing the lead in a French production of the Emlyn Williams play *Night Must Fall*. I told the other two to go on to Paris without me, and I would join them by train in a couple of days, so that I could see the production and take Nadine to dinner afterwards. Then when we did get to Paris one of the wealthy young married ladies dining with Don on his first evening at the Ritz took a great interest in me, and complications ensued.

Thereafter, whenever our holiday together was mentioned by my two companions, I was always referred to as 'The Dark Horse'.

These ladies deserve a few extra paragraphs to themselves.

Vreni Mettler, as she then was, came to Cornwall to stay for some months just before the war. She had apparently strained her heart skiing and had been sent to England to recuperate. This did not prevent her dancing and surfing and playing tennis. And flirting. During the war I heard nothing of her, but after it I heard from her that she had married a lawyer called Réné Wittmann and had two children. Her great ambition all her life was to be a painter. Her father, who lived in St Gall, had been a woollen manufacturer and had made a fortune supplying both sides in the First World War, but, instead of investing in stocks and shares, he bought paintings. Vreni, a teenager coming home from art school, would show her father the results of her work, and he would look at them and then at the Toulouse-Lautrecs, the Cézannes, the Utrillos on his walls and shake his head at her.

When Vreni married during the war her husband, knowing the wealth of her parents, virtually gave up his practice, preferring to live the life of a studious gentleman. Vreni, having produced two children, employed governesses to look after them and took up painting in earnest. She never spent less than five hours a day at her easel and eventually came to have a number of successful exhibitions in Switzerland and Austria. I have two of her paintings.

When her father died her mother said Vreni and her three brothers should share his collection between them, each child having a half-dozen on loan for a year and then changing with one of the others. Old Mrs Mettler kept the best Toulouse-Lautrecs for herself. She was tempted by outrageous offers from American galleries, but she said she found greater pleasure in looking at them in her house than from all the extra money she would have in the bank. Because of the peculiar tax situation in Switzerland (where apparently people are taxed on the value of their possessions) the pictures were never insured. I often wonder what happened to them after she died. Vreni was killed in a car crash some years ago. In spite of the ready brilliance of her smile, she was a sad woman. Her children did well, but her own marriage was a formality and she never quite attained her ambition as a painter. She had the strange arid fatalism of some Swiss, and from what she said the last time I met her I think that death – though certainly not sought – would not have been unwelcome.

The second lady, the one I met in Dijon, was, as I have said, Nadine Alari. After that first meeting, five years before, when we had taken a strong liking to each other, we had met several times, and she had invited me to see the French farce in which she was then playing, and after that to join her and her company for the annual dinner and dance and other festivities, held annually in the Place de la Concorde on the 13th of July, when all the actors and many of the notorieties of Paris congregate for a tremendous party which goes on all night. (I wrote about this in *After the Act.*) It had indeed been a memorable night for me, in more ways than one. So finding her so unexpectedly in Dijon was a special bonus, and I rang her and, as I have said, we had a happy reunion.

Since then Nadine has had a successful career on the French stage and in the French cinema; but as far as I know she never did do a film in English. She spoke it fluently. Had things turned out differently, with her playing the lead in *Night Without Stars* and partnering Paul Scofield, who knows what might have happened, or how much more successful the film might have been?

The plan when we reached Paris – I two days late – was for Don to meet his new girlfriend, who was coming from England to join him, and they would stay at the Ritz. Neither Nigel nor I fancied ourselves as gooseberries overlooking this new romance; and in any case the Ritz was far too expensive for our pockets. So we took rooms at the Hôtel d'Alsace in the Rue des Beaux-Arts, in the heart of the Latin Quarter. The Hôtel d'Alsace was run by a crippled lady called Madame Gely, and it was at this hotel that Oscar Wilde had died. Those who passed the test of her approval – as we did – were shown the first-floor bedroom and the actual bed. After making suitable comments in our broken French, we tiptoed reverently out.

For my part I would in any case far rather have stayed at the d'Alsace than the Ritz. It was totally, marvellously French; nearby were the famous cafés, Le Flore and Les Deux Magots. Michael Ayrton told me a splendid story of when as a very young artist he had gone to Paris with a French friend and stopped for a drink at Les Deux Magots.

After they had been there a few minutes his friend gripped his arm and said: 'Look! Picasso!' And there was the great man himself with three friends, seated at a nearby table. They watched with fascination, while trying not to watch.

Then again Michael had his arm gripped. 'Look, just look and then glance away. He's sketching something!' There was Picasso, pencil in hand, drawing on the paper tablecloth.

And then: 'Don't look again. I think he's drawing you!' Michael Ayrton was a good-looking young man, but he was transfixed at the thought that the great Picasso should think him worthy of a sketch. Sure enough, one more glance showed the great man's eyes fixed thoughtfully on him as he worked with his pencil. After a few minutes he stopped, then he paid the bill and the quartet left.

What was more amazing was that Picasso had actually left his sketch behind. Quickly, before anyone else could take the table, Michael and his friend rushed over, sat down and looked at the tablecloth. On it was written: '2 café filtres, 8 f., 1 cassis, 6 f., 1 absinthe, 8 f., pourboire 2 f., total 24 francs.'

Faithful to his old friends, Don invited us both to dinner at the Ritz to meet his girlfriend, but at the last moment Nigel was unwell, so I went alone. It was a glittering company. I remember by name only the Earl of Dudley, le Comte et Comtesse de la Fregonnière, Sir Duncan and Lady Mitchell-Clegg, and of course Don's girlfriend, of whom much more later. Both the foreign ladies seemed to take a fancy to me. Dickie de la Fregonnière's fancy was innocuous. She was American born, middle-aged, jolly and gnarled. Anoushka Mitchell-Clegg's fancy was not. She was Duncan's third wife, thirty years younger than he, sultry in a way only a Russian woman can be sultry, and very, very beautiful. We looked at each other aghast.

During the next few days I lost touch with Don and his girlfriend and, emerging daily from my artistic slum, was caught up in a whirl of social engagements: cocktail parties at the Meurice, luncheon parties at the de la Fregonnières' house in Neuilly, dinner parties at the Crillon. It was a world I had never moved in before – a world in which money was never mentioned because it was so abundant that it was unimportant. (One does not discuss water when all one needs to do is turn on the tap.) Health was much talked of, particularly one's liver. A Brazilian I met was flying back to Rio on the morrow to see his dentist because one of his teeth was giving trouble. Social engagements were discussed, and 'a little trinket' from Cartier's, and hunting, and one's liver, and the place one had on the Riviera, and occasionally the misbehaviour of chefs – and one's liver.

It was a supremely sophisticated society, and supremely decadent. I remember discussing this once with Prince Chula Chakrabongse, the then senior prince of Thailand and the king's uncle – and himself half-Russian – and he said: 'I am a millionaire but I am not welcome in that society. I am not sufficiently sophisticated for them.'

However, a young Englishman, *un*sophisticated but temporarily unattached, and agreeable, was welcomed – literally – with open arms.

Sir Duncan Mitchell-Clegg was a Canadian millionaire. He was large and gruff and elderly and suspicious. He accompanied his wife everywhere. We took dinner together, as a threesome. We took tea together in their hotel suite, as a threesome. It was very trying for two of us. Then the day before I was due to leave, when things were coming to a terrible crisis, I was struck down with a remnant of Nigel's virus. It saved me – at least temporarily – from a fate much better than death.

However, a few weeks later the Mitchell-Cleggs came to London, and Sir Duncan had business to attend to, and I had not; so Anoushka and I saw quite a lot of each other after all.

To prepare the way I sent a bouquet of red roses to her at Claridge's. Before filling up the card I asked Monja Danischewsky, the witty film director, how I could put *Welcome* in Russian on this greeting card. He drew himself up to his full five feet six inches and said: 'In my contry der is no soch vord!'

Don's girlfriend in that eventful weekend was a very pretty and vivacious blonde called Maureen McKenzie. An ex-Wren, she had just got in at the tail end of the war, and was sent out to the Far East, where she met Earl Mountbatten, who took an immediate fancy to her and they developed an intimate friendship. They used to picnic together and for a time, until Lady Mountbatten turned up, were close companions. Maureen says it was platonic, and, since she was a supremely frank person and had nothing to hide, there is no reason to disbelieve her. A North Country girl of good family, she had been a child music prodigy, and at the age of eleven had played Grieg's Piano Concerto at the Free Trade Hall in Manchester. Soon after the war she married and had two children, and when she met Don she was twenty-nine. In order to join Don in Paris she had had to tell her husband that she was visiting her mother in South-port – who had agreed to cover for her. It was intended on both sides just as an exciting weekend and no more, but it quickly developed into a long-standing and serious affair which ended in two divorces, the first marchioness at last having been very reluctantly persuaded to file a petition, and Don and Maureen were married and lived together in Switzerland until his death in 1975.

Maureen could claim the extraordinary record of having a father-in-law who was born eight years after the Battle of Waterloo. The fifth Marquess lived from 1822 to 1904. The sixth – Don – was born in 1903, when his father was eighty.

One of my most vivid memories of this remarkable sojourn in Paris was of the first dinner I had had at the Ritz – where I first met pretty Maureen – and gnarled Dickie – and beautiful Anoushka.

Chapter Three

The year I was born and the day I was born, at 08.00 hours on the 30th of June, the largest meteorite ever to strike the earth, indeed the greatest cosmic impact of at least the last 2,000 years, landed in Siberia. To quote Dr David Whitehouse, the BBC Online Science Editor:

> The impact had a force of 20 million tonnes of TNT, equivalent to 1,000 Hiroshima bombs. It is estimated that 60 million trees were felled over an area of 2,200 square kilometres …
>
> … The first expedition to reach the site was led by Russian scientist L. A. Kullick in 1938. His team was amazed to find so much devastation but no obvious crater.
>
> So began the mystery of Tunguska. What was the object that caused such destruction and why did it leave no crater?

When I read this piece to Gwen Hartfield, my housekeeper, she said: 'It does bring you down to earth with a bump, doesn't it?'

Naturally I disclaim all responsibility, and I have never been to the site. I rely on hearsay.

I rely on hearsay for everything that has happened in the world before I was born, and the world, as I know it, will end on the day I die. When I become part of 'the dull, the indiscriminate dust' there is nothing to prove to me that anything will still go on, any more than that anything existed before I opened my eyes and blinked up at my doting parents. Nothing can prove to me that the world and all it appears to contain has an objective reality. I know it has a *subjective* reality but no more. 'There, sir, I refute it *thus*,' Dr Johnson said, when in an argument with Boswell over Bishop Berkeley's theory of the essential non-existence of matter, as he kicked vigorously at a stone. But what did Dr Johnson refute or disprove – if he ever lived, that is? Only that his foot felt the weight of the stone as it rolled away from him. I burn my finger and I feel the pain. I feel nothing of the horrible pains of a thousand martyrs who have been – it is said – burned at the stake for their beliefs, or disbeliefs. Even among my nearest and dearest there is no transference – can be no transference – of experience. One can feel empathy for someone suffering, but one cannot feel the suffering. We are all *alone* – desperately alone. What are we in this world? A conjunction of subjective impressions making up something that is accepted as reality?

I have long been convinced of the illusory nature of all human experience; but where does it lead me? – To Plato and his parable of the cave? Or is it just back to *Cogito, ergo sum*?

I have always been secretive about my age, therefore there have never been any great celebrations on my reaching any of the ever-more-lonely eminences of life. Such secrecy, of course, runs totally counter to modern practice. Every newspaper demands it. '39-year-old, old Etonian, ex-Guardsman, former trombonist John Smith-Brown was yesterday charged with …'. Every official form, however trivial, has a space for 'date of birth'. Any casual acquaintance will suddenly come out with 'how old are you?'

Reticence over age is very much a family failing, and I can't explain why. I remember when I was twenty being embarrassed that I was so old and preferring not to mention it. I never knew my mother's age or my father's age until just before they died.

But my aunt the violinist carried things a bit far. Taken with acute appendicitis at the age of seventy, she was asked how old she was by the doctor accompanying her in the ambulance to the hospital. 'Sixty,' she replied, and ever afterwards her official age was economical of the truth by ten years. Since she had not contributed to a state pension and in those days it was not obligatory, the deception did not deprive her of a pension, for she would have received none anyway.

When she died, aged eighty-five, she left instructions that her age was not to be put on her coffin or on her tombstone.

For a person such as myself, who has achieved a certain notoriety, it is of course much more difficult to keep one's privacy on this matter; but on the whole I have had a certain amount of fun in deceiving people. In *Who's Who* I don't give my birth date, and in four other similar publications around the world I have given different dates, all of them wrong. So what? Does it matter? Who profits but the idly curious?

In *The Black Moon*, when Aunt Agatha lies dying at the age of ninety-eight, her last conscious sensation is of her kitten's fur as it rubs its head against her hand. I wonder what mine will be. I remember my *first* conscious sensation is of my grandfather jokingly putting his specs on my nose and my crying in indignation because the world I looked out on was all prisms. I can't date that precisely but he died when I was two.

My uncle Jack, the one who died at eighty-four, was a newspaper editor who married a lady called Emily Towler. They had a son, who died, and then seven daughters, all good-looking and all of abounding health and vigour. They were called Emmie, Edna, Marjorie, Winifred, Kathleen, Millicent and Dorothea. Em, their mother, put on weight and then more weight and still more weight. She never went out, being embarrassed by her size, but was very extravagant, ordering things through the post, and constantly ran my uncle into debt. I remember going to see her once as a very small boy and being compelled, as it seemed to me, to crawl up a feather bed to kiss her. It must have been almost true, for when the family moved houses it was found she was too stout to get into a taxi, and she had to go in the furniture van.

Thus do music-hall jokes impinge on real life.

Chapter Four

One day during the first year of the war, when I was still waiting for call-up, I went to Truro by train and sat opposite a young RAF officer who told me he was convalescing after a crash. He had a substantial, barely healed scar from temple to lower cheek.

'We were only on a diversionary op over Abbeville,' he said, 'and some lucky fool with an ack-ack gun blew half my wing off. Thought I could get home but then the gas started leaking. Ditched near the Isle of Wight, and nobody saw me for a hell of a time. Must admit it was raining.'

While convalescing he had been visiting his parents near Padstow, but he couldn't wait to be operational again.

'It's a different life. A good crate is a joy to handle. You're in a new dimension. Grounded you're like a beetle. Up aloft you're a bird.'

'Do you like actual air combat?'

'When it's over, yes. And the prospect of it. Yes, I suppose I do. With luck it's fighting one to one, and that's a challenge.'

A very tall bony good-looking young man with a high-strung disquiet about him that made a great impression on me. And a depth and darkness that lay behind the frivolity of his air force language. He was not at all nervous, but one guessed that strong nerves contributed to his latent urgent vitality.

At that time a hazy picture of the character who was to become Ross Poldark had already formed, and I was writing about him while his appearance and character still grew.

Some friend told me once that there was an element of Heathcliff in Ross Poldark. A Cornishman, Peter Pool, more perceptively, I think, saw an affinity with Captain Hornblower, at least in his capacity for self-criticism. It's impossible for me to take a detached view of Ross's origin and character. All I know is that the young airman, his general appearance and my perception of his character, provided the basis for what followed.

In the early years of my time in Cornwall I became very friendly with a young chemist called Ridley Polgreen, who died at the grievously early age of thirty-two. When I began to write the first of the Cornish novels, I thought to write about a man called Ross Polgreen – which itself is a rare name in the county; but after a few chapters the name Polgreen seemed a little too floral, a little too gentle. I wanted something a bit more formidable, darker. *Darker*, that was it. And so the name came into being. There never was a Poldark before. Since then various institutions have borrowed the name. There is unfortunately no copyright in titles. Though I suppose use of the name is a form of flattery.

During the filming of *Poldark* Ross's scar was the subject of an occasional joke. One morning everyone arrived on the set, which happened to be out of doors, with a scar on the cheek exactly like Ross's, cast and technicians alike. Shooting began twenty minutes late that morning.

I wish I could be as explicit as that in considering the creation of Demelza. Obviously there have been borrowings, chiefly from my wife. I took her sturdy common sense and judgement, her courage, her carthy ability to go at once to the root of a problem and point the answer; her intense interest and pleasure in small things; and particularly I have used her gamine sense of humour. As for the rest, most of it seemed to come from within. A romantic man's perception of an ideal woman? That was maybe how it began, but I have had no more than parental control over how she has developed.

Sometimes a name is a great help. While the first book was still in its preliminary stages I was driving across Bodmin Moor, and not far from Roche saw a small signpost marked DEMELZA. Until then she had no name; after that she could have had no other.

Warleggan, taken from another village on the moors, was also a help in formulating the characteristics of that clan. Incidentally it was reported to me that one evening in Pratt's Club the doyens of two distinguished Cornish families were heard to be arguing as to which family had provided the model for the Warleggans. Each claimed it. Which is a little surprising considering the character of the family portrayed.

In fact, elements from both families were incorporated, but my interest was chiefly centred on the Lemon family, which dominated Truro at the end of the eighteenth century. F. L. Harris, the historian, said he always thought of the Warleggans as 'Bad Lemons'.

Jud Paynter's character I took from three men I knew: Dick Hill, Fred Sampson, and George Murray. From Hill I got the appearance and the drunkenness, from Sampson the apocalyptic indignation and sense of injustice, from Murray the mispronunciations. The latter two were coastguards, and Sampson I have already referred to.

Dick Hill lived with his sister Florrie in a cottage in Tywarnhayle Road. Florrie was the perfect model for Prudie. Lank black hair, powerful voice, ponderous figure, I used to see Dick Hill cycling to the pub every evening and wondered, as the distance from his cottage to the pub was not three hundred yards, why he bothered to cycle there – until I saw him returning home one night and realized he used his cycle to lean on.

Florrie Hill took part in one of the one-act plays I wrote for amateur production at that time, and, in so doing, betrayed some of the extravagances which may have stemmed from the part she played or was hitherto unexpressed from within her own nature.

One day, when the second series of *Poldark* was being filmed, I was sitting on a deckchair watching the scene – this was in Boconnoc, near Lostwithiel. I was approached by a local man, probably in his sixties, bald-headed, two-toothed, battered hat, which he kept taking on and off, corduroy trousers, tattered jacket, and he sat down beside me and started talking. It was Job, I believe, who said, 'A spirit passed before my face and the hair of my flesh stood up.' My hair wanted to stand up. Here was Jud, conceived by me thirty years ago but now incarnate, sitting beside me in a stable yard in the thin May sunlight. Most of his declamation, which was nonstop, was speaking of events from which he had emerged triumphant. His most-used phrase was not 'Tedn right, tedn proper' – stemming first from Fred Sampson – but 'How 'bout that, then? How 'bout that?'

I never saw him again. I sometimes wonder if he ever really existed. Assuming he was real, it came as a reassuring shock to me to discover that the Cornish strain of eccentricity still runs true and that I had not unduly exaggerated it.

Those who have read *Poldark's Cornwall* will remember the occasion a few years after the end of the war when a trim black-bearded young man in shabby clothes called at Treberran and asked me if I owned the Stamps Land in Perrancombe. I said I did. He explained that he was starting a small mine entirely on his own at Mithian and that parts of the waterwheel and the heads and lifters would be useful to him. Could he buy them? Although reluctant to part with this picturesque ruin, I told him he could have them without cost to himself except the transport. He was pleased at this, and we chatted for a few minutes. He was upset at the way Cornwall was getting spoiled, and felt it was largely the result of up-country folk coming into Cornwall and developing it for their own profit. He also expressed a grudge against up-country writers who wrote about the county and made money out of it all. Interested in this, I asked him if he had any particular writers in mind? He replied: 'Well, this chap Winston Graham, for instance.'

A quicker-witted man would no doubt have led him on; instead I blurted out my guilt at once. He did not see this as amusing, but neither was he at all embarrassed. After a few seconds of thoughtful staring he explained accusatively that he lived at Mingoose, and that since the early *Poldark* novels were published he had been much troubled by people coming around looking for Mingoose House, where in the novels the Treneglos family lives. 'They come round my place Sat'day af'noons, Sunday mornings, looking for Mingoose House. There isn't no Mingoose House. There isn't no such place. Tis a proper nuisance!'

I did not tell him that, even if it had now vanished, there *had* been a Mingoose House. It is marked plainly on William Tunnicliffe's map of Cornwall of 1791, and the house is shown to be in the possession of one John Harris, Esq.

Instead, I apologized for being who I was, and he came to take a more favourable view of me. Had I ever been down a one-man mine? No, I said. 'Then come Sunday af'noon, I'll show 'ee.' Which he did. It was clearly part of an old mine which he had redeveloped. The ladders were shaky and so in the end was I. Later we went back to his cottage for tea, and he played me hymn tunes on the organ he had built himself into the wall of the cottage.

In the *Poldark* novels he was Ben Carter, son of Jim and Jinny, who was in love with Clowance.

I wish it were as easy to pinpoint other characters I lifted from life. In a canvas as wide as the twelve *Poldark* novels, the number of characters is enormous and their variation, one from another, is enormous; but, looking back, there are relatively few cases in which I have drawn from a living original. It's as if, in the course of my life, I have encountered thousands of people and they have descended into a sort of cauldron of the subconscious, and some part of one or another has been selected or has surfaced to the conscious at the suitable time to be made into fictional flesh. I don't ever remember looking around in search of new personalities; they have always been available. But of course you must have an understanding of a character, you don't just feel *with*, you have to feel *in*. Empathy, not sympathy, even though what you find there is dislikeable.

Stories are another matter and are the subject of weeks, sometimes months, of agonizing indecision. That aunt of whom I have already written once said to me: 'Oh, how I envy you. Stories come from you like plums falling from a laden plum tree.' If she but knew.

Names are often difficult. I have already written of how I came by the names of Poldark and Demelza. And Warleggan, from a village on Bodmin Moor, was a name which felt immediately right.

The area round which Nampara is centred is St Ann's, Perranporth, and partly of Crantock, chiefly West Pentire. It is meant as a composite picture, not to put onto an Ordnance Survey map. Various maps have been drawn by enthusiastic readers, and some of these have been brilliantly accurate. But while approving of them, I have never endorsed them without a disclaimer of responsibility. On the other hand, where actual towns exist, such as Truro, Falmouth, Redruth, I have tried to make them as accurate as research can achieve.

Digressing slightly, I often think that a good novelist is never altogether a free man and never quite a whole one. The stuff of his life is the stuff of his writing, and vice versa, and he can't escape. That is why, if things are going badly with his work, it is a constant nagging worry, however much he may appear to be enjoying himself. Conversely, when things are going well, it offers a constant warm retreat of the mind against boredom, annoyance and discomfort.

It could be said that an author is the most harmless form of schizophrenic. He lives for a substantial part of his time in a world of his own creation, even fantasy, but never – one hopes – loses track with reality. When he is the participator he is also, willy-nilly, the observer. While being attached, he is also detached. In one of his diaries Arnold Bennett confesses that when he went to see his mother when she was dying, parallel with his absolutely genuine grief some part of him was taking in the texture of the blankets, the smell of the oil lamp, the drip of liquid on the edge of the medicine bottle, the fly buzzing against the windowpane. In different mood Goethe admits that in the middle of one of his numerous love affairs he found himself tapping out the hexameters of his latest poem on the backbone of his new girlfriend.

The Cornish novels, twelve in all, not far off two million words, have occupied for better or worse a considerable part of my life. Over long periods they have been entirely quiescent, though never forgotten. After the first four, which covered in the writing only about eight years, there was the long gap of twenty years before I took them up again.

I was very doubtful then whether I could ever get back into the mood in which I had written *Poldark*, even if I wanted to. Life moves on. One becomes more cynical, more sophisticated – and one's work mirrors it. All through two decades I had received letters from readers asking me to continue the story. Friends similarly

– especially, of course, Cornish friends. And the memory of that 'possession' which had taken hold of me once or twice in the writing – especially in *Demelza* – still stirred. None of my modern novels had created this haunted sensation. But the modern novels gave me a lot of satisfaction in other ways, and were much more successful.

Since I returned to England I had had one success after another, and was still oppressed by the levels of taxation. I badly wanted to leave England again for this reason, but knew I could not – or would not. England, somewhere in England, I knew now, had to be my home. So after *Angell, Pearl and Little God* I found myself under a number of pressures. I had no need to make money for some years; my new publisher, Collins, were ardent admirers of the *Poldark* novels – readers' letters still came; and over and above all this, far more important than all this, was a growing desire and a curiosity to know what all these people would do after Christmas 1793, where I had left them for so long.

So a new novel, *The Black Moon*, was dated to begin on the 14th of February 1794, seven weeks after the end of *Warleggan*. Only in reality was there a gap of twenty years.

It was hard going to begin. The style seemed to be lost. I was trying to return to the eighteenth century and a family saga, a different, slower tempo, a rebirth of characters long since left behind. And although I didn't take too much account of this, I knew that by changing styles I should be disappointing as many readers as I pleased.

I have somewhere, writing before, described the return to Poldark as being as difficult as breaking the sound barrier. This is an exaggeration, but for some months I told no one except my wife what was going on, lest I should find the attempt beyond me and give it all up.

But after a few months the momentum came back; the characters had clearly only been latent, for they were active and lively from the start, almost as if they had never been neglected at all. They sprang up around me.

And the momentum increased, and the preoccupation took over. Halfway through I called to see my accountant one day and told him cheerfully that for a year or two I was 'returning to my non-profit-making activities', meaning the *Poldarks*. I told Ian Chapman, and he was delighted, for he and his wife Marjory had long been admirers of the first four books. (Not so the reps, who, for all their enthusiasm, rightly foresaw the difficulty they would have reselling a new/old style Winston Graham to the booksellers and the public, whose memory is usually short. And so it proved.)

Towards the end the novel seemed to take over my life – even though it was being written in Sussex, not Cornwall – and the intense absorption, exciting but exhausting, reached a climax in the last two weeks, when I sometimes wrote 4,000 words – in longhand – in a day.

When it was over and done with and after a decent interval, I began the sixth *Poldark*, *The Four Swans*. Irrespective of what reception *The Black Moon* might receive, there was no question now but that I must complete another sequence of these novels – though this time it was to be three books, not four; and my feeling was to write these straight through, not intersperse them with modern novels as had been done with the first four. A whole set of new characters had flooded into *The Black Moon*, and they demanded time and space to work out their own destiny.

For some years in a desultory way there had been interest shown by the film industry in the first four *Poldark* novels. A firm called Hemway – part-owned by David Hemmings, who later starred in the film of my novel *The Walking Stick* – had considered taking out an option and had tried to get a production team together. Then Ian Chapman handed the books to Robert Clark, the millionaire chairman of Associated British Pictures, and he at once declared an interest, which he never abandoned all his life.

I should say in the years that had passed since the first four were published, Ward, Lock had continued to keep them in print, and they had been selling, though very slowly. In 1950 I met Max Reinhardt, then married to Margaret Leighton, but soon after we met his marriage broke up, and in 1956, being a temporary bachelor, he invited me to go as his guest to the Publishers' Annual Congress, this year to be held in Florence and Rome. I accepted, and we had a wonderful time – the Italians, regardless of cost, putting on all the possible panoply of their rich country for the world's publishers, from a Palio staged specially for us at Siena and an opera in Florence at which Victoria de los Angeles sang, to an audience of the Pope in Rome.

I did not realize until too late that in fact the one species not represented at this teeming conference was an *Author*. I was the only one there, and I had no business there. I'm sure Max didn't care. We laughed and joked our way through eight days of festivities. Of some slight embarrassment to me was the assumption of the authorities that, as I was Mr Reinhardt's guest, I was probably Mrs Reinhardt. Publishers wore red labels, their wives received purple. I wore the purple. I had invitations to dress shows, beauty salons, hair stylists. I told Max I ought to be considered one of the Congress tarts.

With us on this adventure went Denys Kilham Roberts, Secretary General of the Society of Authors, and his wife Betty. Their marriage too was wobbling dangerously near the rocks, but at the time all went well.

A few weeks before leaving England I had sold the serial rights of my latest novel, *The Sleeping Partner*, to *John Bull* magazine. Just before I left, the editor wrote to tell me he liked the book so much he had decided to increase the payment by an extra 200 guineas. Talking to Max and Denys when we were in Florence I told them of this and added, 'It's enough to destroy one's lack of faith in human nature.'

The same day they were discussing the huge success Ralph Richardson and Peggy Ashcroft had recently had at Stratford in *Titus Andronicus*. I said, 'With a cast like that, it's money for old rape.'

So, briefly, I earned a reputation for wit. Two days later Denys Kilham Roberts introduced me to Marghanita Laski and said: 'You'll know Winston as a novelist, of course. But he is also a very witty man.'

I was so embarrassed by this introduction that even my general tendency to see the funny side of things deserted me, and she and I talked soberly of Gothic and Renaissance churches and the Italian tendency to architectural flamboyance. Then she said magisterially: 'Are you a member of PEN?' I said, no, and she said, 'Oh, you *must* be.' So I meekly joined there and then. I have never regretted it, but I am sure no one can have guessed that my membership, stretching now over forty years, springs from a desire to appease Marghanita for turning out such a dull and unfunny man.

One day we were walking across the Piazza della Signoria and Max said to me: 'You see that man ahead of us, that's Stanley Unwin. He's selling The Bodley Head. They say he wants £80,000 for it. Ridiculous!'

Three months later Max bought it.

Earlier he had said to me: 'As you know, I own two publishing firms. They are agreeable occupations, and I have enough to live comfortably on and to treat them as a side issue. Or I could buy a large established publishing firm and take it as my full-time profession.' His purchase of the Bodley Head told me he had made his choice.

Less than a year later he came to stay with us in Cornwall, and walking on the beach one day he said: 'The Bodley Head has a fine backlist but I would like to add to it. Do you have any of your earlier novels which have gone out of print and would like to see republished?'

It happened that Ward, Lock had become discouraged by the falling sales of the four *Poldark* novels and had written to tell me they felt these books had reached the end of the road and they were allowing them to go out of print. The rights had therefore reverted. I hesitantly told Max of these books and invited him to have a look at them. He promised to do so. I told him that, as my other novels were doing so well, I would be quite happy to allow him to put them out on a little or no royalty basis if they suited him, because I was fond of the books and would like to see them in circulation again. When he returned to London and read the books he said he would be happy to publish. Of course he gave me a fair royalty.

This digression is to make the point that, had the first four *Poldarks* not been republished by Bodley Head in an attractive new format, they would have been out of print for years before Collins eventually decided to do them in Fontana, and much less likely to catch the eye of Robert Clark and other film-makers.

As I have said, the late George Hardinge, an editor at Collins, was a great admirer of the *Poldark* novels, and his prophecy that in paperback they would be 'a licence to print money' was proved to be true.

In this climate, Robert Clark took an option on the books and set in motion a plan for a huge and expensive film covering all the first four books, intending to make of them a sort of Cornish *Gone With The Wind*. Kenneth Harper was to be the producer and Vincent Tilsley the scriptwriter.

Jean and I went down and met them in Cornwall, and we had an exciting five days looking for locations. The March weather was horrible, drizzle and mist every day, but I was able to show them many of the scenes that the film would expect to include.

I took them to Port Isaac and Roscarrock and Port Quin and to Trevellas Porth. At Trevellas the mist was thick and ghostly. We slithered our way down in two big cars almost to the edge of the sea. It was not a pretty road, having been used for more than twenty years for test trials on the London to Land's End motor rally: hairpin bends and surfaces of loose stone and rock. The old mineshafts loomed in the mist, the sea muttered on the rocks, a solitary gull told us of its bereavement. Vincent said he would like to go off on his own for a bit. He was obviously inspired, and we waited for him there in the damp, clammy mist, not speaking ourselves, listening perhaps for the tramp of long-dead miners, for the hiss and suck of the long-silent engines; for the clang of the long-fallen changing bell. Nothing had altered here except time and weather, turning it all to rubble and to waste.

The following day we went to St Day, the very centre of the old copper-mining belt, to Redruth and Camborne, stopped at South Crofty, where a mine still worked and was in profit, and then to St Ives and Penzance. In the few days we saw much, and then we all returned to London.

Vincent Tilsley wrote a very good script, but inevitably the story had to be hideously slashed. And even more would have had to come out, for his script as written would have run for at least five hours.

However I need not have been concerned (if concerned is the word). Unknown to us, a financial battle was developing in London with EMI trying to take over Associated British Pictures. After months of conflict they won, and, it being the invariable custom of incoming moguls to axe any projects initiated by outgoing moguls, *Poldark* was axed.

At about this time I was approached by Donald Wilson, one of the BBC's foremost producers, with a proposition of his own. He had been the moving force which had finally got *The Forsyte Saga* to the TV screen, and he was looking for some other project to follow it up. He did not want a historical subject, he wanted it to be about modern life, and thought its setting should be Bristol.

In 1497 Giovanni and his son Sebastian Cabot had sailed from that port under letters patent from Henry VII, and had discovered Nova Scotia. The family of Cabot had been in and around Bristol for most of their lives but had left no apparent heirs. Donald Wilson's idea was to suppose that in the twentieth-century a family called Cabot was still living in Bristol. A good writer, he thought, could produce a long saga about this family bringing in whichever occupations and industries and cultures he fancied to use from the Bristol of today.

It was a clever idea, and I was not untempted. But it would be a very big project, and I had done nothing like it before. As usual lacking confidence, I tried to get out of it. I had never written a script, I said (which was only true of TV). It would involve the creation of an enormous range of characters, and I was not sure I could do this.

Donald said: 'Why not go there and scout round for a few days, see if anything appeals to you? I can lay it on.'

So after humming and ha-ing a bit more I agreed to go.

It was February. Bristol in summer has a very pleasant climate. Sometimes in the winter it is like Alaska. For the first three days I was there it was like Alaska.

I arrived at Temple Meads to be greeted by Brandon Acton-Bond, the head of BBC Bristol. A first slight shock. Accustomed to the chauffeur-driven Rolls-Royces of the film industry, I blinked twice at the careworn Hillman Minx and at Brandon's shabby overcoat.

He drove me to the hotel and we had dinner. He was a man of fifty-odd, dark, thin, pleasantly intellectual. We got on well. Before he left he told me of the sandsuckers which, like other shipping in those days, came directly into the centre of Bristol, and whose duty it was to keep the channel from silting up.

'I'll show you them tomorrow,' he said, 'and you can meet some of the captains and crews. But first we'll go round the docks.'

Next morning it was grey with a bitter east wind. I shivered at the thought of the ordeal to come. My overcoat had felt like paper last night. Eventually I decided to keep my thick pyjamas on under everything else. I went downstairs feeling a little constricted but protected against the worst.

Brandon drew up in his Hillman. 'You looked pretty cold last night,' he said, 'so I've brought you an extra overcoat.'

We went round the docks. Only my nose suffered in the east wind. We went aboard a sandsucker and I met the captain and crew. This part was really interesting. (A member of the Cabot family working as mate on a sandsucker?)

At lunch I was able to shed the two coats, but the restaurant still seemed oppressive. After lunch Brandon took me to the Theatre Royal to see the Old Vic Company. Leaving one coat in the car but lugging my own along, I took a cramped seat in the third row. By the end of the act I was melting away like a wax candle.

'Excuse me,' I said and went off hurriedly to the lavatory, where I all but had to strip, dragged off my pyjamas, tore back into the rest of my clothes and was just in my seat in time for curtain up with the pockets of my overcoat fairly bulging.

The rest of my stay was surprisingly stimulating. I went back to the sandsuckers twice more, saw another play, went round the Wills factory, saw where the Bristol car was made, etc., and all the time ideas were tugging at me.

The girls in the cigarette factory were great fun. I went back a second time. They were jolly, uninhibited, very frank, didn't seem to mind my company at all. One of them told me that until last Christmas she had always believed that Jesus Christ was the first man and that Adam and Eve came after.

I went home, talked it over with Jean. I consulted the few notes I had made. After all, it would be fun to create another, modern saga, after writing *Poldark*. I rang Donald Wilson and said I would have a shot at it.

He said: 'Good, good, I'm delighted. Could you let us have a synopsis of the story.'

I said: 'Sorry, I've never written a synopsis in my life, and it's too late to start now.'

Embarrassed pause. 'Well, before I commission this I have to show something to my superiors.'

I said: 'Things only grow as I write. But look: I'll be happy to write you six chapters – that may be about 100 pages of type – happy to do that. Will that suit?'

He agreed at once.

I can't recall how long this took me. The characters were formulating themselves quite quickly, so it may have been less than six weeks. I sent a copy of the chapters to Donald and a second copy to Brandon.

A couple of weeks elapsed and then Donald came on the telephone to me to say how delighted he was with the piece, and Brandon, he said, was equally excited.

Unfortunately between the time he first approached me and when I delivered there had been a turnaround in the higher echelons of the BBC. Donald Baverstock had taken over as head of drama and had decreed that serials were 'out'. The new fashion was for a 'series', in which the author creates a group of characters and writes each week a separate story for them. Of course there could be continuing interest from one instalment to the next, but each one should have a separate beginning, middle and end.

I said: 'That's a form of short story. All right for them as likes them. But I don't write short stories.'

We argued, amicable to the end, but I refused to budge.

He said: 'Please think it over for a week or two.'

'I will,' I promised, and I did.

The outcome was still, regretfully, 'no'.

It is the only time in my life that I started something and then aborted it.

Inevitably it was not all lost. The character of Angell, based on a solicitor at the Savile Club and whom I had had in mind for some time before, moved over to a novel I wrote later using his name. The character of Deborah I used in the novel *The Walking Stick*.

Chapter Five

In the meantime things had been moving elsewhere. Robert Clark, deprived of his position at Associated British Pictures, had bought London Films, which had continued to exist since the death of Korda solely for the purpose of exploiting the many famous films the great Hungarian had made in his lifetime. Clark had other ideas, and he bought another option on the *Poldarks* and tried to set it up in the television world.

I remember we had been on our annual September visit to Venice, and when we returned I was told that London Films had made a deal with the BBC to produce the first four books. I could hardly believe it – or believe my luck. My admiration for the BBC's costume drama productions knew no bounds. *The Forsyte Saga*, the adaptations of Henry James, of Jane Austen, of George Eliot, of Anthony Trollope had conditioned me to such a high standard of excellence that I was wholly confident in their ability and their goodwill to put a faithful interpretation of my novels on the small screen. Surprisingly, apart from *Night Without Stars*, I had been pretty faithfully served by the producers and the directors of the cinema. In spite of all their appalling reputations for taking a novel and distorting it after their own fancies, *Take My Life, Fortune is a Woman* and later (though I was not to know this) *The Walking Stick* had all stuck closely to the story of the novel. How much happier, then, was I to feel that these books were going to be entrusted to our own BBC, whose reputation for integrity was so high, indeed impeccable.

In due course I met Maurice Barry, who was to be the producer of the whole sixteen episodes, and Simon Masters, the script editor, and Christopher Barry (no relation), who was to direct the first four episodes covering the first novel, *Ross Poldark*. We had a jolly lunch, discussing scripting, casting and locations. Jack Pulman was to write the first four episodes, and I could not have been happier about this, as he had adapted many of the classic novels screened, with great tact and with great skill. I was really in good hands.

A few weeks later – uninvited – I went down to join the unit which had gone to Cornwall to scout for locations. Chris d'Oyly John was the production manager, and it was clear that, although he did not know much about Cornwall, he much preferred his own investigations there to receiving unwelcome suggestions from the author, who happened to have lived in Cornwall for thirty years. (The only way to get his cooperation, I found, was to be fiendishly clever and put the idea of a location into his head in such a way that he believed he had thought of it himself.)

On the second day of our tour we stopped for a snack lunch at Portreath, and I paid for the group. Softened by this generosity – I discovered it was really the only way to his heart – Maurice Barry drew me aside and told me that 'of course' there had had to be some alterations in the early scripts, that is alterations from the storyline in the novel. Knowing the film industry, and knowing how much more scrupulous the BBC was bound to be, I replied that I was used to the changes necessary to present a story in picture form, and we left it at that.

When I first sold an option to Robert Clark I had made it a condition of the sale that they should oversee and vet any production they had a hand in and would preserve the story and the characters without unnecessary distortion. Leslie Baker, the managing director, had gladly given me his personal assurance.

However, I had no qualms. It was further a condition of any sale that I should see the scripts and be able to comment on them. (Script *approval* is virtually never given, and it is unrealistic to ask for it.)

Partly for reasons of time, a different scriptwriter had been assigned for each of the four books, and Simon Masters, as script editor, was to oversee them and keep an eye on their continuity. The writer allotted for *Ross Poldark* was, as I have said, Jack Pulman.

What was my surprise, as bad novelists say, when the first two scripts arrived and I found the story totally distorted, Demelza's

168

character changed, and my carefully studied Cornish dialect swept away, and in its place a sort of phoney Zummerset which only exists inside the close confines of television studios.

Indeed, not a line of my own dialogue was retained. It was as if the scriptwriter had read the book through a couple of times and then thrown it away and told the same sort of story in his own words.

I would make it clear that I was not some middle-aged novelist who had had no experience of the cinematic or dramatic world and considered his precious creations sacrosanct. I had had two full-length scripts made into feature films, and I had contributed substantial parts to half a dozen others. I had had six of my novels filmed, and I was completely aware that in any translation from novel to film there must be abbreviation and broad strokes. Above all, dialogue must be *understandable*, and dialect can only be used sparingly and with that stipulation in mind.

(Where dialect was used in these scripts it was no more understandable, and it was as Cornish as haggis.)

What stuck in my crop beyond all swallowing were the ridiculous liberties taken with the characters and with the stories. Hitchcock at his most egocentric could hardly have done more. (And in fact had done less.) It was a cold April morning, if I remember, when I called to see Leslie Baker, of London Films, reminded him of the undertaking of his firm to see that these novels were fairly presented, and told him that I wanted the whole project cancelled. They must tell the BBC that the deal was off; and I would repay the money that I had so far received.

He was naturally full of apologies and consternation. He had noticed the changes, of course, and certainly did not like them, but he rather thought that I had been consulted over them. I said I had not, and I wanted the whole thing cancelled, wiped out, forgotten. He looked at my face, which must have been white with anger, and said he would consult his fellow directors, particularly Mr Robert Clark, the chairman, and approach the BBC and see what he could do.

I remember walking down St Martin's Lane and into Trafalgar

Square, trying to breathe out my fury. It wouldn't go. If anyone had offered me a helicopter and a bomb, I should have leapt at the chance and should have known just where to drop it.

Though I have never been appraised of the details, I gather that there was a great deal of telephoning and consultation, and meetings in the BBC and threats of resignation here and there. However, the outcome was that London Films welched on me and, while making my angry protests known, had felt the production was too far advanced for it to be cancelled. Further, this was the very first joint venture between them and the BBC, and for it to end in disaster would prejudice any future cooperation between them.

So the production went ahead. In view of its enormous success it was as well. However, the ruction I caused was not in vain, for after Episode 4 the scripts kept much more closely to the books (except for the final episode, No. 16, where the whole thing went haywire again. In this episode, apart from scenes of the miners being driven from their homes by cruel bailiffs, and the burning down of Trenwith – incidents which no doubt could have happened in Ireland or in France but never did in Cornwall – Maurice Barry wanted Elizabeth to go mad, and was only restrained from this enormity by the terms of the contract, and no doubt the apprehension of my wrath).

One of the difficulties of my position was that I never dealt directly with the BBC on the first series; all my communications went through London Films. Probably things would have been much easier had I been able to have the personal contact.

Anyway, when the script for Episode 5 came along and I thought well of it, I let London Films know and said I would like to go down and see some of the shooting in Cornwall. Producer Maurice Barry sent word through London Films that I would not be welcome on the set, and if I came to their location I would be treated as an ordinary member of the public.

This was not a general feeling. Christopher Barry who, as the first of the three directors, must have been very much involved in the early squabbles, wrote to say how disappointed he had been not to see me during the shooting. And when, much later, I recognized Clive Francis (who played Francis Poldark) at my club and made myself known to him, he put his arms round me and said: 'But why haven't you been to *see* us? We thought you didn't *like* us!'

'Not *like* you?' I said. 'The very reverse! I like and admire you all!'

However, Maurice Barry's spite kept me away, and, although meeting and coming much to admire Kenneth Ives, the third director, I saw none of the shooting of the first series.

There were of course other, though minor, annoyances. I never know why TV companies pay such scrupulous attention to material detail – every little item of clothing and furniture has to be true to the period – yet are so slovenly about the spoken word. Of course, all period dialogue is a compromise. In *The Fifth Queen*, a novel by Ford Madox Ford about Catherine Howard, the author uses dialogue as nearly true to the time as it is possible to get, and very impressive it is. Rose Macaulay in *They Were Defeated*, a novel about Herrick, also uses language faithful to the time.

This is no longer really acceptable – certainly not on TV, and rightly so. But use of the language of today can be controlled and stripped of its more modern idioms. Before I began to write any of the *Poldarks* I would always read Sterne, Swift, Gay, Chesterfield, Sheridan, in order to get something of the flavour and cadences of the speech of those days. I believe one can achieve a sense of the eighteenth century without using archaic words or words of old-fashioned meaning. *But* the fashionable catchphrases of today should be avoided like the plague.

In the very first scene in *Poldark*, when they are jogging along in the coach, someone says: 'You must be joking.' I drew attention to this, but my letter was ignored. In the second (or third) episode Elizabeth comes to Ross and tells him she is going to divorce Francis because of his infidelity. I pointed out that until the Act of 1857, divorce could only be achieved by Act of Parliament, usually took two years and cost about £10,000. This they very grudgingly altered. In the second series (yes, the second, which generally was so much, much better), at a dinner party at Tehidy, Caroline Enys asks Sir Francis Basset if he thinks there is going to be war. I pointed out that at this date England had been already at war with France for several years, and it was like someone in 1940 asking if it is thought there is going to be a war when Hitler controlled virtually all Europe.

It was, less grudgingly, changed because I was on the spot. But in the first episode of the second series Ross Poldark is returning from Holland and is seen galloping home across the sands. This was well done, but a research girl pointed out that in 1796 an army officer did not wear his hat peak over nose, like Wellington later, but peak ear-to-ear like Napoleon. So the whole morning's shooting was scrapped and reshot next morning with the hat correctly worn. That all seems a little disproportionate.

So far as the Cornish dialect was concerned they did not of course consult me, but instead engaged a dialect coach, from *Liverpool*, who had been to Cornwall *twice* to direct productions at the Minack Theatre. In fact neither he nor I should have been necessary. Actors are such quick and clever mimics that those who needed an accent could have been shipped to Cornwall for a week, and they would have picked it up, and it would have been near enough to the genuine thing.

I disliked the series so much that when it was about to be shown I seriously considered wintering in Jamaica to avoid it. But then Episode 5 came along, with an even better 6 and 7, and I began to be reconciled, even excited. And from a fairly slow beginning the series was proving enormously popular. Audience viewing grew from five to ten million. The Attorney-General gave word that no social or other appointments were to be made for him during the hour that *Poldark* was on. Church services were advanced so that parishioners should be able to get home in time. Later people went mad about it in Spain and Greece. In Israel, I was told, when it was shown on Tuesday nights, the series was the chief topic of conversation in the shops on Wednesday morning.

Naturally I was more than delighted with the success of the series in England, and strove hard to overlook the enormities of the earlier scripts. Then there came from the BBC the proposal that a second series should be made. *The Black Moon* was already published. *The Four Swans* was finished. I was just beginning *The Angry Tide*. It had somehow come to someone's notice in the BBC that I had not been quite enraptured with the way the first series was done, so they sent down one of their best producers, an Australian called Anthony Coburn, to see me and to find out the reasons for my objection. He came and I let him know them. A jolly, bluff, candid man, he took my views aboard and reported to the BBC. He then wrote inviting me to lunch with the executive producer of the day, Bill Slater, and himself. I went along.

Bill Slater was a very pleasant, civilized man, and we had a pleasant, civilized meal. He soon raised the question of a second series, and told me that Tony Coburn had passed on to him my dissatisfaction with the first.

'Nevertheless,' he added, 'the series has been a tremendous success.'

'It has,' I agreed, 'and I'm truly delighted about that. Both delighted and excited. And nothing, I assure you, would give me greater pleasure than to see a second series made ...'

'Then?'

'But if you want the same producer; or any of the same directors; or any of the same scriptwriters, we'll just enjoy this meal together and then go home and forget all about it.'

He seemed startled. 'I'm sorry, I don't understand. Can you be more explicit?'

I was more explicit. He looked a bit pale. 'I knew practically nothing about this. I'm very sorry it happened.'

We went on with our lunch.

'Look,' he said. 'Thinking over what you've just said ... I'm not in a position to write any of your stipulations into a contract for a second series, but if I gave you my word that I'll personally see that they're met, then will that do?'

'Gladly,' I said.

We shook hands on it and the meal ended happily for us all.

Tony Coburn was appointed producer for the second series of thirteen instalments, and, probably feeling they had been remiss in not involving me more actively in the first series, London Films appointed me their representative on the coproduction, so that if needed I always had an official justification for being about. But in fact I was always made welcome. I kept my active interference to an absolute minimum.

There were exceptions once or twice. At the end of Episode 5 (the last part of *The Black Moon*), Ralph Bates, playing George Warleggan, is told by old Aunt Agatha, played by Eileen Way, her reasons for believing that he is not the father of the son just born to his wife Elizabeth. In the novel he stares at her with bitter hatred and goes out, slamming the door behind him. In the script he takes her by the throat and shakes her. Legitimate dramatization. But as it was directed it looked unquestionably as if George had strangled her. I objected that this was contrary to the intention of the book and a distortion of George's character. So it was reshot.

Incidentally in the film, Ralph Bates' progression from room to room of the house as the old woman's venom sinks in was one of the finest pieces of acting of the series.

All the scripts were discussed with me, under Tony Coburn's supervision, and then the final scripts were sent to me for approval. Tragically, Tony Coburn died of a heart attack with the series half done. His replacement, another Australian, was taken ill with overwork – he was producing another series, *The Plantagenets*, at the same time – so the final episodes were produced by Colin Tucker. Unasked, we had three producers on this second series, as well as two new directors and three new scriptwriters.

It is difficult to know how much, if any, difference the ordinary viewer detected between the two series. Obviously the second series, being a sequel, lacked some of the original impact of the first, and – not knowing the characters or the storyline in the original books – deviation did not worry them. (It worried and offended many who had read the books first.) It was very pleasant to see some of my own dialogue surfacing and being as speakable and audible as the rest.

Perhaps the acid test is audience viewing. Ratings for the second series were higher all through and were still rising at the end.

In the light of this, perhaps it is not surprising that the BBC wanted a third series. About Episode 8 or 9, they sent down Graeme

McDonald, the head of drama at that time, to Cornwall – where shooting was in progress – to put the proposition to me that I should write a third series, which could go into production next year.

My reply was simple but sad. I had enjoyed very few things in my life more than being involved in this second production, in becoming personal friends of most of the actors and actresses, of the production teams, of seeing my own stories, my own characters, and – some – of my own dialogue reproduced with enviable spirit and dedication. My wife and I had almost become mascots of the cast, and they seemed sometimes not to want to start until we were there. We had parties in the evenings and happy lunches sitting in canvas chairs or on the steps of caravans, joking and eating and establishing a wonderful camaraderie. Several of the professionals said they had never had such an enjoyable time – it must go on.

'Graeme, I'm *really* sad about this,' I said. 'I would have had no conditions to make this time. In fact, to continue the series I'd be perfectly willing to contribute the next thirteen or sixteen episodes free. But where are they coming from? The story – my story – ends with the death of Elizabeth. There is no more.'

'Think it over,' he said gently. 'We'll gladly lend you a couple of scriptwriters to help you through your blockage.'

I said: 'Dear Graeme, it isn't a blockage, it's an endage.'

As indeed it was. The death of Elizabeth brought the whole conception full circle. There was nothing to add. And even if there were still plenty of loose ends from which new ideas would develop (as I found in due course) they couldn't be forced, they couldn't be contrived, fitted together like a Meccano frame. Whatever quality or lack of it the *Poldark* novels possess, they are organic, they have to grow; forcing them would have distorted history and the doings of a family, both of which were too dear to my heart.

'Think it over,' Graeme McDonald urged again. 'Don't decide at once. We'll meet in London in a few weeks when you have had time to reflect.'

'One or two of the leads in the cast,' I said defensively, 'have told me they're tired out and don't want to go any further.'

He said: 'Don't you worry about the cast. We'll deal with them.

You just give us the material. Don't say any more now. We'll meet for lunch in London in a few weeks' time.'

Graeme McDonald was too nice a man ever to play the devil's role, but I suppose if there were ever a time when I was taken up and shown all the cities of the plain, this was it. Another series, as dizzyingly enjoyable as this second one; the tremendous notoriety I had achieved – not displeasing to one's ego, however much one might physically retreat from it, the temptation to carry on, to hold the viewers in the palms of one's hands, to work with stimulating advice, to know of twelve million viewers waiting for it: surely one's creative urges would work at double speed to satisfy such a demand? Had not Dickens written his books in instalments, to be published at regular intervals and to be soaked up by an eager and doting public?

Looking back, and seeing the situation from the perspective of the years, it is very surprising to me now that I scarcely felt the temptation. I met Graeme McDonald in London and regretfully told him no. Perhaps it is a measure of the attachment I felt for all the *Poldark* characters that I hardly seriously contemplated providing the *material* for another three or four books. The seven published books had not come that way. Nor could any others.

The fact that five years later I began again is quite another matter. An author can be influenced in his choice of what he writes by the knowledge that his public wants more about a particular character and nothing else. (Conan Doyle, to his own great chagrin, found his public very little interested in his excellent historical novels such as *The White Company* and calling only for more Sherlock Holmes.)

What did influence me, in the end, apart from the enormous continuing popularity of the *Poldarks*, was my own enduring preoccupation with this scene and these people. To go back to them and open yet another chapter in their lives was something I found myself gradually impelled to do, even though I had thought the story finished with the seventh book. Of course I was aware it would pleasure many other people, but mainly I was pleasing myself, as I had done ten years before when turning my back on successful modern novels.

By the time the first of the new quartet, *The Stranger from the Sea*, was published, Graeme McDonald had left the BBC and moved to Anglia Television. Almost all the people connected with the television production had left or been moved, and the newcomers were not interested.

Among the many totally enjoyable events of that happy summer when the second series was being made, two events particularly stand out. Christopher Biggins, who came into the second series and who made such a hit as the lecherous parson, Osborne Whitworth, is a very talented, amusing, gregarious man, full of laughter and bonhomie. Discovering that he had no part to play in Episode 6, he thought to take a holiday. A rich friend of his had offered to lend him his villa in Minorca for ten days, so Christopher invited Jane Wymark, who was his downtrodden wife (Morwenna) in the production, Julie Dawn Cole, her pretty sister (Rowella), Julie's boyfriend, and another rather mysterious half-French girl called Janique.

Then he said: 'Why don't you and Jean come along with us? *Do!*'

It could have been a disaster. We were at least thirty years older than the next oldest member of the party. None of the others did we know at all well; two we had not even met. We assembled at Heathrow to meet together for the first time and to catch the 11.30 p.m. plane for Minorca, with a traffic controllers' strike due to begin at midnight. We sat in the plane nervously waiting, making what jokes we could, and hoping for the best. We took off at five minutes to twelve.

Two and a half hours later we straggled sleepily out of the airport at Mahon. Christopher said he had ordered a self-drive car or cars to meet us. There was no one anywhere about. But in the car park two very battered Fiat 500s were standing, and on each windscreen was a big placard marked 'Biggins'. The keys had been left in the ignition. We had to help ourselves.

Christopher drove one and I drove the other. He presumably had some idea where we were going, so I followed him. I do not know how long it took, but presently we arrived at a luxurious villa, with eight bedrooms each with its own bathroom, built round a large private swimming pool. Christopher triumphantly switched on all the lights – we made tea, were allotted our bedrooms and dropped into bed.

I suppose it was lucky that we all liked the same things. Casual breakfasts, a drive to spend a long day on a beach somewhere, with lunch at a beachside cafe, endless bathing and sunbathing, then home to change and out to dinner at one of the numerous restaurants dotted about the island. In the ten days I do not remember a disagreement, a cross word or a complaint. All I remember is the laughter.

Of course Christopher was the supreme organizer and the catalyst. He it was who sought out the restaurants and, since few of them were on the telephone, buzzed over in his rickety Fiat to make the reservations. The swimming pool, elegant as it was, was simply not used. With complete accord, every day we sought the sea, and laughed and joked our way through the day. Only towards the very end of our stay two members of the party said they were exhausted and wanted to opt out. They were the two youngest.

The evening before we left to return to England we were late back to the villa, and Jean whispered to me:

'Quick, quick, Christopher is still with the car. I want to get into his bed without anyone seeing!'

So off she limped to the other side of the villa, me trailing behind her, and presently when she was happily abed, having redonned her sun hat, I slipped away, and waited for the arrival of Biggins. A chorus of good-nights followed and then a scream that would have put a banshee to shame brought everyone out of their rooms again to discover what more laughter was to be had so long after midnight.

Jane Wymark, writing to me many years later, sums up: 'If C. Biggins Esq. never does anything else I feel he should be given a medal for organizing that holiday in Minorca. I remember Jean in her wild bathing hat covered in roses and wearing her water ring. What if a stroke leaves you with a bit of trouble on one side? – swim round in circles and enjoy yourself! Then the evenings with the whole lot of us clean and content if slightly sun-struck, and Jean smartly dressed for dinner with the odd rich jewel carelessly sprinkled around. And everyone, everyone jolly together.'

Chapter Six

Soon after the second series was started various members of the cast got together and insisted that I should make an appearance on the screen – à la Hitchcock – so the director was prevailed upon to put me in as a member of the church congregation waiting outside the church to greet the arrival of the Revd Mr Odgers. I was dressed up in suitable yeoman-style clothes and when Mr Odgers appeared I was to touch my hat and say, 'Mornin', Vicar,' in a good Cornish voice. This took place and I fancied I delivered the lines without forgetting a single syllable. However, when the episode was shown I was not in it. I raised this with the director, Philip Dudley, who said: 'I thought you might notice that. Sorry. The episode was running long and you ended up on the cutting-room floor.'

We were now about to start Episode 12 (of 13), and he went on: 'Let's see, there's not much left now. I could put you in this episode as a drowning miner …'

'Thanks, no, all the same.'

'Wait a minute,' he said, 'I could put you in another church scene, the last. Where Morwenna marries Drake. You can stand outside the porch and kiss her as she comes out.'

'That sounds more promising,' I said.

The following night we attended an Old Cornish Dinner at Lostwithiel, and just before going I sprained my back. I spent the evening in acute pain, and was tremendously relieved to collapse into bed in Lamellyn Vean, the house we had rented for the duration in Probus; but conscious that on the morrow the wedding would take place, where I was expected to play a part.

The next morning my back was no better, but determined not to miss my eighty seconds of celluoid immortality, I asked Jean if she had any sort of corset she could lend me.

She said: 'I don't wear them, as you know. Not the sort of thing that would be any help to you, anyway. I'll go into Truro and see if I can find anything there.'

She was gone a long time, and when she returned she had a large white suspender belt, which duly went on and offered me some minimal support.

It was time to go. By merciful good fortune my dear friend F. L. Harris had arranged to come with us, and it was relative bliss to sit in an upright car instead of the low-slung Alfa.

After a canteen lunch it was time for the next scene, and the call came. I went over to one of the caravans to be dressed and made up.

As it happened, the dresser was a pleasant little chap I had seen about quite a bit. He had dyed carrot-coloured hair, a safety pin through one ear, and read girlie magazines.

'I've a lovely brown jacket for you 'ere,' he said in his twittering voice, 'an' a pair of breeches to match.'

Reluctantly I took my trousers off, when I was seen to be wearing an old-fashioned white corset with four suspenders dangling ...

Later that afternoon, in the porch of the little granite church of St Braddock, I duly kissed the 'bride'. It was a misty, drizzly day, and for some reason the director could not get the scene just as he liked it. We went through it four, five times.

As I dutifully kissed Jane Wymark once again I whispered: 'I believe I'm getting more fun out of the wedding than the groom.'

She smiled through her teeth and replied: 'Yes, and more than he's ever going to get too.'

The other and particularly happy recollection concerns an event at the very end of the outdoor shooting. Because the scriptwriter of the first series had, bizarrely and with complete disregard for my story, decreed in Episode 16 that Trenwith should be burned down, a new house had had to be found for the Warleggans to live in in the second series. Godolphin, in the west of the county, near Helston, had been changed to Boconnoc, in the east, near Lostwithiel. The owner of Boconnoc, a Major Desmond Fortescue,

age was enormous and included a cricket ground where
iel occasionally played, allowed himself to be persuaded
a cricket match – for some charity, I don't remember which
e contestants being the Poldarks against the Warleggans, the
ams composed of most of the cast and any of the technicians who
fancied making up the numbers. It was thought that two or three
hundred spectators might come, and suitable provision was made.
Over six thousand arrived.

It was a lovely day, sunny and fresh. I had had to go to London
for something, so I travelled back to Cornwall by overnight sleeper,
bringing my car, the pagoda-yellow Alfa, on the same train. Bleary
with the inevitable rackety, bumpy night, I arrived in Penzance at
7.30, took the hood down, drove to Probus, where we had the
house, changed, had breakfast, rested a bit, then drove with Jean to
Boconnoc,where we had lunch at the Dower House with Desmond
Fortescue and our old friends Nancie Tresawna and John and Molly
Corbett. Then we drove to the cricket match.

Mayhem reigned. But it was altogether a happy, good-tempered
mayhem. I forget which side batted first, but the game was constantly
subject to what are now called pitch invasions – whenever, in fact,
an important member of the cast was sent near the boundary to
field and was at once surrounded by people anxious to talk to them
and to get their autographs. I remember Judy Geeson (Caroline
Enys) arriving late and wandering onto the field of play. She was
so surrounded, almost overwhelmed, that I stood guard over her so
that she should not totally disappear in the friendly scrum.

The Poldarks won the match. The highlight of the game, perhaps,
was when Robin Ellis (Ross Poldark in person) was batting and had
scored freely all round the wicket. Ralph Bates (George Warleggan)
asked Jill Townsend (Elizabeth Warleggan) to bowl an over. Jill, who
is American, had only the faintest notion what to do, but followed
the instructions so well that she bowled Ross Poldark first ball.

I do not know whether it has been quite clear in the course of
these pages that my criticism of the producer and writers of the
first series stopped entirely short of the actors and technicians. For

them I had only admiration. And if my criticism of the original producer has been very forthright, it does not include criticism of his casting. In some cases it was inspired. From the beginning they were a wonderful group: Robin Ellis, Angharad Rees, Ralph Bates, Clive Francis, Jill Townsend and Norma Streader made a brilliant sextet round which the other actors congregated to create their own *Poldark* world. Paul Curran as Jud Paynter, Mary Wimbush as Prudie, Richard Morant as Dwight Enys and Judy Geeson as Caroline Penvenen were added to in the second series by Christopher Biggins as Osborne Whitworth, Jane Wymark as Morwenna, Kevin McNally as Drake Carne and David Delve as Sam Carne. For the second series, which was separated from the first by two years, only one big cast change had to be made. Dwight Enys was played in the second series – and played equally well – by Michael Cadman. Of the technicians also I cannot speak too highly.

We had one day of very bad weather at the beginning of Episode 1 of the second series, when Ross, returning from Holland (where he had been sent by the previous scriptwriter), had to gallop across Porthluney Beach in his full regimentals. Torrential hail showers drifted up, flooded and drenched everybody and were succeeded by a cold, fitful sun, gleaming before the next shower. It was very trying. Everything was spasmodic and damp and chill. Walking back after one huge shower, I passed a cameraman called Chris, just emerging, dripping, from the hibernation of a piece of tarpaulin. I said to him: 'Frightful weather, isn't it.'

He looked at me judicially and then said: 'Oh, I don't know. It's not too bad. I'm alive. I'm well. And I'm working.'

It's a wonderful remark and should be studied by us all.

The reason the BBC gave for their lack of enthusiasm when the further books were eventually written was that they did not wish to repeat old successes. The new executives wanted to make their own impression on the screen, not to seem to be copying their predecessors.

Even so, there have been any number of attempts to continue

the series on TV. In 1981 Robin Clark, who had inherited London Films together with a large fortune from his father Robert Clark, bought an option on the next three novels (with a fourth promised to follow). He paid handsomely for a twelve-month option, and immediately gave a large cocktail party to mark the event and invited all the old cast and a number of top BBC executives. At this party not one representative of the BBC turned up.

Nevertheless he went ahead and invested considerable funds in the preliminaries of a production. At the end of the year he felt he had made some progress, so bought another year's option. During this second period he brought in two experienced producers to work on the production, particularly to estimate its costing. He also published a glossy booklet advertising his intentions and listing the number of countries in which the previous series had been shown and with handsome pictures of scenes from *Poldark One* and *Two*. When the second year was up he took still one more option – this of six months. But nothing he could do could persuade the BBC to move an inch.

During this period there had been stirrings in the commercial network too, and when the Clark option finally expired, John Edwards, a freelance entrepreneur, paid a similar large sum for a further twelve months' option. Nothing came of this either, but Edwards continued to have faith in the books, so I gave him a further option – this time free – to run for another year.

In the meantime Robin Ellis (Ross Poldark) had read the by-now four unfilmed *Poldark* novels and was very enthusiastic about their potential as a continuation – or climax – of the saga. He discussed it with one of his friends, Jackie Stoller, herself a distinguished TV producer, and in early 1992 they approached me telling me of their plans for getting a film mounted and asking me for a twelve-month option, another free one. John Edwards' second option had now expired, so I gladly agreed to this. Between them, I thought they would produce an admirable series.

The last *Poldark* novel, *The Twisted Sword*, had been published in 1990, and it seemed that despite the big gap of time which had passed since the end of the two TV series, interest in *Poldark* had seldom been greater.

After early 1992 when this last option was granted, nothing material happened for a long time. I was in touch with Robin, who kept me appraised of the situation; but by the time the year was up there had not been any real progress. They therefore asked for another year's option, which I again gladly granted them.

Towards the end of the second year I was approached yet again by John Edwards, who by now had interested HTV in the *Poldarks* – or perhaps more correctly reactivated their interest – and he said they would consider taking an option themselves. When the property became free at the end of Robin and Jackie's second year I agreed with John Edwards that he should have a free option for *six weeks* only. This was greatly to the disappointment of Robin and Jackie, but I thought such a short option could hardly do any harm.

At the end of the six weeks, HTV said they were prepared to buy a year's option, paying less than a third of what Robin Clark had paid, but it was definitely an earnest of their interest.

The rest (as they say) is history. HTV took up the option and announced a production due to start in May 1995. This, following the new fashion, was to be a two-hour film based on the eighth *Poldark* novel, *The Stranger from the Sea*, and if this was as successful as everyone expected, it was to be followed (at an interval) by the three remaining novels in twelve hourly instalments, rather on the BBC model. The actors in the two previous series were all approached, and all the main actors were delighted to accept the offer to play their old parts. (The exception was Ralph Bates, who had played George Warleggan in the previous series – one of the most charming of men – and whose untimely death we all mourned.)

I was recovering from a minor operation, and one Tuesday all the main participants in the HTV production came to lunch with me at my home. John Edwards, Stephen Matthews, Geraint Morris, Sally Haynes. They could not have been more charming or more enthusiastic, and they left me with a feeling of happy anticipation.

Except that I had urged them to change the format, making four one-hour episodes of the book. The *Poldark* novels are not written for blockbuster films, they seem ideally made, however accidentally, for a long-running serial. I was assured that HTV could do nothing whatsoever about this. It was a condition imposed by the ITV moguls, who had got this idea from America and who made it a condition of providing the finance that it should be made in this form.

The one important person missing from our luncheon was the scriptwriter, who they said was too busy on the adaptation to attend. They said she played over one of the old TV tapes each day before beginning work on the new book.

In the meantime while we waited – and waited – all was optimism among the old cast. Robin went daily to the gym to reduce his weight and get in trim. Angharad glowed rosily at the prospect of portraying the part of Demelza which she had made triumphantly her own. My own enquiries to HTV of Sally Haynes, who was to produce the film, were met with reassurances that the script had had some amendments but had now gone back for the final polishing.

At length – very late – it came, with production scheduled to begin in a month's time. There was just time enough to go full steam ahead. When I read the script I was once again shattered and deeply affronted. The scriptwriter apparently had felt free to use my characters but almost to write a different story. Or if the bones of the story were adhered to the flesh had completely changed. Important incidents in the book were totally omitted, important incidents which were not in the book were inserted. It didn't read right, it wouldn't speak right. Any resemblance to the 'feel' of the novels was coincidental. I rang up Sally Haynes and told her it was an insult. It just wouldn't do. Fortunately Stephen Matthews, the executive in charge, didn't like it either.

So the script was thrown out, and after a pause another scriptwriter, *equally unknown*, was engaged. This meant that the whole rumbling mechanism of production was brought to a stop, at great cost, and a new date, in September, four months hence, was chosen. At this stage John Edwards, whose role was now only supervisory, wrote a treatment which kept closely to the book while paring off inessentials. Robin and Angharad went to see Geraint Morris and Sally Haynes, and they beat out together a rough idea of how the film should be approached. If only it had happened three months earlier, we thought – and if it was adhered to – it would have saved all the trouble.

But it was not, in the outcome, adhered to at all. Sally, a talented young woman, but a person of great obstinacy, had her own ideas: she had engaged an unknown director called Richard Laxton, and as the summer went on she more and more leaned towards the idea of featuring only Robin and Angharad and otherwise making a clean sweep of the earlier cast. Technicians who had worked on the BBC production, and who had been provisionally signed up to begin in May, were told that they would no longer be needed in September.

By this time I had become aware of a curious dichotomy in HTV's approach. As a group they could not have been more eager, enthusiastic and determined to make this into a resounding success. I remember Sally saying excitedly to me once: 'Won't it be wonderful to see Robin and Angharad reunited on the screen again after all these years!' There was no question in her mind, in anyone's mind, that they should not play.

But underneath the enthusiasm was a total blind ignorance of what *Poldark* was really all about. Even before the two series on television there must have been many thousands of people all over the country able to answer all their questions and to correct all their misapprehensions. After the TV series it must have been numbered in millions.

Yet there was this *enthusiasm*, there was this *commitment*. *Nothing* was going to be too expensive or too much trouble to ensure that the new production was as good as, or better than, the old.

And unlike certain people who might try to sit in judgement on HTV, I have a long memory. I remember the total ignorance of the BBC when it all began in 1975. They had the first four novels, which a lot of people had read, and many hadn't. The great saving grace, then, was that it went on week after week regardless, and they learned in the process. By the end of Episode 4 things were changing. This may have been partly because of my raging disgust at the first scripts; partly, I believe the actors created a spell along with the story that gradually worked for all.

So when the *second* script came along from HTV, the entirely new script by an entirely new writer, I was delighted and relieved by the enormous improvement this showed. Remembering the awful travesty of the first four episodes that Jack Pulman produced for the BBC, this was not to be gagged at. I accepted it in its entirety, hoping that when it came down to the ultimate shooting script, minor and gently insinuated criticisms could iron out the too obvious faults.

I understood from all I heard that the top brass at HTV approved the new script, also that Robin and Angharad liked it, and I felt happy that at last this big expensive new project was about to go on the road.

In July I went on holiday with my daughter, Rosamund. We drove (in great heat) to Geneva and from there took the short flight to Nice and stayed at the Hôtel Metropole, Beaulieu. Then a week or so later we returned by air and car (in great heat) to England. We had been away less than three weeks, but in that period things had turned very sour. On the last day of the month Robin rang me to say he was withdrawing from the production.

It is not easy to relate the sequence of events which had led him to take this drastic step. Before I went away I knew there were certain elements in the second script that he did not like (and I entirely agreed with him) but, as I have said, I believed that these would be ironed out in the course of ordinary consultation. The official reason for the complete break was that the sums offered to him and Angharad for six weeks' work on the film just weren't enough. But I have never believed this was the whole of the story. It was probably the last straw.

Robin and Angharad had always believed that their participation in the next *Poldark* on TV was an absolute essential. They had created these two characters on screen from the characters in my novels. For weeks and months in the Seventies they had worked together, projecting themselves into these two eighteenth-century people, thinking and feeling like them. They had themselves been as close as lovers (which I don't believe they ever were), consulting, arguing, agreeing, working with the relevant director (and sometimes against him). They had presented these characters to the world, they had travelled together, to Spain, to America, etc., perpetuating the image and the dream.

They had been feted everywhere; twenty-two countries knew them. After the furore of the Seventies and early Eighties things must have begun to quieten down. The excitement was subsiding. Then in 1981 the BBC had reluctantly decided to show the series again – at the mildly insane time of 5.30 p.m. on Mondays. It had nevertheless roused much new interest, and out of this new excitement the Poldark Appreciation Society was born. Founded by Val Adams, it had rapidly grown in membership and at the annual luncheons, to which the stars and I were invited, there were people from all over the world. I greatly appreciated the warmth and admiration with which I was treated, but the largest number of admirers quite naturally centred on Robin and Angharad. I was the author, but they were actors, both young people with great charm and good looks, and they were the centre of the main attention. I fully approved of this, but it may have added to Robin and Angharad's impression, their conviction, that the new series stood or fell by their approval, that they were totally irreplaceable.

Most people, including me, felt they were. Not so the TV company. In their enthusiasm and eagerness to put on a fine series, they took it for granted that Robin and Angharad would be the stars; but they, the TV company, had to be in charge. With infinite error they had chosen an executive producer, a producer and a director, and – for the second time – a writer, the last three of whom were untried and certainly had no *real* knowledge of what *Poldark* meant. They all *wanted* the participation and the help of Robin and Angharad, but it was to be an ITV production and *they* were putting up the money and *they* intended to be in the saddle.

In the matter of the money the two stars were offered £30,000 each for six weeks' work, with pro-rata payment if the time was exceeded. HTV assured me, rightly or wrongly, that their offer was the top rate that was paid to TV stars. They were well aware that in the hard cold light of the TV world neither Robin nor Angharad had continued their fame by appearing in other comparable productions in the eighteen years that had passed.

When this offer was refused there was consternation at HTV and it looked as if the production might founder for a second time – and this time for good. The big people with the big money in the TV world were appealed to, were adamant that the top salaries offered was all there was to offer. So at an emergency meeting at HTV a package was contrived – for which later they were sternly reprimanded – whereby the two stars in addition to their salaries should each receive a percentage of the profits. This was also turned down.

Two well-known actors to whom I spoke at this time both said that Robin and Angharad were unwise to refuse such an offer.

Personally I greatly fault Robin's and Angharad's agents for not going into this matter thoroughly at the *very outset*. For God's sake get these two key people agreed and signed up before *anything else* begins. Even a relatively unbusinesslike type like me knew that much about the world – particularly, of all professions, the film and TV world! HTV's accountants were equally to blame. Did both sides quietly think 'Oh, *they*'ll agree when the time comes'? Was there already an element of bluff on both sides?

As I say, I have never believed that money was the whole cause of the break. From the beginning Robin and Angharad gave me the impression that because this was commercial television it might be slightly lower grade than the BBC. From the beginning HTV gave me the impression that though Ross and Demelza were the major stars, it was the story of their children that they wished mainly to concentrate on.

I don't know if either of these attitudes became perceptible to the other side, but neither of them would have mattered without the clash of temperaments which had grown up and which finally came to a headlong battle over the second script.

While I was away with my daughter, Angharad went to stay with Robin at his house in France, and one afternoon the two sides had a violent argument by telephone which lasted over two hours. I have heard both versions of this telephone call, but I gather that tempers were lost on all sides, that halfway through Angharad retreated into the garden and would take no further part in it, that Sally Haynes was in tears, that Richard Laxton had accused the actors of wanting to take over the film. Mistakenly, Sally thought that Angharad had joined forces with Robin in France in order to 'gang up' against them. Richard said it would be near impossible to direct them, since they wanted to direct themselves. (From time to time they had done just this in the earlier series, with benefit to the production.)

But Geraint Morris, the executive producer and in my view the only film-maker of repute and experience in the team, summed it up when he said: 'To me making a television play should be fun; otherwise the thing is not worth making. I don't see much fun in this. We are going to have to recast.'

What Robin and Angharad were chiefly complaining about in the second script was that the writer had totally misunderstood the characters of Ross and Demelza. (A lot of these mistakes were lost, as I had hoped, in the final shooting, but enough were left to spoil many of the scenes.) Whether, if Robin and Angharad had been playing the parts, they would have been able to influence the director or writer on the set we shall never know.

It is only a slight exaggeration to say that the break up of the entire production was chiefly a matter of chemistry.

When the news broke the fury of Robin and Angharad's admirers knew no bounds. A factor in all this which has been overlooked was that about two years before HTV began to mount the film the BBC after so many years decided reluctantly and timorously to release the twenty-nine instalments on videotape. Following a careful weighing of the pros and cons they had decided that it might just be financially viable to take this enormous risk. In the event the *Poldarks* went straight into the best-seller top ten, and over the next twenty-four months sold about two million copies. So that, along with the memories of the fifteen million-odd people who had watched the series twenty years before, there was a whole new mass of people to whom the series had just come fresh and in whose minds the original enormously engaging cast were still vivid and new.

To this was added the noisy voice of the Poldark Appreciation

Society. Perhaps 4,000-strong, it had formed itself as a band of fervent admirers of the original books and the original cast. As that admirable actor John Bowe, who came to play Ross in the HTV version, said: 'It should really be called the Robin Ellis and Angharad Rees Appreciation Society.' Which was perfectly true. I had seen this all along, and had never regarded it with anything but great pleasure – until the break took place.

Many of the members took up an angry attitude, changing in a trice from happily pro to extremely hostile to HTV, and a number of them wrote to every newspaper they knew, staged demonstrations in Bond Street, paraded in Cornwall, etc.

Most of these good people were ardent admirers of the books too. Often and often they had come over to me and told me what the books meant to them in terms of sheer pleasure, and (God help me) uplift, succour in ill-health, comfort and relief in times of personal distress. Many of them had read all the novels three or four times. It has always been a genuinely heart-warming experience to meet them.

But what of those idols, those who had come to portray visually characters hitherto only alive in their imaginations? Were they for the sake of a few extra thousands of pounds to be cast aside for a set of new idols, slowly obscuring the lineaments of the old?

They were not willing that this should happen. Val Adams must have felt unable to unknit her strong allegiances. All the same, it would have been more becoming to have kept a lower profile out of some consideration for the author of the books.

For the most part I was the one to keep the low profile, though behind the scenes I did everything humanly possible to heal the split. Some people, notably among the Poldark Appreciation Society supporters, thought that if I had aligned myself alongside Robin and Angharad the TV companies would once again have backed down and invited Robin and Angharad to return. This was a complete pipe dream. ITV were quite adamant. So I was left with a choice, disagreeable though that was. I faced the facts. HTV had bought the rights of the last four *Poldarks*. Although in some ways they had behaved like infidels, they were in deadly earnest, they had, chiefly because of my disapproval, thrown out the first script and brought the whole production to a stop, at great expense; more than the BBC had done when I raged at them. Now HTV, however wrong-headed they were in some things, had produced a second script which, for all its faults, was better than Jack Pulman's for the opening of the first series ever. In those days, though, there was no Poldark Appreciation Society to throw up its hands in horror, nor did the leading parts 'belong' to any actor or group of actors. No one knew where they were going. The BBC was at least as unfaithful to the intentions of the novels to begin. The redeeming feature was that Maurice Barry and his associates had been so generally inspired in their choice of cast. And the BBC had commissioned a long one-hour weekly showing of the four books so that they were able to stagger through the first episodes under a hail of criticism from the snide press. HTV, under the orders of their masters, were committed to an enormously expensive two-hour blockbuster to 'test the water'. Even if the reaction was overwhelmingly favourable it would have been another year before the beginning of a proper series was shown.

But my full commitment to HTV was not until I was invited to a meeting at which all the new cast was present and we sat, thirty round the table, technicians standing in the background, while Geraint Morris read the agreed script from beginning to end. I was tremendously impressed by the sheer look of quality of the new actors engaged. And nothing thereafter shook my intent to go along with this new production of my novels through thick and thin.

After the shooting in Cornwall was completed, where we had been dogged by foul weather, there was a big ballroom scene which was to be shot in the Pump Room in Bath (standing in for London). I had returned home for a couple of days and was taking two friends back to Bath to see the shooting. The day before I left the *Mail on Sunday* came down by appointment for a feature interview at my house in Sussex. The *Mail*, among whose staff Val Adams had some friends, had consistently supported the old actors and published all possible news derogatory to HTV; so I awaited the interview with lively interest.

In it I answered all their questions as truthfully and in as detached a way as I could, trying to keep a level between what was good on one side and what was good on the other. At about noon there was a break for coffee, and wandering into my study I found the chief interviewer – a very pleasant chap – on the mobile to his editor. I heard him say: 'But he favours *them*.' 'Them' being presumably HTV. The interview ended about 2.30 and the chief interviewer said: 'There'll be a full-page spread tomorrow.'

The next day I drove to Bath with my friends and watched the magnificent ballroom scene being shot. When I met Geraint he said that news had got around among the cast and technicians that there had been this interview, and every *Mail on Sunday* sold out the moment the papers arrived.

In fact there was nothing in the paper at all. Because my view had not been unfavourable to the HTV production and therefore did not fit in with his policy, the editor had killed the interview.

I have written at some length of the failure of this – possibly – final attempt to put *Poldark* back on the screen, because it was so widely discussed, so widely written about, and yet with the issues so widely misunderstood. Everyone had a different version of what they thought were the facts. As the one who stood to lose or gain most by this enterprise and who, feeling sympathy and impatience with both sides, yet for the most part I could only stand by and watch the lemmings carefully plotting their own fall.

Many of the scenes in the HTV film were magnificent and almost all the acting was of a high standard.

Quite the most important contribution to the failure of *Poldark* 3, even outweighing the change of cast, was ITV's bull-headedly stupid insistence on a first two-hour film to be made, to ensure it was going to be a success. This had the double-edged disadvantage of an all-or-nothing throw on the one showing. (ITV would certainly have given up if they had taken account of the adverse notices of the *first* episode of the *first* series). But also it meant that they had compressed the whole of one *Poldark* novel into quite a bit less than two hours, while the BBC had allotted four instalments of fifty-five minutes for each of the novels they used. The HTV film had far too much to say in too short a time.

Of course *Poldark* was so closely and affectionately associated with Robin and Angharad that without them much of the old magic was lacking. But I am pretty sure that, had it been presented in the way the BBC presented it, the public, while hating the changes, would have become absorbed in the progress of Ross and Demelza's children, played as they were by Ioan Gruffudd and Kelly Reilly, and would reluctantly have switched on in increasing numbers as the series went along.

Chapter Seven

My wife had had her first stroke – a slight one – in April 1967, when she was fifty-four. Our local doctor had taken her blood pressure a couple of months before, had noted it was over 200, but had not bothered to tell us.

One can hardly believe the strides medicine has made since then. Control of blood pressure was in its infancy. She went into University College Hospital where the head physician, John Stokes, was an old friend of mine. They gave her Esbatal tablets, which brought the blood pressure down most effectively. Unfortunately the BP reading was too dramatically different when the patient was lying down to when she was standing up. The result was that although the pressure was satisfactory when she was in bed, the minute she stood up she fainted.

She successively survived the spring and our daughter's wedding and the summer – during which we went twice to Ireland and then a tour of America (of which more later) – and the early autumn, taking a few of these pills which in small doses kept her blood pressure within safer limits but which were always inclined to make her dizzy and feel faint. In the September we went to Crete, hired a Volkswagen and drove round the island, ending up at Agios Nikolaos, where we spent ten days at the Minos Beach Hotel, bathing and sitting in the sun. The slight weakness in her left arm, which was the only visible sign of her illness, had quite gone, and she seemed well enough.

On the way back to Heraklion, where we would spend another day or so before flying home, we stopped at a little hotel called Grammatikakis at Malia, where we had spent a night on the way out, but this time only for a bathe and a picnic lunch.

As we were about to get out of the car, Jean said: 'I feel queer. A nasty sensation in my head.'

Hoping it was just the effects of the sun I said: 'Well, sit still a minute. I'll get you a brandy.'

When I came back she said: 'Oh, God, I think I'm losing the use of my hand.'

We both knew what that meant. I most particularly because I had observed it too closely in my father. We had two choices: go straight into this hotel and take a room and see what happened; or drive the thirty-odd miles into Heraklion. We knew from our previous visit that they spoke no English at this hotel, only Greek and German, also that the beds were like boards and that when dark fell the lights were hardly as bright as candles. At Heraklion we should be in relative civilization. I shut the door on her and we drove on.

I shall not forget that on the way there – although she must have known as well as I did what was happening – she commented on the scenery, pointed out things of interest, never referred to how she felt. It was a brave foreshadowing of the way she would face this illness which she had to face for the rest of her life. When we got to the Hotel Astir at Heraklion they had to carry her out of the car.

Up in the bedroom, her left arm seemed to improve a bit and she sat up in bed and insisted on making our luncheon sandwiches, which we tried to eat while waiting for a doctor. Dr Xekardarkis, when he came, confirmed what we already knew, gave her more pills, which from their effects must have been similar to Esbatal, and said we should try to manage in the hotel; he would not under any circumstances recommend the hospital, which in his view was appalling. (Unknowing of this insult, the Cretan proprietor of the hotel said to me next day: 'I wouldn't trust that doctor too far, he's a Greek.')

So we managed somehow for a week. Everyone in the hotel was supremely kind. Three sturdy chambermaids gave Jean regular blanket baths; food for her was sent up. The first night, in the middle of the night, she wanted to go to the lavatory. I got a chair and levered her on to it, then dragged it screeching into the bathroom, transferred her and left her there. When I went back she had fainted. I could not lift her but dragged her back along the floor and eventually, somehow, heaving and pulling, I got her back into bed. Her eyes were open and staring; she did not seem to be breathing; I thought she was dead. Then, as the Esbatal-type drug ceased to have its dire effect, the blood came back and her eyes flickered and she smiled up at me. Again it was typical that she should smile.

The next morning I went to buy a bedpan and some knickers. Knowing no Greek and the shopkeepers knowing nothing else, these purchases involved a difficult, even comical, negotiation. Suggestive gestures on my part produced the bedpan at the chemist's fairly soon, but no one in the lingerie shop seemed to have the least idea about knickers. The three pretty girl assistants produced girdles, suspender belts, petticoats, sanitary towels, bikinis. In the end in despair I found a smart fashion magazine and scrabbled through it. On about page 42 a girl stood in elegant underwear. I pointed, and the three girls simultaneously cried 'A-a-a-h!' and thereupon opened cupboards upon cupboards and produced every kind of the desired object, from flimsy panties to voluminous drawers.

It was very hot in Heraklion and there was no air-conditioning. Apart from reading, and the doctor's assiduous visits, Jean's only occupation was watching the weddings which constantly took place at the church in the square outside. October seemed the fashionable month. After a couple of dismal beach visits on my own, I occupied my time trying to get more money from England (since in 1967 currency restrictions were still in force and my traveller's cheques would not begin to suffice), in returning the hire car, in reading beside her and to her in the bedroom, and in making what preparation I could for a return to England.

Dr Xekardarkis, who, in spite of the hotelier's warning, was proving an efficient and helpful doctor, said he thought it would be safe for Jean to travel in a few more days. The left arm and leg were completely paralysed, but the internal haemorrhage seemed to have stopped. She could just move her hand. Life in the hotel was becoming insupportable.

In those days there was no direct flight from Crete to England: one had to change planes at Athens. In order that she might lie down

I booked three seats for her. Then I arranged for an ambulance to meet the plane at Athens and take her to some convenient place where she might await the plane for London. I also arranged for an ambulance to meet us at Heathrow to take us to the University College Hospital, who were warned to expect us. It was five more days to wait.

On the Thursday, the day before we left, the doctor came at midday and said Jean's blood pressure was much better. I paid him, we said friendly goodbyes, I packed, I paid the hotel. We couldn't wait. Then at 5 p.m. BEA telephoned that they would not take us. Their medical officer at Heathrow had decided that it was too soon for Jean to fly. She was, he said, too young to be subjected to the risk.

We shall never know how far this distant medico was concerned for my wife's health and how far concerned not to have an invalid aboard who might be taken ill and cause the flight to be interrupted. I can only say we took it very badly indeed. If a competent Greek doctor who had attended the patient for ten days thought it safe for her to fly, why should a man who had never seen her and was a thousand miles away presume to decide otherwise? We were faced with an indefinite sentence to stay on in this hot foreign hotel in this small Cretan town. I went to see the travel agent and besought her to find us some other way home. She was wonderfully, wonderfully helpful. Although it was closing time she kept the office open and rang here, there and everywhere. Eventually Olympic Airways agreed to take us, but at a very early hour, and then there would be a longer wait in Athens. I hastened back to tell Jean the good news.

Up at five, breakfast at six, the plane left at eight. At Athens, where we arrived at 9.15, there was no ambulance, because the arrangement had been for a later plane. Two porters carried her down the steps of the plane in a blanket, which they used like a hammock. We were deposited in the main concourse, and she lay there for three hours while travellers milled around her.

Through it all, though paralysed, Jean kept her good spirits.

A well-meaning American tourist saw her lying there and came up and said: 'Aren't you feeling very well, dear?'

She replied: 'I'm fine, thank you, it's just that I like travelling this way.'

Other problems arose. I got a snack and drink for us both. Then I said:

'You've got to find somewhere to spend a penny.'

'I'll be all right,' she said.

'Nonsense, it's three hours to London even when we're off.' I went in search of somebody who could speak English and found one – a security man, as it happened – and explained the position to him.

'I will see to this,' he said, and we went together to see the doyenne of the women's loo. Under pressure she emptied the lavatory of all its women clients. Then two security men picked up the blanket and carried Jean into the loo, I following with the bedpan which I had kept among the hand luggage. Then they all trooped out until she had used the pan and I had emptied it. A few minutes later we returned in triumph to our place in the concourse and normal traffic in the ladies' loo was resumed.

Again, there was no ambulance waiting at Heathrow for there had been no time to tell them of our change of plan; but one did arrive later, and we drove off crazily over what seemed all the broken roads in London to the University College Hospital.

I never used BEA again – not, that is, until it amalgamated with BOAC and became just British Airways, by which time my anger had run its course.

Towards the end of Jean's four weeks at UCH I had a long chat with John Stokes.

He said: 'You can see how much better she is. She has full movement in the leg and quite a lot in the hand. Of course her arm and leg will always be weak, and she'll need to wear a caliper to support her ankle for the rest of her life. But you're lucky that the stroke was on the left side – it seldom affects the speech, and for a right-handed person is much easier to adjust to.'

I said: 'That I'm delighted about; but I'm chiefly concerned as to how we can prevent another stroke.'

He said: 'There's no way. She should lead an easy, balanced life, and we'll control the blood pressure as far as we can. You might get five years. You might even get ten.'

The day before she left he said to me: 'I can see how devoted you are to each other. I think – if I may say so – you must try to distance yourself from her.'

That was November 1967. After a year Jean threw her caliper into the dustbin and never used one after – though sometimes she needed it. It would be absurd to claim that she enjoyed good health. She had chesty coughs, and periods of sickness when her appetite was nil. Sometimes she was dizzy. Often she tripped and fell. She was unable to swim, dance, play golf, play the piano, or walk anywhere without a stick. Also, having known a few people with strokes, I am aware that this is not an illness which (like, say, tuberculosis) seems to breed hectic high spirits. The tendency is all for depression, and, if anything, overcaution. The easy, balanced life. Above all, take no risks. Don't subject yourself to pressures or stresses. A quiet life.

Well, with the help of my pocket diary, I have made a list of the number of places we visited in the twenty-five years from 1967 to 1992.

Switzerland	19 times
Venice	15 times
France	10 times
Austria	8 times
India	7 times
Majorca and Minorca	8 times
Corfu	6 times
Canary Islands	5 times
United States	5 times
Ireland	4 times
West Indies	3 times
South Africa	3 times
Greece	2 times

and:

Morocco
Kenya
Australia
Hong Kong
Bangkok
Egypt
Bermuda
Nepal
Argentina
Brazil
Canada
Hungary
Sweden
Seychelles
Finland
Denmark
Portugal
Turkey
and
Venezuela

In that time my wife:
Was piggy-backed by a native up the precipitous side of an island in the Seychelles.
Rode on an ostrich in South Africa.
Tried unsuccessfully to surf, with a lame leg and a weak arm, among the great waves of Port Elizabeth, Rio, St Lucia and Bondi Beach.
With a rubber ring for support repeatedly bathed all over the world, including sitting on beaches in Cornwall while the icy water swirled around her.
Was carried out to, and sailed in, a catamaran in Barbados.
Went out in pedalos in Venice, Majorca and Nice.
Took a day-long motor drive across the mountains and dust roads

of Nepal to see the sun rise over Annapurna. (Accommodation for the night was at a guest house which could only be reached by crossing a river on a wooden raft built on oil drums.)

Climbed down to the Iguaçú Falls in Brazil.

Jogged endlessly and uncomplainingly hour after hour in old motor-cars in the heat and dust of India.

Flew in Concorde. (With the extra ear pressures involved.)

Took the dawn flight round Everest.

Neither of us had ever ridden as children, but just after the war we took lessons and did a bit of riding. After the second lesson the instructor sidled up to me and said: 'Your wife is a fearnaught.'

Perhaps that was a good summing-up.

I have to confess – though it does me no credit – that only about 10 per cent of the many trips listed were undertaken to promote my books or to gather material for a future novel. All the rest have been taken in pursuit of pleasure. I have always loved travel abroad for its own sake. War, and lack of the financial resources, prevented me from travelling much until the early 1950s, but from then on it was four or five times a year. Indeed one of my publishers once speculated sardonically that I must write my novels in my spare time.

I have never, in fact, gone abroad seeking material for a book (though several times I have gone to check over details). But in spite of Shaw's remark that travel narrows the mind, I have found the pursuit of hedonism (more sun, exotic food, warm seas) has in my case opened my eyes to new experiences and I have encountered characters of different dimension, some of whom have figured prominently in my novels – see Madame Passani in *The Green Flash*, the lonely man who told me the story of his life that wet day in Terrigal Bay, Australia (same novel), my French publisher in Paris in *Night Without Stars*.

However, there was one trip which resulted in a novel; though as far as I remember it was undertaken entirely for pleasure. Certainly it became one of the rather more hazardous.

One day I said to Jean, 'We've never been to Morocco. D'you think it might be a good idea?'

I knew her answer before she spoke. I have never known her turn down a new venture, nor did she ever have doubts about it before we went. (As I frequently did.)

So we flew to Gibraltar, and after a couple of days seeing the Rock, took the ferry across to Tangier. There we spent three days mainly bathing and sunbathing, then hired a self-drive car to take a look at the hinterland of Morocco.

We were warned not to go by a consular official. 'You're safe enough as far as Ceuta. Even Tetouan is fairly quiet. But certainly avoid the Rif Mountains. There are some Berber tribes in revolt. The government in Rabat is too weak. There was a kidnapping last month.'

The first day we drove to Tetouan the car was searched perfunctorily at the border, but we were soon waved on.

The car was an extremely old Ford 8 (not cylinder, horsepower). The battery seemed a bit flat, but we thought a good run would top it up.

After the night at Tetouan we set off again for the hinterland, driving towards the Rif Mountains in the general direction of Fez. The roads were superb here, all laid down by the French before Morocco gained its independence.

A lot of the early part was desert, and about 12.30 we stopped the car in the sparse shade offered by an argan tree and prepared a picnic lunch, most of which Jean had bought that morning in the Tetouan market before we left.

We were shortly joined by a Holy Man, in tattered black djellaba, with shaven head and a long twisted stick. He squatted about six feet away from us and made a number of observations in the Berber tongue. Presently Jean offered him a sandwich, which he gratefully accepted. Two more followed during the course of our meal. I began to feel horribly uncomfortable, for the sandwiches contained ham.

Later two yellow mongrel dogs arrived, but the Holy Man would not let us feed them, not even with the crumbs that were left. Presently we were able to pack our luncheon basket in the back of the car and prepared to leave. The Holy Man became very vehement, telling us quite plainly by extravagant gestures that we should not go on.

I said in clear tones: 'We are making for Fez. Fez,' I repeated, 'Fez.'

I think he got the message, but his own message was unchanged. We should not go on. We must turn back. For reasons unknown we must not go any further into the desert.

I smiled and nodded and smiled and shrugged and made gestures, while Jean slipped unobtrusively into her seat.

I got in, shut the door. The car reluctantly fired and we were off, steering an apologetic course round the old man, and drove away. His shouts could be heard for miles.

We had filled up with petrol in Tetouan, and the car had used hardly any, so we were comfortable on that score. We had been driving a further hour into the desert when we saw a large white city in the far right distance shimmering through the heat haze. It was obviously an important place, with high-rise buildings one behind another and marble pillars among palm trees. It looked at least as important as we imagined Casablanca might look.

Jean opened the map. There was Rabat, but that was on the coast and at least a hundred miles away.

We drove on. Our road was not leading towards the city, but we got slowly nearer. As we approached the entire city faded away.

Then ahead of us we saw the roadblock. We would have welcomed the thought that this too was a mirage. But no such luck. A tree trunk stretched across the road, supported at each end by a heap of sandbags. There were six armed men guarding it. I was not sufficiently versed in such things as to know whether the guns they carried were Kalashnikov AK47s, but they looked newer and in better order than the men who held them.

We stopped at the barrier. One of the men, who wore a sort of armband of office, strolled across and peered in at the lowered window. A stream of Berber being listened to without comprehension, he switched to a stream of guttural French. Never before had I regretted my total lack of ability to learn other languages. What the hell use would my mathematical talents ever be to me except to add up bridge scores or understand tax tables? During the war in spare hours I had relentlessly taught myself to read French. But speak it? The requisite words tumbled together in my brain but refused to come out.

At length I mentioned Fez. My wife and I wished only to drive to Fez. We were on holiday. We were driving to Fez.

Another flood of French. I shrugged helplessly and repeated what I had already said. Then another man strolled across. He was heavier, older, wore a sort of khaki tunic which had probably belonged to someone else. He had a look at Jean. He appraised her carefully. She smiled at him. He smiled back.

'*Américaine?*' he asked.

'*Non,*' I replied. '*Anglais.*'

He tried again.

'*Allemand?*'

'*Non,*' I said. '*Anglais.*'

'*Ah!*' he exclaimed, as if I had never before mentioned the word. '*Anglais! Entendu.*'

He conferred with the younger man. A couple more of the other men came up. The younger man indicated that we must get out of the car. Reluctantly we did so, and they looked at Jean's legs as they were briefly exposed. They searched the car, but it was perfunctory. Then they opened the two bags, leafed through a few things, drifted off and allowed us to close them. The older man grinned again through his beard, called an order, and two men went to lift the barrier just far enough to allow the passage of the car.

'*Avancez!*'

We beamed gratefully and got back into the car. I looked at Jean to see she was all right, then pressed the starter button. Nothing. I tried again. The engine turned over once reluctantly like an old man turning over in bed. I tried a third time. Nothing. The Berbers were watching us with considerable interest.

I lowered the window again. '*La batterie! C'est fini! Cassé! Vide!*'

The bearded man blinked and passed the message on to his friends. They all began to laugh. Even the two holding the barrier laughed. They hurled advice at us; at least I hope it was advice.

206

The leader put his head in the window, bringing with it the strong smell of goat.

'*Kaput?*'

'Yes! *Oui! Ja! C'est morte.*'

He gabbled something that I did not understand, but if I read his eloquent gestures aright he was suggesting I might like a push.

We would very much like a push.

Three men with rifles dangling came to the back of the car. I put the car in second gear. We lurched forward in a great spasm of forward propulsion, the engine fired, and we were off. The soldiers cheered – or jeered – it was impossible to say which, but as the little Ford gathered momentum a couple of soldiers discharged their rifles. But it was only a salute, into the desert air.

It took an extra day to reach Fez. Then we traversed the Moyen Atlas Mountains and stopped for the night at a little town called Beni Mellal which was even more 'undeveloped' than Fez, and it lacked Fez's wonderful interest and charm. After dark the streets were feebly lit and almost empty. Tall men in long flowing black djellabas moved here and there, casting shadows twice their length, and yellow dogs crawled in the gutters looking for scraps. A ghostly little town, out of another world.

Jean was tired after the heat of the day and after supper went to bed. I said I would look around a bit, but in the end, oppressed by the dark, was content to drift into the bar.

A man in a shiny brown suit, a sallow-skinned Latin with sleek black hair, smiled at me and spoke in a flood of French. I succeeded in conveying to him that I did not understand.

'*Anglais?*' he said. '*Eh bien. Je ne parle pas l'anglais. Mais regardez! Je suis Anglais aussi.*'

He fumbled in an inner pocket and took out a passport. Its stiff blue case was unmistakable. I hardly needed to see the gold lettering or read the words 'Her Britannic Majesty'. He opened it and showed me the photograph of himself. His name was Carlo Vianelli and he had been born in Malta, a British citizen. Even so, though of course he spoke Italian and French, he knew virtually no English. He was what in those days was known as a commercial traveller – later a rep – and covered the whole of Morocco selling and taking orders for one single commodity.

'*Le soutien-gorge*,' he explained, and then translated. 'The brassiere.'

Later I was to observe these items of feminine underwear hanging in rich profusion in every other market stall, and in a startling array of materials and sizes. However out of favour the brassiere might be in France, in Morocco M. Vianelli was on to a good thing.

The car was now limping along. Every time I switched off the engine I had to leave the car on a slope so that momentum would start the engine. In the villages it was not quite so difficult because there were always a half-dozen boys somewhere around who with shouts of delight would give us a shove.

In this condition we reached Marrakech, and, after a day there during which the battery was put on charge, we essayed the enormous massif of the Atlas Mountains. It was soon clear that the battery was in terminal decline. The direction indicators now failed, and it would clearly be fatal if we were sometime to be overtaken by the dark. It was a great relief when, after eight hours' driving, we reached Agadir.

Agadir is not at all like the other Moroccan towns, being a Europeanized seaside resort built around one of the finest beaches in the world. When we first saw it, it was all freshly rebuilt or still rebuilding after the momentous earthquake of 1960, when over 12,000 people died, and within a few seconds the entire town could as well have been struck by an atomic bomb.

Rooted there for three days while a new battery was at last procured, we had ample time to observe the scars and to hear the stories of people who had undergone the nightmare of the earthquake yet somehow survived.

It was a very suitable subject for a novel, and I decided that when the novel I was then writing was finished, I would write this.

When that time came, however, I was put off by a disinclination to write a novel about a number of disparate people, whose separate stories come together only because of how they are affected by the earthquake – their lives terminated or their problems otherwise resolved. Thornton Wilder in his *Bridge of San Luis Rey* had used this form to great effect. But I tend to write the sort of novels I like to read, and such composite stories have never greatly appealed to me. So I shelved it, and it was only some years later that I finally used the idea. Of course I went back to Agadir twice more then, and *Tremor* was published in 1995.

Some years before this I had been with Jean to Saas Fee with our children, and after a jolly week there we left them to their skiing and flew to Beirut. I can't remember for certain, but I think my idea was to combine winter and summer in one holiday.

But soon after reaching the Lebanon I went down with a particularly nasty flu bug and spent a couple of days in bed. (Unusual for me on a holiday.) After dinner on the second night Jean came upstairs, eyes glinting.

'I've met some very nice people downstairs – three of them – and they've asked me out for a drink. D'you mind if I go?'

'Are they English?'

'One is. But they're all very respectable.'

(Herewith a typical example of my iron discipline. Can't deprive my loved ones of their simple pleasures. What had I to offer her, stuffed shakily in bed?)

'Have a care. Don't forget we're in the Middle East.'

'I will.'

Later I was to learn that they went out in two cars on the inland road towards the mountains and stopped at a little hotel, where they had more drinks and agreeable conversation. Then the first couple left to go home, and after a suitable interval the other man said he would drive Jean back to Beirut.

On the way back he stopped in a lay-by and became amorous. Having no success, he suggested that they might both get out and 'lie down' among the palm trees.

'I'm married,' she said.

'He would never know.'

'I would.'

After a few more words, he attacked her. She pushed him away, and he knocked her glasses off and hit her in the face. After a short but bitter struggle he found her as strong as he was, so he pushed her out of the car and drove off. She was able to locate her glasses in the dark and was faced with a seven-mile walk home.

She tried to flag down the occasional car, and at the third attempt was terribly lucky in finding two French people who drove her back to the hotel.

I did not hear the full account of what had happened until about a month later, but the long scratch down her forearm could not be minimized, nor the bruise on her cheek, though powder hid most of this. And the following morning she went out to get the side-piece of her glasses straightened.

When she came back, she said: 'Races are on this afternoon.'

'What races?'

'The races you said you would like to go to.' She looked at me. 'You wouldn't … ?'

'Not wouldn't. Couldn't.'

'D'you think I could go?'

'It's mainly a male pastime in this part of the world. D'you feel up to it?'

'Oh, yes. And it would be daylight. Pretty safe.'

When she returned, she was looking pleased. 'I won £21!'

'Were there many women there?'

'No, I think I was the only one on her own. But everyone was very courteous.'

She paused a moment. 'A good-looking young sheikh spoke to me. He invited me to go round tomorrow morning to see his stable of Arab horses. I refused.'

'Oh? Why?'

'I said my husband wouldn't like it.'

'You surprise me.'

Chapter Eight

Including the novel published last year, *Bella Poldark*, I have written, I think, forty-six books – forty-three of them novels, one book of short stories, *The Japanese Girl*; the others were *Poldark's Cornwall* and *The Spanish Armadas*, an illustrated history of the Anglo-Spanish war of the sixteenth century. Of the forty-three novels, only sixteen have been historical, the twelve *Poldark* novels, and *Cordelia, The Forgotten Story, The Grove of Eagles* and *The Ugly Sister*. Yet it is for the *Poldarks* that I have become best known.

There are historians of repute – and of course critics – who, while just admitting to the validity of the modern novel (which must be 'emotion recollected in tranquillity', or, at least, experience so recalled), consider the historical novel, in anyone's hands, a spurious art form per se, because it imposes the writer's usually ignorant, possibly warped, probably over-romantic, over-coloured view upon a past time, that it presents history in a – to them – unconfirmed or unhistorical way. But a lot of this is true of any novel, either modern or historical. Any writer, any good writer, takes a set of events and imposes his own view on them. If there is no personal view there is no art. As Cézanne said of his paintings: 'I have not tried to reproduce nature, I have represented it.' And that is what any good writer does. And if he is good enough he creates a world of his own which the reader comes to inhabit and finds it comparable with life rather than identical with it.

And if one is to downgrade the historical novel, what is one to make of such trivia as *War and Peace, Vanity Fair* and *Wuthering Heights*, all historical novels in their time?

Historical novels as such divide easily into three classes. First, there are those which use actual historical personages as the chief characters of the books, such as Robert Graves' *I, Claudius*, and Helen Waddell's *Peter Abelard*. Second, there are those in which historical personages are substantial figures in the story but have as their main characters fictitious persons – very often, as it were, standing beside the historical characters. Such are Rose Macaulay's *They Were Defeated* and my own *The Grove of Eagles*. Third, there are those which use entirely, or almost entirely, fictitious characters set in a recreated historical time. Such are Stevenson's *The Black Arrow*, or H. F. M. Prescott's *The Man on a Donkey*, or the *Poldarks*.

There has been a tendency in critical circles over the last half-century to rate these categories in descending importance. The novel featuring solely historical characters is rated higher than the novels in which historical characters play only a part; and the novel in which historical characters play a part is rated higher than those in which all the characters are fictional.

This is pretentious nonsense. Every type and quality of historical novel from fine to awful has been produced in all three categories. In any case you only have to regard the first three novels mentioned above and consider in what category they belong.

But in all three classes of novel one has to attempt a degree of historical truth as well as a truth to human nature. Man has not changed, but his reaction to certain life patterns has. Unless the writer can understand these and transmit his understanding to the reader, his characters are simply modern people in fancy dress. Similarly there must be a geographical truth. Cornwall has particularly suffered from the writers who have spent a few months living there and have decided to write an epic set in the county; in fact it could just as well have been set in Kent, Yorkshire or Cumberland for all it matters, but Cornwall, they think, is more romantic.

I believe it to be most important in the third category (where all of the characters are fictional) to deal as much as possible in historical fact. I have an inventive brain, but I could never have devised all the events which fill the pages of the *Poldark* novels. It would be tedious to enumerate all the sources – indeed it would mean hours of research in reverse, tracing the origins of this event and that, back from the novel to the manuscript, the old newspaper, the map, the out-of-print book, the contemporary travel book, the parochial history, the mining manual, the autobiography.

As a selection: Jim Carter's arrest for poaching, his imprisonment in Launceston Gaol; fever, and blood incompetently let by a fellow prisoner, Jim's subsequent death. From a line in *Wesley's Journal*.

Description of Launceston Gaol. From Howard's *State of the Prisons*, 1784 edition.

Ross's attempt to start a copper-smelting company in Cornwall to compete against the companies of South Wales which used to send the coal and take the copper away by sea; and the failure of the attempt. Not precise as to detail, but accurate in general terms about such an attempt which was made at that time.

The two wrecks at the end of *Demelza* and the rioting miners on the beach. Taken from a report of such a double wreck on Perranporth beach in 1778.

The voting procedure at Bodmin for the election of two Members of Parliament in 1790. Factual.

The occasion when a rich young woman, Caroline Penvenen, calls in Dr Dwight Enys, and when he gets there asks him to attend to her dog. The further occasion when he is called in to the same young lady because it is believed she has the morbid sore throat, and what he finds. Both are related by Dr James Fordyce in his book on fevers which had a limited circulation in 1789.

The smuggling in *Warleggan*. Most details are factual; also the way in which Ross, apparently trapped, escapes detection.

Conditions in the French prisoner-of-war camp at Quimper are chiefly taken from accounts given by Lady Ann Fitzroy, who for a time was imprisoned there.

The struggle for power in Truro and the quarrel between Lord Falmouth and the Burgesses supported by Sir Francis Basset is almost all derived from the contents of a single letter written by Mr Henry Rosewarne, the MP newly elected in defiance of the Boscawen interest, addressed to Lord Falmouth, explaining the reasons for the Corporation's defiance and defending his own actions. Corroborative information came from Cornelius Cardew and others.

The riots in Camborne, Sir Francis Basset's suppression of them, the death penalty for three of the rioters, two reprieved, one, Peter Hoskin, hanged: all factual.

The character of Monk Adderley was based on a character in the original William Hickey Diaries. Details of the duel between Adderley and Ross came largely from the life of John Wilkes.

The run on Pascoe's Bank in Truro, the pressure by the other banks, the anonymous letters deliberately circulated to create a panic. All factual, except not exactly as to date.

Dwight Enys saving the injured miner by giving him what is now called 'the kiss of life'. From a case related in John Knyveton's *Surgeon's Mate*.

So in the case of the Penzance lifeboat.

So in the case of the stagecoach. The original excerpt from the *Morning Post* for Monday, 23rd of November 1812, is printed in *The Miller's Dance* in its entirety. As far as I know, the mystery of the robbery was never solved. I went up to Gloucestershire to examine an eighteenth-century stagecoach in detail and worked out, at least to my own satisfaction, how it could have been done.

As for Bella Poldark, I do not think I would have ventured to tell her extraordinary life story, were it not for the history of Charlotte Cushman, who was born in Boston in 1816.

There is, naturally enough, the converse risk of becoming too preoccupied by history. One can so easily detect the midnight oil, the desire to instruct. But novels are about life. If a reader wishes to pursue a particular subject, textbooks by the thousand exist. An author tends to be reluctant, once he has discovered something, at great trouble to himself, not to make the best of it. But the temptation must be resisted. It is a recurring discipline which should be exercised by every novelist who does research, whether the research is into the Peninsular War or into modern techniques of assassination. What is not relevant is irrelevant.

In my view, the historical novel at its best is not a spurious form of art because the past of itself is not a shard that one can dig up and measure and piece together. No one can do this, however conscientious, because history is not an objective science. Historical truth is not mathematical truth. The past has really no existence other than that which our minds can give it. Even the pure historian is at the mercy of hissources, and his sources usually are other fallible, or prejudiced, or forgetful human beings.

In my one book of short stories there is a story about the death and the burial of William the Conqueror. All the material facts for that came from a contemporary account by Ordericus Vitalis, which is as near as even the most conscientious historian can get to the truth of that matter. If I had written this as an essay and punctuated it with numbers and asterisks and then notes at the bottom saying Ord. Vit., page 231, and following with *ib.*, *ib.*, *ib.*, people would no doubt have been more impressed. But in fact Ordericus Vitalis was thirteen when William died. In other words he probably depended on an eyewitness, or possibly even hearsay, and who knows how good *his* information was?

I am not trying to equate the good historian with the good historical novelist. Each has different aims. The latter, in pursuit of these aims, is more likely to err than the former. But each, in a subjective profession, is fallible.

And the pure historian – like the good novelist, though in a lesser degree – moulds the past, whether he intends to or not; he colours it with his own personality. All good historians set their personal impression on the past: Thucydides, Gibbon, Macaulay, Froude, Rowse – go through them all, and they all do that, for it can't be otherwise.

Probably the only way of judging a work of art is to try to measure or judge the integrity of intention. If it has that, it may be a masterpiece. Or it may be a very poor and flawed work. But with such integrity it can't be all bad, and it can't be all lost.

Chapter Nine

When I wrote the first *Poldark* it was suggested to me – though not by my publishers – that I might have it put out under another name. I rejected this, preferring to take all the blame – or all the praise – without the shelter of a pseudonym. Also, for such a purpose, I have never written quickly enough. I have a very long list of publications, but this is because I started young and have been writing for a very long time. At the height of my production I came to write a novel about every eighteen months. Now it is about two years. Three novels have each taken three years to write. (I have been fortunate in that, once I began to earn a living from writing, I always earned enough to be able to take my time. In my earlier years I would have eagerly accepted some other literary activity to help augment my pitiful income, but it was not offered. When it was offered I was able to turn it down, so I have virtually never done any peripheral literary work in my life.)

From the earliest years I have always felt that it was up to the public to buy me by name rather than style or subject. This arrogant view has only partly been vindicated. Had I kept to one style I know I should have become a richer man. But so what?

Distributors, booksellers, and, alas, the public (who are the final arbiters) all like to be sure of what they are buying. Why should a shop that has developed a substantial clientele with a taste for Wilkins' marmalade be expected to try to sell them the same firm's strawberry jam instead? The remark made by Wilfred Lock, about my fifth novel being ten years ahead of the others but that commercially he could shake me, has been confirmed and reconfirmed through the years.

Collins were delighted when I returned to *Poldark* after a

lapse of twenty years. *The Black Moon* was launched with great acclaim. I remember meeting their chief London rep a few days after publication and, along with his continuing – if a little forced – enthusiasm, his dropping into the conversation the fact that the book was piling up unsold at Hatchard's and Harrod's.

There has been a lot of stimulus and relaxation in moving from one style to the other. Ideally, perhaps, one should have used the styles alternately – and this happened for a time in the early Fifties – but one can't discipline one's impulses – or I don't. The sparse, fairly taut story-telling of a suspense novel, with its stronger frame of events and its sharp conclusive ending, is just as much fun to write as the longer, more leisurely, more exploratory style of the historical novel. Why should I have given up either? Or why crouch in one's study endlessly writing too many books when there is so much else to be found in life?

The 'so much else' has been largely hedonistic. Until well past forty I played tennis to distraction. With no natural talent for the game whatever, and no coaching, I became fairly good out of sheer application. I never played for Cornwall, though twice invited to do so – the deterrent being to drive to somewhere like Criccieth in North Wales, to spend each day playing competitive tennis for one's county and each evening dancing until the small hours: a normal young man's dream of delight, but not mine; I never had the stamina.

But I came to play with a number of county players from other counties which were much stronger than Cornwall, and not a few of the near-top English players, people who got usually to the second or third round at Wimbledon though never beyond. Of course I could not have lived with them at singles, not even the women. At doubles I was good enough not to spoil their game.

Perranporth at that time attracted a wonderful collection of good tennis players – the knowledge that some were coming would attract others – over a period of about eight weeks a year, beginning mid-July. Three hard sets of men's doubles on a sunny summer morning, with kindred souls, is one of the rare pleasures that I would ask for again if I ever get to heaven.

In the earlier *Who's Whos* to which I contributed I used to list one of my hobbies as 'beachcombing'. My love of the sea, especially the Cornish sea, has already been made plain. It seems to run in the family. My brother had no greater ambition than to sit in the sun on some Cornish strand. My son once said that if windsurfing had been invented when he was a boy he might have chosen not to be an academic but to be a 'beachcomber' instead. I don't know how serious he was.

On the north coast swimming is rarely possible; surfing is all. Before the Malibu, body surfing was the universal occupation. In *Poldark's Cornwall* I have described some of the peculiar joys of surfing. I will only repeat briefly some few moments of the wonderful summer before my son went to Charterhouse in the September.

All through that splendid decade, if a summer's day broke bright I would begin to write immediately after breakfast and go on until Jean let me know, about noon, that the picnic was ready. Then we would bundle the things – including the children if they were home – into the car and dash off to West Pentire or Treyarnon and spend the day sitting in the sun and surfing when the time and tide were right, returning home about seven, for me to do a little desultory work before a late supper.

That was quite a reasonable arrangement in most summers – I could seize the good days and work in the bad – but in that summer there was no let up. The fine weather set in on the 9th of July and went on until the end of September. Not merely did I neglect my work, but Jean got utterly sick of cutting sandwiches and packing picnics. But as summer did not relax, neither did we. The difficulty about our English summer, and more particularly about a Cornish summer, is that one can never, never take the next day for granted. So often one has been deceived by a halcyon two days and stayed in the second day, knowing exactly how to enjoy the third, and the third dawns with grey skies, a strong wind, and a 20-degree drop in temperature. We didn't trust it that year, and the summer went on and on. So for virtually ten weeks we picnicked and sunbathed and surfed every day, gradually turning more and more boot-polish brown.

My son was due to be delivered to his new school on the 18th of September. The 17th was largely taken up with preparations and packing, but in the early evening he and I escaped onto Perranporth beach on an incoming tide. An almost breathless evening but the sea was monstrous. It was one of those seas when a surfer catches one wave, is borne along a dizzying way, then dropped upon another, and so upon another, and even sometimes on a fourth.

As we staggered together out of the sea joyfully exhausted after our fifteenth run, Andrew said to me: 'Daddy, people who haven't done this haven't lived.' He was about right. It is my second request from Paradise.

I have driven cars ever since I was eighteen. The number has not been great because I prefer to live with a car and get to know it. First was a Morris Minor, a small four-seater with a folding roof and an engine given much to piston wear (one always seemed to be discussing 'rings'). It was the only car I know that, being delivered to us new, was used for six months before I noticed that the number plate on the front differed from the number plate on the back. It was also delivered with the footbrake only just working; the handbrake itself, operated only on the transmission shaft, being the only means of bringing the car to a stop. I decided to take my mother to the cinema in Newquay. On the way a herd of cows was crossing the road in leisurely fashion. I applied the brake and nothing happened, except that we drifted into a cow. Everyone was very courteous; the cow was not hurt, the car not damaged, the farmer was apologetic, and I more justifiably so. We continued on our way, saw the film and got in to drive home. By then it was night, and we found our headlamps to be squinting skywards at the stars.

The following day I slithered up and down the hills to Falmouth to get the brakes seen to. It was not a good beginning for a new driver. In those days, of course, there was no driving test to pass. 'If in trouble put both feet down,' directed presumably, and hopefully, to the brake and clutch. I had had an unlucky career as a cyclist, and my brother and sister-in-law came to the conclusion, which they gladly imparted to my mother, that Winston 'would be no good with a car'.

The second was a Wolseley Hornet, that triumph of British engineering which had a very small six-cylinder engine noted for its excessive cylinder wear and no compensating increase in quietness. It also had a 'twin top' gear specially suitable, they said, for overtaking. Unfortunately the two top gear ratios were so close that, going up Cornish hills, one was often forced to drop into second and grind up at a funeral pace.

Third was a Standard Flying Twenty, a handsome car for those days: probably it would be rated as a three-litre now. I bought it secondhand from Ronnie Neame, who directed my first film and who had had it from a naval lieutenant who had kept it unused during the war, so that the engine and all moving parts were in very good condition. But the bodywork was poor, so I arranged to have it overhauled and resprayed. I remember picking it up in London: it was transformed, beautiful and black and shiny. But the engine was missing badly. I drove it to Piccadilly, where I had arranged to meet my film agent and Anthony Kimmins, the film director, who had a project to put to me. I parked outside – one could in those days – but my attention to his proposition was a little absent-minded, as I wondered how I was going to be able to drive this shiny black beast back to Cornwall on the morrow if the engine was going to run as if fifteen out of the twenty horses had glanders.

I should, no doubt, have had a better sense of proportion, for nothing came of the meeting, and when I returned to the car it refused to start at all. I got the bonnet up and discovered that during the respray three out of the six plugs had had their operative ends playfully – or accidentally – hammered down so that there was no gap left for the plug to spark. I was eventually able to buy a new set and, when installed, drove the car back to my club where I took a late dinner and bed. The car had been parked at a busy part of the north side of Piccadilly for five hours.

The Standard served us well and it was years before I sold it and bought a three-litre drophead Alvis. This was also a four-seater, but two-door and not so roomy.

The Alvis became the pride of our lives. Its suspension was very hard, but its roadholding and acceleration were superb. Without any attempt at all to go faster, I knocked an hour and a half off trips between London and Cornwall. It was in this car that I took my family on an annual holiday from Cornwall.

It was seven years before I could bring myself to change the Alvis, which I eventually did for a 3.4 Jaguar Saloon.

It was extraordinary to find a return of my travelling time between places to something like that of the old Standard. The new Jaguar, however good-looking it was and however silent and reliable the engine, however comfortable to ride in at modest speeds, was to me like a coffin on wheels. Coming from a car that glued itself to the road, I had a number of narrow escapes, not of hitting another car but of going off the road at a corner. The suspension was woefully soggy, the roadholding, in a fast car, really dangerous. But provided you didn't actually drive it into a ditch, it was very trouble-free, and we kept the car for quite a while, along with a secondary car of assorted kinds: various Minis, a Riley (new style, alas), an Austin Healey Sprite.

When I sold the Jaguar I bought an Aston Martin DB6. This was the fastest thing I have ever driven. Its road-holding was still not as good as the Alvis but it was infinitely faster. At over 90 m.p.h. the Alvis began to smell of engine oil. The fastest I ever drove was in the first Aston: 140 mph on the Turin autostrada.

The engine was beautiful – none of that nonsense spread by envious rivals that after one crossing of London it needed a retune. You could drive it very fast indeed on the Continental motorways, yet the next day would be in the choked traffic of Monte Carlo, and it would crawl along the Riviera without a vestige of snatch. But the clutch was a brute.

After eighteen months I took the car back and ordered an automatic. In the jargon of the fashionable motor world, this new car would, they said, be built specially for me, my name on it, so to speak, from the beginning. But the automatic Aston was not a great car. It was as powerful as its predecessor, and at speed seemed to settle its back down securely on the road, but it was too low geared. At 120 m.p.h., which it would reach quickly and effortlessly, the rev-counter would be showing 6,000, in the red zone. It was also too low slung and grated on awkward dips (such as crossing King Harry Ferry). And it burnt out exhaust systems at a great rate. The new Avon tyres with which it was fitted lasted 9,000 miles, then I had seven punctures in five weeks. (The Pirelli tyres with which I replaced them not only improved the roadholding, they lasted almost for ever.)

About this time I started buying Alfa Romeos as a second car. I went to look for a Lancia in a showroom on the Bayswater Road, and saw a drophead Alfa Spyder in the window. I never got any further. The salesman, seeing my interest, said: 'It's a fun car, sir.' I thought this a piece of conventional salesmanship, but in fact it proved to be the truth. Insofar as driving a car is ever anything more than a means of getting from place to place nowadays, the Alfa provided it. Though, of course, a much smaller and lighter car, it had almost all the qualities of the Alvis, with a more comfortable ride and fewer foibles. It is the car by which I now judge all others for suspension and roadholding. In the course of the years I had three of them: white, pagoda yellow, and dove grey.

When I sold the second Aston I fell for the new Jaguar XJS twelve-cylinder model, and kept it for nine years before buying a second. The early XJSs had a very bad reputation for unreliability, but apart from one recurring fault, which took a time to sort out, it did me extremely well, and the second was even better. It is wonderfully quiet, with none of that throttle roar of the Aston (which some people love), very powerful, very easy to drive, and very fast. I have done 125 in the last one, and there still seemed a little more in it. It still does not corner as well as the Alvis and the Alfa, but I have no other complaint.

In addition to my own car I have rented many in different parts of the world, the United States, North and South Africa, Australia and most countries of Western Europe. On my first visit to Hollywood I hired a car to drive down the coast as far as La Jolla and San Diego, requesting a 'compact' car, as they call them. The car was late arriving and they apologized for this and for the fact that they didn't have a compact. They awarded me a Chevrolet Bel Air, which measured 17 feet 9 inches. It was the first automatic car I had ever driven. They didn't even bother to turn the engine off: I signed the papers, they bundled our luggage into the enormous boot and edged me into the driving seat. Then they leaned in at the open window and said: 'That's OK, Mr Graham, just don't use your left foot.'

Driving on the opposite side of the road has seldom troubled me. (I remember once leaving Compiègne and taking the wrong way round a roundabout. In England this would have resulted in a barrage of flashing lights and blaring horns. The French just ignored me until I came to my senses.) But being launched out into the Los Angeles traffic and trying to ignore one's left foot was another matter. At the first lights we jerked to a violent halt. Both our heads tried to go through the windscreen. We proceeded in a volley of jolts and jerks – and here again the American drivers, though I was driving an American car, seemed to sense that I was a Limey and merited their forbearance, for I never heard an impatient horn.

Presently we spotted a sign pointing to the required highway and we were really off. Even this did not imbue any sense of confidence or ease, for we found ourselves part of a convoy of enormous automobiles all proceeding together down a four-lane highway at sixty miles an hour. There was no way of getting out of it. We could not accelerate without breaking the law. We almost came to be on nodding terms with our fellow travellers to right and left. At long last the congestion began to thin out.

I said to Jean: 'What's that noise?'

'The radio,' she said.

'Who switched it on?'

'They must have. It was on when we left.'

I hadn't heard it. Imminence of death concentrates the mind wonderfully.

When *The Walking Stick* was published in America, Double-day invited me to go over to publicize the book. When issuing the invitation Ken McCormick, the most distinguished editor Doubleday have ever had, said to me: 'Mind, we shall expect you to work hard.'

I said OK, and despite this Jean, who had just had her premonitory stroke, chose to come with me.

It was an interesting experience. I gave a talk (lecture) and four interviews in Washington, six interviews – two on television, two on radio and two to the press – in New York, a similar number in Chicago and rather more in Detroit and San Francisco. It isn't an experience I want to repeat, but I saw it as a challenge.

In Washington the lecture was to the English-Speaking Union, and I had taken a good deal of trouble to prepare what I was going to say, which was to be fairly wide-ranging and including speculation as to the future of the novel both in America and in England. Five minutes before I went on the platform the editor from Doubleday said to me: 'Make it nice and folksy. And don't forget to talk about your new novel.'

Swallowing my script, I began by saying that I had originally intended to talk about the novel in general but it had been suggested to begin that I talk first about one novel in particular, etc. etc.

It was a full house, and there was one tall middle-aged lady in the front row who fixed me with an eye and shook her head disapprovingly. After going on a couple of minutes more I hastened to add that nevertheless I wanted to make this lecture fairly wide-ranging, and shortly I would be broadening my approach. I glanced down and saw the lady shake her head disapprovingly at me again. I made a fairly good joke, to which most of the audience responded, but she still didn't like me at all.

I went on, trying to avoid her gaze and consoling myself that there were about 299 people in the room who didn't necessarily feel as she felt. Nevertheless it was disconcerting. It took me about another five minutes to realize that disapproval was not the expression on her face, and that she suffered from a nervous tic, causing her head to jerk negatively from side to side at irregular intervals.

One thinks of the Maugham story in which there is a woman who jerks her head backwards in such a way that she seems to be inviting every man she meets to come with her into her bedroom.

As it happened, I almost felt I was receiving such an invitation at the dinner of the Association of American Publishers the following night. I was put next to a really beautiful girl whose father ran a bookstore in North Carolina.

As soon as I sat down she said: 'Oh, Mr Graham, I'm real glad to be setten' next to you. I took you to bed with me last night, but I was feeling sleepy so we didn't get very far.'

I was about to reply on what I thought was the same plane, telling her that it would give me the greatest pleasure to help her to try again, when I gazed into her liquid brown eyes and saw not a spark of humour in them. Not for the first time I remarked to myself on the dangers of a common language. No French girl would have said that, but I would have understood the signals better.

In Detroit my fellow guest on a television programme was Muhammad Ali, or Cassius Clay: that is, we were joint guests. He was then at the height of his powers as one of the greatest of heavyweights, and in the height of his youth and good looks. Quizzed closely by the host about his attitude to patriotism, colour bars, conscription, etc., he was, I thought, very reasonable and very well behaved. None of the bragging, macho attitude one had come to associate with his name in the media.

We shared a taxi back to the hotel and shared a lift to our rooms. The lift attendant was a pretty young black girl. Ali gave his floor number as 5, I gave mine as 12. As he got out of the lift he gave the lift girl a smile. We then went up to floor 22.

I said: 'No, I wanted twelve.'

'Oh, sorry, suh,' she said, 'I was goin' wa-ay up to heaven.'

In Chicago I did my usual round, including the famous Kup's talk show, to which about a dozen personalities were invited and over a period of three hours were casually questioned on this and that, and one was given a cup by the host Kupcinet and told one might have it filled with the liquid of one's choice. Unknown to us in the cloistered circle of the TV lights, a violent storm broke over Chicago while we were there, decimating a carnival procession, organized by the Puerto Ricans to commemorate some anniversary, and flooding the streets. My wife, who had come with me to the studio, had a grandstand view of it all, saw the dancing girls drenched and the long display floats stripped of their hangings. When at last I came out we had great difficulty in getting back to our hotel, and when we reached it the kitchens were six feet deep in water and the lifts had failed. (By a crowning mercy one service lift still operated.) It seems that in their eagerness to cover the whole area of the lakeside city in concrete, the planners had not allowed for drainage to cope with emergencies.

While I was in Chicago I was invited by a journalist I knew to attend the seventieth birthday party of 'one of the last gangsters', a man called Paddy Bauler. He had been a bootlegger and was said to have personally shot and killed a policeman years ago, but nothing could be proved. I have his invitation before me now. It has a Hong Kong postmark and carries a rather splendid frontispiece with a Chinese painting of cloud-covered mountains. Inside it states in large letters:

Neither
    DEATH, TAXES or ELECTIONS
    Can Stop
    PADDY BAULER'S ANNUAL ART FAIR PARTY
    You are commanded to be present at the
    49th WARD CULTURE CENTER
    403 WEST NORTH AVENUE
    on Sunday 11th June beginning at 4 p.m.

The committee was twelve-strong, and included such interesting names as the Illinois Assistant Attorney General Joe Rubinelli and jazz club owner Earl Pionke. Heading the list was Governor Otto Kerner and Mayor Richard Daley. Third was the newspaperman Herman Kogan, who arranged my invitation, so I was in influential hands.

It was a brownstone house in an unexceptional street – except that it had been swept and scoured of all litter, and blue-washed, sidewalk, street and all, and was guarded by armed and uniformed policemen sitting astride motorbikes. You went in through a small hall into a much larger one, with two other rooms beyond and then a backyard, also blue-washed and guarded. We were given chicken legs and hamburgers, and beer to drink. A German band played music and an operatic soprano sang items from the shows of the time, accompanied by a zither. Many influential people were there, including a Catholic bishop, several judges and aldermen, a district attorney or two, and Adlai Stevenson junior.

Although recently having stepped down as an alderman, Paddy was still powerful in the Democratic Party; also he had a rake-off from most of the one-armed bandits in clubs and arcades in the city, so he was very rich. In his later and more respectable years he had developed a passion for things Chinese, hence the appearance of the invitation card. All the names of the committee had their Chinese equivalent in gold leaf beside their own on the card. There were Chinese lanterns in the rooms, and numerous bonsai on pedestals. Fireworks occurred later in the yard.

Paddy was known to give not unvaluable silk kimonos to those who took his fancy at such parties, and he was wearing one himself on the night, with Chinese silk trousers. He was a very small man, and he sat on a high chair surrounded by his henchmen. His face was lined, his head shrunk between his shoulders, his eyes small and a faded blue. Herman introduced me. 'This is Winston Graham, the celebrated British novelist, who is over in our city on a brief visit.'

Paddy took a shrivelled-looking cheroot from between his lips and stared at me belligerently.

Presently he said: 'You look like an egghead.'

I smiled apologetically and said: 'Oh, I don't know about that. Just a writer, I suppose.'

He continued to stare and then snarled: 'Your country starts all the wor-rs.'

This was the end of the interview. I didn't receive a kimono.

San Francisco was chock-a-block with some convention, and my publishers had had to get us accommodation in one of the older hotels instead of at the Fairmont where we had previously stayed. Breakfast in our room proved an almost insurmountable obstacle. Telephone calls were to no avail. Hours seemed to pass. I was due for a radio interview at eleven, and only just made it.

The hotel where we were staying was the one where Fatty Arbuckle, one of the most famous of the earlier film stars of the silent screen, had many years before committed suicide in mysterious circumstances. Arriving at the restaurant (it was to be an interview in a restaurant) feeling frustrated and very angry, I was about to say that I had at last solved the mystery of Fatty Arbuckle's suicide. He had shot himself, at the hotel where I was at present staying, in frustration waiting for his breakfast.

But as the interview began I happened to glance down and see a printed notice on the table saying something to the effect that 'interviewees' were 'personally and legally responsible for any action for libel or slander brought by any person or persons as a result of this interview'.

I have never seen this notice before or since. Perhaps it is everywhere – if so I haven't spotted it. But perhaps it is as well I took heed. Knowing something of the speed of the American law processes, I think if I had spoken out, I might just still have been over there fighting my corner.

Between Charterhouse and university Andrew took a year off and worked for my American publisher in New York, before travelling widely round the States by Greyhound bus. He had done well at school, though was not perhaps *'facile princips'*, as the headmaster of the Cathedral School, Truro, presciently described him. He coasted along pleasantly at St Edmund Hall for a couple of years, but in the third year began to make big strides. It was a time when the National Economic Development Council (NEDDY) was in its infancy, and an official came round seeking likely recruits. His tutor recommended Andrew, who was invited for an interview and offered an appointment before he sat his Finals.

So to the tall new building on the banks of the Thames; but within a few months George Brown created the Department of Economic Affairs and invited Sir Donald MacDougall to lead it and to bring with him from NEDDY a half-dozen of the brighter young economists. Andrew was one of them.

He came home one weekend and told us there was a vacancy

in the Cabinet Office, and it had been suggested to him that he might apply. He did so apply, and was appointed; but found when he arrived that he was not to be in the Cabinet Office but in 10 Downing Street itself, where he was to be the junior in an office of five under the then Sir Thomas Balogh.

In a fairly short time one after the other of his seniors in the office left to take up other posts and were not replaced, and he found himself Balogh's personal assistant. Then Balogh accepted a peerage and came to spend most of his time in the House of Lords, and Andrew was left on his own with two secretaries and five telephones at his disposal.

In the meantime Harold Wilson had taken a liking to him, and he became accustomed to accompany Wilson to Cabinet meetings and subcommittees and sit with Wilson's secretary, taking notes. By this time Henry Kissinger was already emerging as senior adviser to the President. Wilson wanted to send him a résumé of Britain's view of how the world economic situation had developed since the days of Bretton Woods, and he asked Andrew, then twenty-five, to write it. Andrew came home with about thirty pages he had written, and with an occasional notation from the Prime Minister made in bright green ink. In due course this was sent off.

The following year Andrew told me there was a vacancy for an economics fellowship at Balliol, and it had been suggested he might apply. What should he do? I said there was no harm in his applying so long as he didn't expect to get it. So he applied, and got it. He was one of the youngest dons to be appointed to Balliol in half a century.

Later, the Labour Government fell; but they were not out of office for long, and when he came back Wilson immediately applied for Andrew to return as the economic adviser in his policy unit. This he then did for the next two years. New as he was to Balliol, it was a very exacting time for him, and he was not disappointed, I think, when Wilson's resignation created a natural break.

But he expected to be recalled when the next Labour Government came to office – and would have been. He had become personal economic adviser to John Smith, and was a close personal friend, but when Smith unexpectedly died, the top echelons of the Labour Party underwent drastic change, and Andrew was marginalized.

It cannot really be looked upon as a consolation prize that he has now become Master of Balliol.

Rosamund, being nearly four years younger, thought naturally enough that when she left school she too would be entitled to travel as her brother had done. But she did not want to go to university. Going on from Truro High School to Westonbirt in Gloucestershire, her routine as a normal schoolgirl had been abruptly, if blissfully, interrupted by a summer on the Côte d'Azur. This too was a fairly natural reaction. Give any pretty blonde a summer in Cap Ferrat, where she spends hours sitting in the sun in a bikini, surrounded by admiring French boys, then returns after two months to the rigours of the English public school, wearing thick grey stockings, flat-heeled shoes and a plain school uniform, and academic life does not appeal. After a year at a finishing school, the Institut Alpin Montesano at Gstaad, she wanted to take another year in the States, working as Andrew had worked, travelling as Andrew had travelled.

At that time there happened to be a ban on the employment of British secretaries in New York, as the local girls were being deprived of their jobs. So by infinite contrivance I arranged a fictitious job in a publishing firm in Boston. (It did not occur to me at the time that I was arranging for her to spend most of the rest of her life at a distance from us of 8,000 miles, but that, as someone once said, is how the cookie crumbles.)

Rosamund met a tall, good-looking American, and it was love at first sight. Already divorced, Douglas was still in his twenties; and although I have not been able to monitor his life at close quarters, I get the strong impression that he has never looked seriously at another woman since he first met my daughter.

After two sojourns in England, where two of their three children were born, they finally settled in California, where Rosamund has been the linchpin of their family life. Maximilian, Dominic and Anthea are all tall and goodlooking. More important is that they are all jolly, cleanliving, affectionate and highly intelligent, the two boys already married. Max is in law, Dominic is in law-enforcement! Apart from bearing and raising the children, Rosamund has worked all through, first at a Californian university, and more lately she has become Director of Human Resources for the District of Tulare, responsible for the welfare – and the hiring and firing – of 750 personnel, of mixed races, many Hispanic.

Before she was married, she rejected the academic life. Now, having raised a family and all the time lived a life of endless and extraordinary activity, she has recently studied for, and been awarded, a BA.

Both children have now been long and happily married, my son to Peggotty, a remarkably pretty, but not noticeably studious, girl from Somerset. However, since she found they would have no family, she decided to follow a fully academic life of her own, is now an MSc and is at present Dean and Director of Social Sciences at the Open University.

As to the rest of the immediate family, my niece Barbara (my brother Cecil's only child) lives at Haywards Heath, not far from Buxted, and – together with her late husband, Ronald – has provided much appreciated support and companionship. Recently widowed, but ever cheerful and competent, she has often stepped in to help at times of domestic crisis.

Jean's niece, Jacqui, now married to Geoff Williams and living in Newport, Shropshire, I see far too rarely.

Chapter Ten

Slow, slow, fresh fount,
  Ben Jonson wrote,

> Keep time with my salt tears,
> Yet slower yet, O faintly, gentle springs.
> List to the heavy part the music bears.
> Woe weeps out her division when she sings.
> Droop, herbs and flowers,
> Fall, grief, in show'rs;
> Our beauties are not ours.
> O that I could still
> Like melting snow upon some craggy hill, drop.
> Drop, drop, drop.
> Since nature's pride is now a withered daffodil.'

In 1983 my wife began to lose a lot of weight she could ill spare, and her voice became hoarse and croaky. Emphysema was diagnosed, but she refused to believe she had this. She became in the next few years quite tiny and bent: it was strange for me to see her when I remembered her straight back, her sturdiness and her great vitality.

It cannot have gone unnoticed that I think my marriage was an extraordinarily lucky one, because it was such a happy one. The best of marriages have their ups and downs, but in half a century I recall only one serious quarrel, which lasted about half an hour, and in the course of which my wife threw part of our dinner service out of the window onto the lawn, but, when anger cooled, compelled herself to go out and pick up the pieces before the maids arrived in the morning.

For the most part I remember it as an association full of passion and laughter, constant amicable companionship and enduring love.

She died in December 1992, to the last issuing strict instructions as to how her Christmas pudding was to be cooked.

After the loss of a woman with whom one has lived in the greatest amity for much the larger part of one's life, one is not a little bereft. When towards the end she would once or twice become a mite depressed, I would say to her: 'Don't be so selfish. You can't go and *die* on me. Think of *me*. I can't go on without you.' And, although light-heartedly expressed, I meant it – and totally believed it. But I have.

Sometimes if you wear a cheerful face to deceive, the deception begins to stick, and you end up by deceiving yourself. I was of course greatly helped by my family, though necessarily after a few weeks most were far distant. And a few very good friends, the Chapmans, Christopher Biggins, Angharad Rees, and some of Jean's bridge friends such as Molly Burton. But the largest contribution came from a young woman called Gwen Hartfield. My wife had taken her on when Gwen was living nearby with a husband and a daughter of seven. She came to help in the house, but then, as Jean's health deteriorated, she took over ever more of the housekeeping, and when Jean died she became my housekeeper, while continuing to see to her own husband and child, and this has continued ever since. Efficient, humorous,cheerful, witty and eccentric, she offered me friendly yet challenging companionship which I so much needed at that time, and which has never wavered. She has recently celebrated twenty years with us.

A year or two before Jean died we also took on a second helper (replacing one who left) called Tina Creelman, and a new young gardener, Robin Brown. These three formed a young and jolly triumvirate and have continued so ever since, making the big empty house more pleasant to live in and more tolerable to return to after one of my visits to London or my travels abroad.

I dedicated my novel *Tremor* to them, and they were my guests at the Savile Club for a birthday party that was given to me there a few years ago.

So a routine has set in, different and inferior to the one I lost, but becoming more to be enjoyed for its own sake as the years passed. I have usually been able to get abroad about three times a year and to stay at my club two or three nights every fortnight, and this has made for a very pleasant way of life.

Another recent dedicatee is Ann Hoffmann, who, working for me on a freelance basis for upwards of thirty-five years, has been an enormous help both as researcher and typist. Recently that help has become even more invaluable. Very early in my creative life I found it impossible to type correctly and at the same time to concentrate on the exact meaning and perception of what I was putting down. Some subtle communication was lost. (Jean was a great consultant, but no typist.)

I have therefore had a variety of typists of varying quality (or lack of it). Coming to live in Sussex meant losing whatever help I had had before, so I was extremely lucky to meet Ann by chance at a book launch at Elise Santoro's bookshop in Crowborough, and a friendship blossomed. Although primarily a researcher, and a writer herself, she agreed to type for me if required. Thus a very friendly yet half-business association has grown up. I have never met anyone else who can copy a manuscript so error-free. This has been indispensable in view of the untidy nature of my later manuscripts, made ever worse by the cramped and spidery nature of my handwriting, which is showing the wear and tear of the years. Among other publications, Ann is the author of the definitive research manual, *Research for Writers*, which has recently gone into its seventh edition.

I have been under considerable pressure to buy at least a laptop computer. I have always turned the suggestions down for the reason that I have never done creative work on a typewriter. There is to me a lack of empathy. I have been told of the many extra advantages of word-processing, and I acknowledge them. But, apart from other reasons, I find that a sentence, a page, a book, assumes a different nature when it is first in manuscript, second in typescript, and third in page proofs. There is a separate, a welcome change, and each time one is able to see it in a new light.

Ann, of course, has long since become computer-literate.

The friendships which Jean and I made during the shooting of *Poldark* have, happily, continued.

An eminent man, who has had a good deal to do with television, remarked the other day that he had never known so many friendships – and enduring friendships – to develop between the actors in a TV series and the author and his wife. It said something, he added, important of both sides.

Angharad has remained a specially dear friend. She has visited me in a variety of hospitals in which from time to time I have reluctantly found myself. Young, pretty, smiling, bringing flowers or fruit or delicacies to eat, sometimes all three on one visit, she has lightened the eyes of doctors and nurses and, when recently I was in an accident ward, that of other patients. Angharad has just *not changed*. She could still play Demelza – Ross's young wife – as she did in the late Seventies, and one would not notice the difference. A few years ago I invited my eighteen-year-old grandson, who had a terrible crush on her, to have lunch with her at Buck's Club; and when it was over, and we had separated from her, I said: 'Well, has it helped?' He gave a convulsive sigh, and replied, '*No.*'

My popularity at the Savile Club shows a remarkable leap when I invite her to lunch. Men I hardly know, or others who at most would content themselves with a wave of the hand, think up excuses to come over and speak to me.

Robin Ellis was voted the sexiest man of his generation. When he was acting at Stratford, which was between the first and second *Poldark* series, his dressing room would be invaded by groups of adoring girls. Wherever he went, he was followed and feted.

When Clark Gable was between marriages, and rather suddenly and unexpectedly remarried, one of the Hollywood newspapers came out with a banner headline, 'GABLE'S GONE, GIRLS'. Well, Robin 'went' by marrying an elegant and charming American girl.

They had a splendid wedding, which Jean and I went to, and he has now, it seems, retired from acting and lives a quiet life in France, north of the Pyrenees. His friends see him too seldom.

Ralph Bates (George Warleggan) died tragically young, and his wife runs a fashionable shop supplying dresses and costumes for the stage. Their daughter, Daisy Bates, is in the television world and recently played John Thaw's daughter in *Kavanagh QC*.

Jill Townsend (Elizabeth), during and after the filming, had a long association with Alan Price, but more lately it has broken up and she has gone back to America, where I have lost touch with her. (I once played snooker with Alan Price in Luxulyan Church Hall, while a scene was being prepared in the graveyard. It was a strange experience.) I put him up for the Savile Club, of which he remained a member for many years.

Christopher Biggins remains a close friend. It has always disappointed me that he has not received his due as a straight actor. Because of his size, his joviality, his keen sense of humour, he is always much in demand for light comic roles. (He seems to have made a corner for himself as a Pantomime Dame, and for this he is rightly in great demand and rightly renowned.) But casting directors should look again at his acting as Nero in *I, Claudius* and as Whitworth in the second *Poldark* series to see the range of his more serious talents, particularly in a role with a touch of the sinister, and they should make use of them.

Jane Wymark (Morwenna) is also a good friend. Shortly after the end of the series she married a man in the diplomatic service, and they have two children. Since they returned to England she has appeared in a number of TV plays. She is Patrick Wymark's daughter, and although in *Poldark* she was required to play a quiet, gentle girl, trapped in a hateful marriage, she has, I am sure, the capacity to play dynamic, aggressive parts. Such as a woman barrister?

Paul Curran (Jud Paynter), alas, died.

Mary Wimbush (Prudie) is fortunately still with us.

David Delve (Sam Carne) has been on the stage a lot since *Poldark*. He played an important part in *The Phantom of the Opera* at Her Majesty's Theatre, Haymarket, and stayed in it for two years.

The last time I saw Kevin McNally (Drake Carne) on the stage was when he played opposite Dame Maggie Smith in *The Lady in the Van*. Kevin played Alan Bennett, who wrote the play, and his personification of the author was pinpoint perfect. Years ago, on the set of *Poldark*, Robin Ellis said to me that Kevin McNally was the best actor in the production.

Chapter Eleven

I have recently rediscovered, having long thought them lost, the pocket diaries covering my early twenties. To read them one would think me a gardener and not much else. Occasionally a particularly good and exciting game of tennis is recorded, but most entries deal with sowing seeds, planting bulbs or herbaceous plants, picking or spraying or feeding roses or tomatoes, even cutting grass. Reading these diaries I astonish myself. Not perhaps for the preoccupation, but for the priority I gave that preoccupation in my diary.

When we lived in Manchester we had a normal town-size garden which my father would plant each summer; usually, in depressing conventionality, with geraniums and marguerites. Occasionally he would try to urge me to do something in the garden, but apart from regularly cutting the grass I paid only sulky attention to his proddings. (I remember once running over a frog with the cylinder lawn mower, discovering it eviscerated by the blades, and retreating into the kitchen to be sick while the maid cleared up the mess.)

Yet I did have a stirring of interest at an earlier age than this – about nine – when I picked up a book of my father's called *A Primer of Biology & Nature Study*. I began to examine and identify the sombre trees of Victoria Park, and still have the book with the pressed leaves I picked to match the illustrations on the pages.

When we moved to Cornwall all was made over anew. A tree in Perranporth was a rarity. Up the valleys you could find the may trees, the nut trees, a few long elms, all shaven by the prevailing winds, but within a mile of the sea nothing. Low-growing shrubs and flowers were riotous, and in endless variety and number. The bungalow that my parents rented for eighteen months had a rockery crammed with strange new plants, things I had never seen or heard of before; things I would hardly bother to grow now, but then strange and exciting, really exciting.

When we transferred to the house we bought in Perrancombe we were about a mile from the sea and there were apple trees in the garden (all uprooted one screaming November night a few years later). Not infrequently in the winter the foam from the mountainous seas dashing against the cliffs of Cligga two miles away would drift over our garden and fall like soapsuds. The soil was hideously shallow because of the washing floors that had been there in the last century, but it was to this garden, of about half an acre, that all the early diary entries refer. My sister-in-law, seeking something derogatory to say about me at this time to my mother, would say: 'He spends all his time with his head in a seed catalogue.'

It would be difficult to infer from these early diaries that I was an aspiring writer, a working writer, someone striving desperately to achieve a breakthrough and get something published, and so justify his existence. In later years – certainly for the last forty – I have always entered the approximate number of words written each day, and the total in the week. This isn't possible when one is struggling with intractable problems in the early stages of a novel or later doing extensive revision, but, once launched, a record of work done in any day has a hypnotic effect. You are stuck on a page, stuck on a page, stuck on a page: movement comes at last, so one works for an extra couple of hours to keep up the average for the week. Romantics who are surprised by this method should refer to Trollope (who of course ruined his reputation for many years by confessing that he counted the words in his output).

When we bought Treberran, I brought leaf mould and soil in dustbins in the back of the Alvis from the other side of the county to make a bed for rhododendrons and camellias. Following the success of this, and aware that protection was all, I built two sunken gardens where the land sloped abruptly away and put up cement-block walls eight feet high and about a hundred and fifty feet in length. It was heavy work and frequently my stomach muscles protested. It seemed at times to take on a bizarre similarity to building the Pyramids: one could not lift the blocks high enough, so pushed them up sloping planks and at the top rolled them over and allowed them to clomp into place. In these protected hollows many attractive small shrubs grew and flowered. I believe they still flourish.

Moving to Sussex, I hoped for lovely rich soil and was deceived by the rhododendrons growing in the garden of the house we bought. In fact the soil is thick Sussex clay, and we lost every Himalayan rhododendron we tried – and that is pretty well all of them – and dozens of choice shrubs besides. But camellias have been wonderful and the less particular rhododendrons, of which there are many. We have probably the largest free-standing *Magnolia grandiflora* in the county, masses of azaleas, hydrangeas of every variety of blue and pink and white: lace caps, oddities like quercifolia and tricolor; tulip trees, judas trees, strawberry trees, fossil trees, nyssa trees, gunneras and liquidambars.

I have used this interest in gardens in only two novels – if you except Demelza's garden at Nampara: in the 1992 novel, *Stephanie*, and an early novel, *The Giant's Chair*, later republished as *Woman in the Mirror*.

I have often been asked why I will not allow the early books to come out again as they originally were.

Many people must have suffered from time to time the frustration of having discovered a novelist, new to them, of enjoying enormously this first book, and of next picking one up on some airport bookstall by the same author and finding it horribly inferior. In annoyance they turn to the front page and discover it was published twenty or thirty years ago. The novelist's writing has improved. Many novelists do so improve. I have. A few hardly need to, they come to their craft fully equipped, like Graham Greene or Rudyard Kipling. Good for them. If my first book were half as good as *The Man Within* or *Plain Tales from the Hills* I would be happy to see it in reprint on any bookstall. As it was not, even relatively not, I refuse to take people's money for what virtually is a con.

Rewriting I know is confusing for the bibliophile, but I am not concerned with the bibliophile. I am concerned for the reader and for myself. One or two of the earlier novels, though lacking much, had good central ideas. Good ideas that could have been treated better. So it has suited me to try to treat them better. It has been a stimulus to try. And a stimulus is what makes one write.

My friendship with other authors has not been extensive, in spite of seven years on the Committee of Management of the Society of Authors, plus two years as its chairman. Through this I came to know many writers superficially, and a few better, but these mainly are from the Savile Club: Compton Mackenzie, J. B. Priestley, Nigel Balchin, John Moore, Eric Linklater.

I first met Somerset Maugham at the Savile when he was a guest at the club. At that time I was a tremendous admirer of his work – still am, if to a less absolute degree – and when introduced I told him what a rare pleasure it was to meet him.

'As it happens,' I said, 'I was in Istanbul last April when you were there, but we didn't meet. Then I was in Athens a month later when you were there, and we didn't meet. And oddly enough, last October, I was in New York at the same time, and we have the same publisher but we didn't meet.'

He looked up at me, screwing up small keen eyes in a small keen face, and said: 'It seems to me you have been tr-tr-trying to avoid me.'

The last time I saw Maugham was when Denys Kilham Roberts, then Secretary-General of the Society of Authors, invited him and Compton Mackenzie to lunch at the Savile, and asked me to make up the four. With a mischievous chuckle he said he thought we should have a rich entertainment. He was wrong. These two men, roughly contemporaries, Maugham nine years the elder, had seen and experienced so much of the writer's world as companions, as rivals, as overseers of the literary scene, that they must have had a hundred things to talk about and discuss. Not so. For some reason they were suspicious; they eyed each other like unacquainted cats, Maugham monosyllabic, Monty talking to Denys or me; even *silences* occurred now and then. Of course it was fairly friendly, but it was a guarded courtesy more than anything else.

I was at Mackenzie's seventieth birthday party and his eightieth.

After the first he went off to a night club with Eric Linklater where, legend has it, Eric was heard to be calling for black women. At 10.30 the next morning Monty was in his favourite seat at the Savile, dark blue pinstripe suit, crimson bow tie, clean, well-shaven, spruce, having already done a broadcast that morning at the BBC, and was now giving us his verbal plans for what he would write in the next ten years. The morning after his eightieth birthday party, having in the previous decade completed his schedule, he was in precisely the same spot making plans for the next ten years. He completed nine of them.

Monty Mackenzie was a great talker, a great raconteur – sometimes one dared to harbour the heresy that he was a better talker than he was a writer – but of all his reminiscences only one sticks in my mind, and that is an account he gave me of a visit to Henry James at Rye. James had known Monty as a child, and after lunch they talked for a while about the technique of the novel. James said:

'Ah, you young men. You throw the ball of narrative against the wall of literary truth and it rebounds effortlessly into your hands. I … I, on the other hand, throw the ball of narrative against the wall, and it rebounds here and there, hither and thither, this way and that, until, my old bones creaking in every joint, I must stoop laboriously to pick it up again.'

Anyone, I think, starting a Henry James for the first time will understand exactly what he meant.

It was at the Savile that I came to draw a line between the anecdote and the funny story. In the club – and I suppose it may be true of most of the great clubs – anecdotes are all; the invented funny stories virtually never told. I don't think I have heard a half-dozen dirty stories told at the Savile in fifty years. Nor is swearing indulged in. There is nothing censorious about this; simply that it is looked on as immature and childish.

I sometimes wonder in fact where all the cursing exists, except on the stage and in novels. *Are* writers immature and childish or simply hoping to shock? Like a schoolboy of eight coming home triumphantly as I did with his first four-letter word? Maybe I have lived a sheltered life. No swearing was ever used in our home, not even by my brother when he returned from two years of war. It didn't seem to occur to any of us. At school there were a number of foul-mouthed characters, understandably enough, but that was where the immaturity came in. During the Second World War I mixed with a fair number of sailors, and I remember nothing very untoward. After the war I was pitchforked into the film industry, and neither among actors nor among technicians did it seem substantially to exist. I heard nothing in the *Poldark* series. Similarly in the play I wrote, which was produced twice with different casts. Of course F-ing goes on with boring regularity among groups of working men, in the army, and in what George Gissing called 'the mean streets'. And of course there are exceptions among the educated, and the half-educated. One gravely afflicted with the complaint was Laurence Harvey. If there were an Olympic prize for obscenity, he would have taken a lot of beating.

Having said this much, I have to admit that since coming to live alone I have fallen into the habit of cursing vehemently – chiefly under my breath – at every minor hindrance or annoyance. In my youth I coined the phrase 'Swearing is the first resort of the vulgar and the last resort of the weak'. I'm not sure where that leaves me now.

Charles Chaplin, Alastair Cooke, Graham Greene, Ralph Richardson I came to know as a result of my friendship with Max Reinhardt and his delightful and distinguished second wife, Joan. They invited me to be godfather to their youngest daughter, Veronica, and Charlie Chaplin was to be the other. When we met at the christening I told him that as a child, and ever since, I had loved his films, but it had never occurred to me in my wildest dreams that one day I should become his godbrother. He replied with an absent smile. Genuine laughter seemed by then to have left the great man.

I met him a few months later when he had just been to the film of *Marnie*, chiefly with the intention of looking at Tippi Hedren for a part in his next film, *A King in New York*. He was very much technically on the ball in respect of the way Hitchcock had made the film. And Tippi was engaged. There was another occasion when we had dinner at the Reinhardts' and after dinner Max showed *The Gold Rush* on his private projector. Charlie was visibly entertained for the first ten minutes, and then slept through the rest of it.

The last time I saw him was at the Venice Film Festival when there was a retrospective showing of some of his more famous comedies, and Sir Charles Chaplin was invited to be present at the showing of *City Lights* projected onto a huge screen in St Mark's Square. After it was over, the diminutive figure appeared on one of the balconies and acknowledged the massive applause of the crowd. I think it was the balcony on which Mussolini had once stood to harangue the people and to receive his acclaim. This time the people were acclaiming 'Il Duce' of the cinema.

Of the other three, Ralph Richardson was the only one I came to know well. He was a member of the Savile, but it was in Cap Ferrat that we really got well acquainted. He had rented Max's cabin cruiser, which I had had the year before, and he was having trouble in making his wishes known to Jeannot, the difficult, tetchy, unagreeable custodian of the boat. I, having suffered the year before, went across to see if I could help, but my French was scarcely better than Ralph's, and if a Frenchman wishes to be misunderstood it's hard to get your message across. However, the struggle enhanced our friendship, and we dined together as a quartet several times during his stay, and in subsequent years I used to go to see him at home, or after lunch at the Savile we would play snooker or go to the cinema together.

Though not quite an intellectual, Ralph had a brilliant, if sometimes eccentric, artistic judgement. He read deeply and widely and had high standards which somehow he managed to assume existed equally among his friends. When he came into a room he had a faculty for raising the status of the occasion without ever attempting to impose himself on it.

One time he met me in the Savile and said: 'Hello, Poet,' (his usual greeting to me), 'care to come a trip on my bike? I have it outside.' I said, 'Fine,' and we went out to his huge red Norton motorbike.

'You'd better have my crash helmet,' he said, so we wobbled up Binney Street and out into the Oxford Street traffic, he with his scanty grey hair straying in the wind, I partly eclipsed under a large crash helmet. Once we were free of the worst traffic we jetted up Bayswater Road and then into the Park, where we roared around madly, eventually coming back via Hyde Park Corner and Piccadilly and so home. Later, in the Savile I was surprised to see strong men blanch at my recklessness.

It was hazardous but it was great fun, as all my contacts with him were. This was about the time when he appeared in the television series *Blandings Castle*, in which he played the Earl of Emsworth. He complained to me bitterly that he had played in the West End for thirty years and could walk the streets unrecognized, but 'one TV series and every little girl I pass knows who I am'. His complaint was of the disproportion of the fame, not of the fame itself. He was not at all averse from being recognized.

He had a passion for unusual pets. He allowed his parrot out of its cage nightly, and one day when he took me back he told me that José was 'in disgrace. He bit Mu last night.' Mu was Lady Richardson. On another occasion he bought a hamster in New York and in due time smuggled it into England. As he left the shop in New York the assistant said: 'Enjoy your hamster.'

'I wonder if the dear girl thought I was having it for breakfast,' he said.

When we went behind to see him after a performance of *No Man's Land*, he demonstrated in his dressing room the fall he had to make each evening on the stage, showing how easy it apparently was, once you had learned the way of it, to fall full length without hurting yourself. He was then seventy-five. I asked him what he thought Harold Pinter meant in a particularly obscure piece of dialogue in the first act.

'Old chap,' he said, 'I've no idea, and I've never dared to ask him.'

Anecdotes about Ralph abound. Donald Sinden told me that one day Ralph was crossing the concourse of Victoria Station when he saw someone he recognized and went up to him.

'David,' he said. 'David Partridge! We haven't met since that play in Birmingham; what is it? – ten, twelve years ago. You *have* changed. You're much slimmer. And you've shaved off your moustache!'

The man looked at Ralph. 'Sorry. But I'm not David Partridge.'

Ralph stared at him as only Ralph could stare. Then he said: 'D'you mean to say you've changed your name as well?'

Peggy Ashcroft said once that she was invited to dine with the Richardsons at their home. This was a delightful Nash house overlooking Regent's Park, but like most such houses it was tall and thin and the Richardsons had installed a lift. Ralph came down to open the door to Peggy, and they ascended in the somewhat creaky lift together.

Ralph looked at his guest and said: 'Peggy, have I ever slept with you?'

'No,' she said.

He eyed her significantly and said: 'Aa-ah.'

At this moment the lift reached the third floor and the door was opened by Mu.

Peggy said she never quite worked out what that 'Aa-ah' had implied.

Most people would say that, knowing Ralph so well, Peggy's uncertainty was a little disingenuous.

The story reminds me of one night at Cap Ferrat when the four of us had been dining together and we walked home from the restaurant in double file, Mu and I in the lead. Halfway home Ralph and Jean, bringing up the rear, disappeared for about three minutes and then took up the trail again. When we had separated and were indoors Jean said: 'Wow! What a kiss!'

I was furious, not because of the kiss but because I had fancied doing something the same to Mu, but, not being aware of the goings-on behind, I had funked it.

When my daughter had made plans to go to America she met Ralph's son, Charles, and they took a liking to each other. Whether Charles was particularly smitten we shall never know, but Ralph certainly was attracted by Rosamund's piquant blonde prettiness. So when Charles took her out he was provided with a large chauffeur-driven

Rolls-Royce to escort her to and from the theatre. By the time Rosamund came home from America she was engaged to marry a Californian.

When Ralph was eighty he was taken ill while on tour and went into hospital and quietly died. Mu, writing to me afterwards, said: 'He just folded his wings and refused to fly.'

I cannot end this section without writing a few more words about Max Reinhardt. Part French, part Austrian, and educated in Istanbul, Paris and London, he was a true cosmopolitan. When we went to Florence to the Publishers' Conference I knew about forty words of Italian; Max, in spite of his father having Italian nationality, knew no Italian at all. At the end of a week I still knew my forty words of Italian: he was speaking it – very badly and rousing companionate laughter, but being understood just the same. A very sophisticated man, easily bored, impatient of indifferent service, especially in restaurants and hotels, quick with his likes and dislikes, but in most other ways tolerant and easygoing, he was a man with a tremendous warmth of personality. Above all he had a supreme gift of friendship. It is one of the higher gifts in man, and I know no one who possessed it in such a degree.

Gilbert Harding, almost a forgotten man, I also came to know well. He used to hold court in the Savile, surrounded by a group of his friends, telling them a quite extraordinary selection of funny and revealing anecdotes about all manner of people he had known, from the lowly to the famous. His memory was brilliant, and his ability to tell a story to its best advantage was brilliant. He would talk for an hour. Andthen another hour. The first time I met him I came to sit somewhat tentatively on the outer orbit of his circle, one of the listening group. Presently his choleric eyes focused on me.

'Who are *you*?' he demanded. 'You look an arrogant fellow.'

I had been accused of a lot of things in my time, but arrogance was not one of them.

I gave him my name and my profession, and he grunted noncommittally and turned to his friends with another story, this one about Dickie Mountbatten, I remember, whom he greatly disliked.

I was staying in the club, and presently went up to dinner and afterwards played snooker. About eleven I went into the lavatory and found Gilbert on his own. His friends had gone and so had the drink, and he was swaying like a large building awaiting demolition. But he remembered me.

'You!' he boomed. 'You say you're an author. What have you written?'

'Well … one called *Take My Life*. That was written first as a screenplay but afterwards it was published as a novel.'

'Never seen it. Never heard of it.'

'And then there was *Night Without Stars*,' I hastened on. 'That was a fairly successful novel, and it was filmed.'

'Never seen it, never heard of it,' he said.

'And there was *Fortune is a Woman*. That was a book club choice in America, and it was also filmed, by Columbia.'

'Never seen it, never heard of it,' he said, finally consigning me to literary oblivion.

At this stage Kean, the porter, appeared on the scene. 'Got a taxi for you now, Mr Harding. Sorry for the delay.'

He helped Gilbert into the hall, and as the big man was so unsteady I took his other arm.

We got him to the taxi, and I was helping him in when he grasped my arm and pulled me in after him.

'Come home with me. I want to talk to you.'

Glass in hand, I went with him.

I did not suppose he was specially interested in me, but he desperately wanted not to be left alone; and later friendly meetings confirmed this. So long as he was projecting this personality he had built up, and he had people to listen to him and to accept it, he could believe in it himself. Under all his bombast was a searing self-contempt, both for what he was and for his way of earning a living. Such self-contempt was undeserved, but you couldn't reason with him about it.

He was in fact a very clever man, and in some ways a very worthy one. Always rebellious, but often rebellious on behalf of people he felt were not getting treated properly, his Vesuvius-like exterior deceived others into supposing he was always looking for trouble. When the drink was in him this was largely true; it was the characteristic that made him famous. But there were those at the Savile who deliberately tried to get a rise out of him and provoke the row they thought it clever to incite. I remember Tony Halsbury (the third Earl) coming into the club one day and, seeing Gilbert sitting by himself, he went up and said:

'Gilbert, you're a Catholic.' (Knowing him very well to be a fairly recent and zealous convert.) 'Tell me, did the Virgin Mary in your opinion use contraceptives? Otherwise, why did Jesus not have a clutch of little brothers and sisters?'

There was an inevitable blow-out, but it was not of Gilbert's seeking.

After that first meeting, he was always particularly courteous to me – and I use the word intentionally, for that was what he was. He admired creative people and despised critics, and this may have been the reason – apart from the fact that he recognized I liked him and took no notice of his brusqueries. Only once or twice, as he was much sharper than most people in the club, I saw him look at me resentfully when I refused another drink. He was conscious that I wasn't going along with him. But he never said anything.

I always found it rather fun to be with him; it was like being with an explosive uncle.

I wish I could say the same about Malcolm Arnold, a true creator in the way Gilbert never was. As a young man Malcolm was delightful, brimfull of talent, laughter, clownish jokes, a musician to his fingertips, unique. But that alas in his later years has all changed. I try to avoid him.

Thinking of Malcolm Arnold, I recall a splendid summer evening at the Savile organized by Gavin Henderson, in which a brass ensemble played wonderful music on the raised terrace behind the club. Malcolm played the trumpet, Jimmy Edwards the tuba.

It was a quiet warm London evening, the sun just setting, and as the music began one window after another slid or screeched open as people in the back rooms of the surrounding houses put their heads out to listen. It was like a film by René Clair.

Apart from schizoids, my allergy for people of unpredictable moods is deep-rooted. My Uncle Tom, as has already been said, was one such. There have been others. My own temper, which can be volatile, rises sharply when I encounter someone who, either by accident or design, is imposing his gloom upon a company or a household. Life to me is too short, and people who spoil it unnecessarily for others are despicable. Even people who, while blameless during the rest of the day, are morose at breakfast irritate me. One does not need to be the life and soul of the party. It's just another day to be lived, and if one is not ill or deeply worried by some outside circumstance, to be savoured from the start.

There are people too whom I describe as psychological bed-wetters, who are for ever making little puddles of trouble that they think they can't help.

> Life is too short to waste
> In critic peep,
> Quarrel or reprimand, or cynic bark,
> Twill soon be dark.

One of the more prominent members of the Savile when I first joined was Richard Graves. A tall, good-looking, austere man with a long and distinguished career behind him – he had been the last British mayor of Jerusalem – he would sit in his favourite corner of the Sandpit, as the 'core' room of the club is called, and regard new members who passed by – and old ones as well – with a cool and dispassionate eye, sometimes of approval, frequently not. He was known to the wits as 'Graves Supérieure'.

For some reason he came to approve of me fairly quickly, and when he heard we were going to Majorca to help Jean recover from a bout of pneumonia he said: 'You must meet my brother, Robert. I'll write to him and tell him about you.'

It was March 1st when we flew over, and all the French countryside was spattered with snow. In Palma the policemen wore greatcoats, white helmets and gloves; our excellent small hotel overlooking the sea, in what now I suppose is called Palma Nova, was run by a Belgian couple who fed us well but failed to cope with the heating of a house built primarily to keep out the sun. We shivered among the white stone pillars and walls, and presently went to see the Poet, who was staying in a four-storey house in the town. He put his head out from a third-floor window, looking exactly like the Emperor Vespasian, and trumpeted to us to come up.

We had a merry meeting, in the middle of which Beryl, his wife, abruptly took Jean off to a ballet class that her daughter was attending – though remarking in passing that there was little chance of her daughter succeeding, as under Franco the tutu was forbidden in Spain. (Shades of yesterday!) I was left to bear the brunt of Robert's erudite conversation, which dealt chiefly with two books he had just written called *Greek Myths* and *Homer's Daughter*. Knowing little about Greek mythology or history, except for some detailed amateur delving into the Trojan Wars, I appropriately floundered. However, this did not seem to matter, and we parted good friends. We met then at irregular intervals through the years when he was at the Savile – not as a member but as the guest of Selwyn Jepson – but much later I heard he had come to England for a prostate operation, so I went to Hampstead to call on him at the house where he was recuperating.

He showed me his almighty scar, barely healed (what advances in surgery since then), and we talked of this literary matter and that. It was a time in his life when his standing as a poet was not as high as it had been, or would be later. Earlier in the winter I had been to a series of lectures at Exeter given by a professor of poetry (I cannot remember what academic faculty he was attached to but he was a young man with his finger, as you might say, on the fashionable pulse), and his theme in one of these lectures was the way in which the new generation of poets had almost totally rejected the old. The only two poets excepted from this anathema and whom they wholeheartedly admired, he said, were W. B. Yeats and Robert Graves.

Thinking this would please him, I told him what the professor

251

had said; but Robert was so insulted that his name should be linked with W. B. Yeats that he was distinctly huffy about it, and talk was rapidly switched.

Perhaps there is a lesson to be learned from this.

After a week or so in Majorca we went by sea to Ibiza (the only way then), accompanied by a young Pole called Casimir Stamirski, a friend of Robert's, who shortly after we arrived introduced us to a big young man from the States called Irving. He seemed to be a typical husky all-American: frank, friendly and fit. Only when we were having a meal with him and I went into his bathroom did I see his medicine chest stuffed with pills. (But maybe this is typical too.) On our second meeting he told me he had written a novel and could I possibly read it and tell him what I thought.

I cursed under my breath. Reading other people's would-be novels in typescript when on holiday is my idea of hell. But I could hardly refuse, and when I read the book I was very impressed. It owed much to Hemingway, but it was a good novel in its own right, tense, terse and tough. I had it sent to Doubleday with a letter of strong recommendation. They turned it down. More fools they, I thought. And sure enough it was later published with considerable success.

Over the following years we kept in touch. Twice I wrote letters of recommendation for him to obtain a Guggenheim scholarship. (Whether anything came of these I never heard.)

The next thing I heard of him was when he was charged with having forged an autobiography of Howard Hughes and sold it to a publisher as genuine. He was found guilty and sentenced to some years in prison.

It was a sort of fame for Clifford Irving at last, no doubt, but hardly what he was seeking.

Incidentally, some years later I met Casimir Stamirski in London, and, since he had an encyclopedic knowledge of the sleazier nightclubs of London, he was very helpful to me when I was writing *The Tumbled House*.

The Green Flash is worth an extra word or two.

As mentioned earlier, I met Gregory Peck's mother-in-law while we were living in the South of France and was much taken with her good looks, intellect and brilliant sophistication. I badly wanted to use her in a novel, but somehow she would not come alive in any circumstances in which I put her.

Floating around in the same creative jelly, as it were, came an idea from some other source – I can't remember what – of a young man who falls in love with a much older woman who disguises her real age until she has an illness and quite suddenly *looks* old. The young man, still young, is bereft. She is still alive, and his memory of her as she was is too potent for him to take other women – on a serious plane – in her place.

These two ideas wanted to come together but I could not decide how. It seemed important that the two chief characters should be in the same world, she senior to him. I was not interested in the commercial world or banking. The film world and the theatre, law, medicine, art, literature, all were thought through, and none seemed to fit the bill, especially where her predominance in her profession was needed for the purposes of the novel. The one calling which seemed to provide absolutely the right ambience was perfumery. Here all the grandes dames of the world of fashion paraded: Chanel, Rubinstein, Arden, Lauder, there was no end to them.

So I proceeded on those grounds. Knowing virtually nothing of the subject, I had to do a lot of research both through books and in the field. I got an introduction to Desmond Brand, the then managing director of Helena Rubinstein, and he put everything I asked for at my disposal. I visited the works, the testing laboratories, the big commercial suppliers, the shops, the beauty salons. Desmond Brand was a very down-to-earth character. He emphasized the commercial, no-nonsense side of the business, but was willing enough to utilize the mystique, the romantic advertising, the bally-hoo that has grown up around the whole subject of perfumery.

I absorbed it all, thought it through again and again – then gave it up. However one treated it, the whole perfumery business seemed to me too light, too trivial for the setting of what had to be – however it eventually turned out (novel, thriller, or whatever) – essentially a sombre story. I gave it up for a year or more. I can't remember what, if anything, I did in the meantime.

Nor can I remember at what stage it was in my struggling with this obstinate novel that I met a man in Terrigal Bay, New South Wales, one wet and dismal morning. Jean and I had flown to Athens, Nairobi, Johannesburg, Cape Town, with a week there, and later taken ship for Australia. In our innocence or ignorance we had imagined these ten days to Perth, followed by calls at Adelaide and Melbourne before coming in at dawn under the famous Sydney Bridge, would be through sunlit seas with flying fish and dolphins, and agreeable days sunbathing by the swimming pool. Instead, we were in the Roaring Forties, with strong cold winds, grey scudding skies and unquiet seas. Furthermore, this was a cruise ship, and though Italian, full of West Germans, English and French taking a round-the-world trip; and, as possibly could have been foreseen by no one, leaving Europe in January, had filled itself with differing kinds of influenza which had cross-bred on the way. When we joined her at Cape Town most of the crew, including the captain, had been down with it and most of the passengers were either recovering or sickening. With the weather so stormy that it was not possible to stay in the open air for more than a few gusty minutes, one spent nearly all one's time in one's cabin or the staterooms, where the air-conditioning relentlessly pumped around the active bacteria. I was the first to go down and sneezed and coughed and sweated through the last half of the voyage and carried the uncomfortable remnants with me as far as Sydney.

Jean, it seemed, was immune, and stumped and staggered her way off to play bridge with various people while I lay in the cabin. February is not the best time to visit Sydney, and we arrived in the middle of a great heat wave: 'One hundred and three in the shade,' screamed one newspaper, 'and to hell with celsius.' We were given a wonderful time by Collins and various associated friends, but in the middle of it the influenza viruses at last overcame Jean's resistance and she went down with a succession of high fevers which, together with the various ailments she carried about with her as a matter of course, raised anxieties about whether she could continue the trip as planned.

Our immediate plan, made in England, was, after ten days in Sydney, to hire a car and drive along the coast as far as Terrigal Bay and then Salamander Bay. The weather pursued us to Terrigal Bay. Intense heat, which made a number of factories in Sydney close down, was accompanied by strident winds. When we arrived there we were determined to bathe; but no sort of protection from the sun could survive on the beach in that gale, so all we could do was to undress in the bedroom of our hotel, tug at the front door until it came open (to slam violently behind us as soon as we had been blown through) and stagger onto the beach, plunge into the warm sea and immediately, to avoid sunstroke, stagger back to the protection of the hotel.

This was the last day of the heatwave. Overnight the temperature dropped from 102° to 52° and all the next day, and for the next six days, lashing rain fell. (At the next place, Salamander Bay, which was a motel, water was running down the inside walls of our bedroom when we arrived. Not the ideal habitation for a woman whose temperature was slightly exceeding that of Sydney when we left.)

Terrigal Bay is – or then was – really little more than a group of hotels and motels and shops and dwelling houses arranged round the rather splendid bay where one may, one hopes, bathe and sunbathe at one's leisure. When it is raining there is virtually nothing to do. Jean, with a true sense of the priorities, decided to have her hair done. While she was in the salon I sat in the bar and got into conversation with another Englishman, similarly stranded, though I never learned what had brought him there in the first place.

When Jean emerged from her salon an hour and a half later and came up to me I smiled at her vaguely and, not at all vaguely, gestured her to make herself scarce. The man was telling me his life story.

It was such an extraordinary story that I should have gone straight upstairs afterwards and written it all down. Stupidly I did not, but enough of it remained in my memory, and some of it was riveting.

One of the problems of life is that truth is so much stranger than fiction that when one uses it as fiction it seems too bizarre to be true.

Among a number of things he told me was that when estranged from his wealthy wife he was invited to her birthday party at the Dorchester Hotel, and he went along feeling this to be the first move towards a reconciliation. When he got there he found all the other eighteen guests were men, and they were all homosexuals.

This scene appears in *The Green Flash*. I hope it convinces. The character of David Abden in the novel owes something to that meeting in Terrigal Bay, but it derives from other men as well. Many have thought him a finely drawn character. Many have disliked him.

So after eighteen months or so I returned to the idea that only a book using the perfumery business as its basis would be suitable for the novel I wanted to write. When I rang Desmond Brand and told him, he was pleased and surprised to hear from me again. In the meantime I had despaired of doing anything with it at all, and had strenuously considered a variety of other stories which might be developed. I would get so far with this or that idea but then across their path would come the story of Shona and David. It blocked the way completely for anything else I hoped to write. I had to get it out of my system.

There were infinite problems, other characters looming, other incidents log-jamming the way ahead. Because of the growth of another character, I had to study fencing and went to fencing schools to see people at work, consulted a master fencer. Scotland featured in it largely, and I did not know the social life and habits of the sort of class from which David Abden derived. The seedy and criminal side of the perfumery world became involved, and Scotland Yard consulted, and the courts. So it went on. But the mere mechanics of research were simple and easy compared to the battle between the characters and the manoeuvring of events so that the characters should have full play.

When I delivered the typescript to Collins their response was more than enthusiastic. Ian Chapman, then still chairman, took the typescript to Venice and rang me from there telling me that this was the novel he had been waiting twenty years for me to write. He said: 'I hope you'll write much more, of course, but if you never wrote another word, this is it.' Others were equally delighted, including

Sam Vaughan, the chief editor of Random House in New York. So all the barometers were set fair.

The first wobbling of the high-pressure system came when the editor who dealt with Random House paperbacks said she did not want it for their own paperback division. And the book's eventual reception both in England and America was mixed. It was well reviewed and pleased a lot of people. I had letters from semi-friends and acquaintances who had never written to me before, other authors among them, and who seemed to see in this book what I had hoped readers would see. But a mass of ordinary readers did not care for it. It was never a big seller even by my standards.

Do I regret this? Of course. Very much. Sales are not all that important; but quite a number of my own personal friends did not like it. Nobody has ever been able to tell me why. The nearest I have ever come to solving this mystery was when a retired film producer friend of mine (who was a tremendous admirer of the book) sent it to a young director friend of his who happened to be one of the successful men of the moment. The director replied to the effect that this was a fine novel but he would not want to make it into a film because the hero was such a shit.

A number of women, especially young ones, have hinted at the same opinion, and one day I made a detailed inventory of David Abden's misdeeds. He is a boy who when he is ten is being bullied by his drunken father and hits his father with a poker and accidentally kills him. This guilt, part conscious, part subconscious, stays with him all his life: he turns to petty crime until he meets Shona and from there on, resentfully, grudgingly, rebelliously, chooses to go straight. Tragedy haunts him and he is involved in another accidental killing; but all through his life his bark is worse than his bite. Having been very much against the police, he comes to work for them. Joining forces with Shona and becoming her lover is all a calculated form of self-advancement, but he finds himself in the end working genuinely for the perfumery business and genuinely unable to separate himself from this older woman whom he finds he truly loves. He is a character, one would think, who seems to merit sympathy rather than dislike.

For many readers it works this way, but for many more it does not.

After the Act is another book which didn't take off in any general way, but I understand why this is and accept it. It is one of my favourite novels. *The Green Flash* still puzzles me. My publishers assure me that it will continue to make its way in the world.

The origins of *Stephanie*, published in August 1992, go back, as usual, a long way. For a good many years I have known two men, both now elderly, who while vastly different in most ways, have one thing in common: they were 'war heroes'. One of them had been parachuted into France, blew up bridges, fought with the Maquis, was captured and tortured, and later was involved in action in North Africa and the Far East. Yet for all the time I had known him, he was the gentlest of men. The other was in the Parachute Regiment, fought with great bravery and the utmost recklessness all through the war and – it is said – ran himself into further debt every leave because he did not expect to survive. He is not now such a gentle man as the first but is quiet, courteous and shy.

It seemed to me that both these men illustrated a peculiar paradox: that for a short time a human being can become a trained killer, and then when that short term is over, can return to the fold, sober, law abiding, reliable, as if nothing had happened. (These are not ordinary soldiers, where the change is not so extreme, but the real killers.) And I put to myself the question: if in later life a situation should arise when violence was again justifiable – not in another war but in their own lives – would they briefly revert to what they had been in their youth?

For some years also I have had a club friend who is the chief police surgeon at Heathrow and deals exclusively with the smuggling of drugs. We talked a lot. Chiefly he talked and I listened. I began to study the drug question, interviewed people, trying to see all around it. On one of my frequent visits to India I happened to meet a drug dealer in Bombay. So it all began.

In the course of the writing I came to use only one of my war-hero friends; the other turned into the man I call Henry Gaveston, who came from a different source altogether. I intended there should be quite a lot of humour in this book, chiefly in the conversations between the two men, but this perished because the novel as it eventually evolved was not suitable for it.

This, as I hope readers will have realized, has not been intended as a chronological memoir. Somewhere along the line – it must have been early 1983 – I was awarded an OBE in the New Year's Honours List.

It was a very pleasant surprise, and I much appreciated being appreciated.

The day the awards were made was sunny but cold. Buckingham Palace was as usual warmly welcoming and magnificent, everything arranged in the most precise detail. The band played its soothing, elegant tunes. The only discordant note came from a tall elderly man next to me who, having received his medal, looked down at it and observed: 'It says here FOR GOD AND EMPIRE. Well, I know the Empire's dead. I'm not sure, but I wonder a bit about God.'

Whatever else, wit at least survives. Recently I was in the Savile Club and got into conversation with two other old men. We fell to discussing prices before and during World War II, and where we were accustomed to stay when we were in London.

The first man said: 'I always went to one of the Waverley group. They were good value and comfortable.'

'Yes,' I agreed. 'I usually stayed in Bloomsbury too. The Lincoln Hall. It was Blitzed during the war.'

Third man said: 'I always stayed at the Cumberland.'

First man gave a guffaw. 'Oh, that was known as the Tart's Hotel. You only had to ring ...'

'I always took my wife there,' the third man said stiffly.

The first man raised an eyebrow. 'Did you have to pay corkage?'

I have called this book *Memoirs of a Private Man*, for this is always what I have wanted to be. In the early days the press were not interested in me, but later sometimes they very much have been, and I have always been intensely uncomfortable under their scrutiny and tried to duck whatever I could.

My second publisher once said to me that if I wanted to avoid publicity I had chosen the wrong profession.

A few years ago I lent some support to Stephen Spender in his pleas for discretion in the publication of his letters after he was dead, urging that they could give unnecessary distress to people still living and to his own family.

I did not know whether Stephen Spender wanted or needed my support. (I had known him to say 'Hello' to for more than thirty years, but oddly enough I do not think we exchanged more than a sentence all that time.)

Kirsty McLeod in the *Daily Telegraph* argued that 'As for the great man himself: be he painter or writer, he has – despite what Spender says – been trying to draw attention to himself from the very moment he first picked up a paintbrush or wielded a pen.' And in a letter in reply in the *Telegraph* I totally disagreed. She did not make – and many people do not make – the distinction between an author's work and an author's private life. Of course authors want publicity for their work – it is their life blood – but not every author wants to parade his personal private doings, or even his personal appearance, before the public. Some do. Some adore it. To be seen about and recognized! To be feted! To be followed by the press! To be asked for their opinion, to go to fashionable dinner parties, to go round publicizing their latest novel! It's heaven. But for some it's hell, and we should be allowed to choose. Some do choose: four such are, or were, Graham Greene, John Fowles, John Le Carré, William Golding.

How far Stephen Spender sought or shrank from personal publicity I do not know; what he was arguing for in this case was that his personal letters, written when a young and no doubt impetuous man, should not be bandied about and analysed by any Paul Pry who came along after his death and fancied displaying his Freudian prowess. I will not, I imagine, ever be famous enough to attract this form of tabloid journalism, but even if I were as notable as Conrad or Hemingway there would be little about my private life which would merit the unearthing. As I have said in the preface, although

I have had a modest share of sinfulness, it has been too ordinary, straightforward and unmuddied by complexes or fixations. I have had one wife, and I loved her and she loved me. I did not terrorize, browbeat or woefully neglect my children. I have never frequented public lavatories. I do not get drunk and disorderly. All very dull.

And I do not want to go to literary lunches, open fetes, give readings of my books, or otherwise appear in the public eye. I have by now written a great many novels, and must through them have surely revealed a fair amount of my own nature and personal feelings. Let that suffice.

Tolstoy says somewhere: 'There is no point in visiting a great writer, because he is incarnate in his works.' Should this not to some extent be true of the less important writer? Even down to the least important of all?

A few years ago, after reading through a novel I had just finished, I wrote these few lines. Maybe they sum up something of my philosophy, and act as a suitable envoi to this book:

> Perfection is a full stop.
> Give me the comma of imperfect striving,
> Thus to find zest in the immediate living.
> Ever the reaching but never the gaining,
> Ever the climbing but never the attaining
> Of the mountain top.

CPSIA information can be obtained at www.ICGtesting.com
Printed in the USA
LVOW11s0926240916

505970LV00004B/117/P